Series: *Language, Media & Education Studies*

Edited by: Marcel Danesi & Leonard G. Sbrocchi

Primary Education:

Goals, Processes and Practices

by

Clare Madott Kosnik

LEGAS

New York   Ottawa   Toronto

Canadian Cataloguing in Publication Data

Main entry under title:

Clare Madott Kosnik
        Primary Education:
        Goals, Processes and Practices

(Series: Language, Media & Education Studies; 6)
Includes bibliographical references
ISBN 0-921252-83-8

Data to come

For further information and for orders:

LEGAS

P. O. Box 040328	68 Kamloops Ave.	2908 Dufferin Street
Brooklyn, New York	Ottawa, Ontario	Toronto, Ontario
USA 11204	K1V 7C9	M6B 3S8

Printed and bound in Canada

For Clive,
my friend,
colleague and mentor

Table of Contents

Chapter Six
Teachers' and Students'
Perspectives on Curriculum 133

Chapter Seven
Drawing on Whole Language Philosophy
and Practice for a Reimagined Curriculum 157

Preface

Primary education: the most important time in children's academic lives or just a time to play. Which is the "right" view? Both perspectives are partially accurate but neither fully recognizes the complexity of the first years of formal schooling. The goals and practices of education in the primary years are not clearly defined or agreed upon. Young children must learn the basics of education; be socialized; be allowed to express themselves; learn about their place in the world; learn to enjoy life; and so on. The mandate is vast and daunting and yet primary teachers must try to balance all the various expectations for young children and themselves. *Primary Education: Goals, Processes and Practices* addresses a broad range of educational issues and outlines a philosophy of education. It offers answers to the basic questions: *what* should be done in the primary years of schooling and *why*.

Primary Education: Goals, Processes and Practices is a comprehensive text which provides a direction for schooling. Educators today face many pressing issues such as the impact of changing families, the influence of media, the changing role of the teacher, the demand for a revitalized curriculum and the evolving yet often troubled relationship between home and school. To address these questions we usually have to go from text to text, each dealing with a specific topic in isolation and offering answers that are often contradictory. Unlike many other texts which tend to be either theoretical or practical, this book weaves theory and practice together in highly readable language. It covers a broad range of topics, is filled with practical examples and discusses theoretical concepts in accessible terms; it offers solutions that are *connected to* and *build upon* each other.

The goals and methods of primary education cannot be detached from those of later grades; the early years are the foundation upon which the whole of schooling (and later life in society) are built. My challenge was to present goals, processes and practices central to *all* of schooling and society yet respect the special needs and interests of primary students and teachers. Although many of the examples are drawn from the primary years this work outlines a general philosophy of education. For example, I argue that well-being should be the ultimate goal for primary education; it should be the aim for students of all ages.

To be consistent with my philosophy of education, which requires attention to both theoretical and practical issues, I wanted this text to be accessible to educators and students of education as well as academics. The text is filled with examples from my own work with children, yet presents a philosophical grounding for the direction of schooling. This overcomes the either/or dilemma of theory and practice. Understanding and solving educational problems requires us to attend to multiple perspectives, which is the only way to move forward with genuine school renewal.

This volume can be used in many ways. It can be the central text in a primary education program or a secondary text in a foundations of education course. It will be of interest to both preservice and graduate students of education. As a main text or as recommended reading it addresses numerous issues central to any discussion of schooling and provides extensive reference to the current literature on education.

But this is also a book for and about teachers. Teachers will find themselves in my stories. It validates their work while trying to make sense of the milieu in which we practice our craft. In telling my story, I describe many years of joys, frustrations, challenges and successes. My experiences reflect the story of many teachers who have been part of the dramatic change that has swept through schools in the last twenty years. I outline goals for education and connect them to my own practice and that of other teachers.

Primary Education: Goals, Processes and Practices does not fit neatly into a typical category of educational writing. It crosses traditional subject lines and speaks to more than one audience. I ask pointed questions, raise different issues and suggest unusual ways of looking at education. If we are to meet the current challenges facing education we need to think differently about our policies, practices, roles and processes. I hope this text will be part of the on-going discussion of education and help both teachers and students in the vital task of educational renewal.

Introduction

I merely utter the warning that education is a difficult problem to be solved by no one simple formula.[1]

Alfred North Whitehead

Education is a complex process: it has both an overt and a hidden curriculum; it must simultaneously address the cognitive, affective, social, aesthetic, spiritual and physical development of students; schools are a place of employment for some and a mandatory requirement for others; for some schooling is an oasis and for others it is torture; schools must respond to society's needs while exercising a leadership role in the community; the political, economic and social spheres of society play themselves out in the educational arena; and the long history of schooling influences this formidable institution. Since on each educational issue there are several distinct theoretical positions and each requires different practical implementation strategies there is tremendous potential for friction. Against this backdrop of multiple agendas and conflicting issues there is the child; each child must be cared for and loved and his or her unique needs, talents and hopes must be cherished and nurtured. Given the complexity of the situation, Alfred North Whitehead was correct when he noted that a simple formula will not work.

Education in itself is not and should not be seen as a problem, a sickness or a blight requiring externally contrived solutions and potions. When we view it this way, we always feel the threat that the illness will reappear so close monitoring is necessary. Education is not a sickness that requires medication, a trial to be endured or an obstacle course to be negotiated; rather, it is a vital part of the fabric of society. Granted, some educational issues may be problematic but education should never be viewed as a problem. To put the point positively, education should be a joy. When we start with our children's needs, hopes and talents and have their well-being as our guide, the spotlight moves away from the many other agendas and conflicts that make education a difficult endeavour. Our approach to schooling must be thoughtful and complex so that education and joy become inextricably linked.

---

[1] Thomas Groome, *Christian Religious Education: Sharing Our Story and Vision* (San Francisco: Harper and Row, 1980), xiii.

General Direction

My philosophy of education book develops a framework for the primary division of schooling. Most discussions of education focus on a single aspect of the process, analyze it in detail and on this basis offer sweeping suggestions for change. Although the ideas presented have some use, the conclusions from the exercise are often separate from the reality of day to day schooling and fail to provide a general direction for education. Both of these factors are critical to educational discussions. A narrow methodology and approach to educational reform lead to a very fragmented education system. Subjects, content, processes, attitudes and goals are often at cross purposes. Further, academics and practitioners are often working in highly specialized areas, unaware of other issues. As a result of this approach to educational reform, our present system is a "patchwork quilt" of objectives, processes and content.

The main problem I want to address is the fragmentation of the schooling system. This fragmentation is found at many levels. On the philosophical level, there are many opposing theories of education. For example, schools have tried to accommodate elements of both behaviourism (Skinner) and progressive education (Dewey), resulting in a highly inconsistent approach. The philosophy for primary education in Ontario is found in *The Formative Years*; although this is in many ways a thoughtful document, it does not adequately address the practical application of its philosophy or the contextual factors of the classroom.

On a second level, curriculum is fragmented into many different subjects, with differing attitudes towards students, processes and goals. Since the links between the subject areas are often not apparent, the curriculum becomes a splintered process. Between school systems and even within the same school, there is not a consistent approach to instruction, content or evaluation methods.

Fragmentation is seen on many other levels: teachers feel disconnected from administrators, school boards and ministries of education; students feel that school is remote from their home lives; and educational theorists have little contact with or understanding of practitioners and vice versa. Many of the individual "pieces" of education are of outstanding quality but they are not brought together into a mosaic of education.

This book develops a philosophy for education, with a special focus on primary schooling. I will use the terms "philosophy," "theory" and "framework" interchangeably. I feel educators need a philosophy to guide and integrate their activities; but the typical "philosophy of education" is inadequate because it is not rooted in day to day schooling. The central principle of my philosophy is that schools must promote the well-being of children; well-being will be the litmus test each aspect must pass. Well-being will be defined in my vision of the educated person.

Central to my position is the idea that this philosophy must be explicit in the community. Further, since teachers are key to the process of education, their involvement in the construction and communication of the philosophy is the only way to avoid repeating the same mistakes. Teachers must understand it, make it their own and clearly articulate it. A recurring theme in the book is the need for dialogue among all members of society. My framework emphasizes and provides for these conversations.

My book adopts a comprehensive approach, arguing that educational reform must arise out of a perspective that considers the "whole" of the schooling process and in its full societal context. It is essential in education to have a framework that guides and coordinates. Accordingly, my discussion is a dialectical interplay between the general and the specific: first, I place schools within the context of our changing society; secondly, I outline broad goals for schooling; and thirdly, I identify the goals and processes for specific aspects of schooling. Using a methodology which moves back and forth between the general and the particular allows me to develop a framework that has a high level of consistency and internal unity. Throughout my discussion I emphasize that aspects of education cannot be considered separately; I show that all parts are interconnected. Change or reform in one part impacts on other elements; for example, I show that teacher well-being is affected by the sense of community in the school, by the type of curriculum that is mandated and by the demands of the neighbourhood community.

My approach to schooling draws on John Miller's concept of holistic education which focuses on relationships. Some of the relationships that Miller identifies are those between mind and body, various domains of knowledge, individual and community, self and Self and linear thinking and intuition. A holistic approach recognizes that education is much more than the acquisition of isolated fragments of knowledge; it acknowledges many different voices, recognizes the importance of the emotional, physical, cognitive, social and aesthetic aspects of the individual and celebrates children thriving in their own way. To help us visualize this holistic model of education, I propose conceptualizing school as a three dimensional object, a cube. Unlike most conceptions which are two dimensional (hierarchy or matrix), a three dimensional image allows for depth and breadth and illustrates the central argument of my book, that the many elements of school are connected. Within the cube there are such "points" as: curriculum, the role of the teacher, the teacher's well-being, the school as a community, the accommodation of special needs students, the impact of computer technology, the relationship with other government institutions and social agencies, the place of values education, the interests of minority groups, the physical layout of the school building and, most importantly, the children's well-being. These points are all linked to one another.

A phrase that is used repeatedly in this book is "keep the conversation going"; it is borrowed from Richard Rorty[1] who argues that our goal should not be to discover truth once and for all or to advance just one view of knowledge, because knowledge keeps changing and many types of knowledge have value. We must avoid a static or narrow approach to the education system which focuses on one perspective, excluding others from the conversation. We must keep the dialogue going between school and society, and between all the participants in the school process. The second significance of the phrase relates to the practical realm of schooling. John Goodlad notes that initially most primary children are very keen about school and rank their experience as fairly positive; however, as students move through the "corridors of the school," their attitude changes to disenchantment,[2] or as Nel Noddings says, alienation.[3] In this book, I show that some of the current practices in the primary division contribute to this changed attitude; the early school experience sets many children on this rather negative path. My approach to education will be one that *keeps the conversation going* between children and teachers.

I do not offer a specific end point for education; rather, I provide broad statements that describe human well-being and an educated person. Unlike the current outcomes based education, with its exit outcomes, or a listing of the texts to be read or courses studied, I look more at the student's attitudes towards schooling and life. My very broad goals describe educated persons as individuals who are able to look back with fondness at the time spent in school, as a time when they felt a sense of belonging and felt that schooling contributed to their well-being. They gained self-confidence, knowledge and skills while maintaining their curiosity and sense of wonder. In school they were able to thrive and as adults they continue to flourish. Like Rorty, I do not ad-

---

[1] Richard Rorty, *Philosophy and the Mirror of Nature* (Princeton, NJ: Princeton University Press, 1979), 377.

[2] John Goodlad, *A Place Called School: Prospects for the Future* (New York: McGraw Hill, 1984), 141.

[3] Nel Noddings, *The Challenge to Care in Schools: An Alternative Approach to Education* (New York: Teachers College Press, 1992), 36.

vocate a single way of life; rather, for each person the school experience and the knowledge gained are different in ways necessary to increase their well-being.

My description of human well-being and an educated person is very broad; to narrow the focus I suggest a second set of goals which I call "intermediate steps." They reveal more clearly the direction schooling should follow in order to produce educated persons who experience well-being. The five intermediate goals are: autonomy/control, which allows for individual development; reflectiveness, which recognizes that children and educators must be thoughtful about the process of education and about themselves; integration, which involves a unified and unifying approach; responsibility/care, which shifts attention to one's role in the community; and mutuality, which recognizes that schools are made up of people who affect us and are affected by us. By having some goals which turn students and teachers inward and some which direct them outwards, I hope to balance the needs of the individual and the community; both are important aspects of well-being. Since schools have often focused on competition and individual achievement, they have neglected to place the individual within the community.

Obviously, my intermediate goals are not simple curriculum objectives; by choosing these goals I am suggesting that schooling is much more than acquiring facts, figures and cognitive skills. I am opposed to the current practice of elevating a standard curriculum to a revered status in schools; rather, I stress that school is a community where children actively participate in meaningful projects, acquire the necessary life skills, live in relationship and feel a sense of ownership over their lives and work. Further, my five goals emphasize the importance of addressing the students' attitudes: it is not sufficient to consider simply what knowledge they have acquired in class. By advocating well-being and thriving, I am stressing that emotional health and physical fitness, as well as strong cognitive skills are all part of the educated person. The whole of the person must be addressed in schools.

Narrowing the Focus to Primary Education

Although there is merit in examining education in general, such a task is so broad that it would be unmanageable. In order not to become lost in vague generalities, it is often wise to limit the discussion to a smaller area. There are two approaches commonly used in discussions of education: either an examination of a specific aspect of education, such as reading and writing, or a concentration on a particular age-group. I

have chosen the latter -namely, a focus on the primary years - because
it still allows me to consider the many facets of education within a
manageable frame of reference (although even studying the primary
years is an enormous task).

There were many reasons for choosing the primary years. First, the
education of young children has long been my passion. Having worked
with youngsters and primary teachers for eighteen years, I feel that I
have done extensive field research. Since I have had the good fortune
to study educational theory *and* be a practitioner, I am confident that I
can blend theory and practice in the dialectical manner which is essential for sound educational inquiry.

Secondly, the old saying "every journey begins with a single step" is
appropriate here because primary education is the first stage of formal
schooling. By focusing on it, and considering education as a journey, we
are then able to identify threads that are common to all periods of our
lives, such as the need to have positive self-esteem or the need to make
informed decisions. This particular metaphor also allows us the flexibility of recognizing that each step is a *special* time. Childhood is a
very precious time and it has an impact on future development. The
first tentative steps on the education path set the tone for the rest of
the journey. Each step is critically important but it does not stand on its
own, it is part of something larger. And further, comparing education to
a journey, we recognize that both require involvement, adventure and
personal interpretation - these are not something that can be "done" to
a person. Nevertheless, I want to qualify the metaphor of the journey,
since it is not my intention to suggest that there is a final destination or
end point, or that we must all follow the same path to the "golden
palace" of knowledge and wealth. I would hope that each person
would construct, in conjunction with the surrounding community, his or
her own "palace" recognizing that each person's treasures are unique.
Primary education, while the first main step in schooling, actually con-
tinues each person's distinctive journey that starts at birth.

We commonly operate under the mistaken view that attitude and
skill development, which are central to education, suddenly burst forth
in the intermediate grades. We overlook the basic "fact" that laying
the foundation, or planting the seeds, takes place in the primary
years.[1] Because young children are often boisterous and their skills are
at the formative level, they are considered with less thoughtfulness

---

[1] The metaphor of laying the foundation or planting seeds is not meant to imply
that we must wait for ten years before there are "blossoms"; rather, I see the
child as living fully at each stage of life. In each period, there are fruits and
flowers.

and seriousness than adults. We often indulge in practices that are inappropriate and not well thought out. In primary grades, we train children to view knowledge as something available from a textbook or teacher; however, in intermediate grades we implore students to "think for themselves." Because we lack a consistent approach we spend a great deal of time having to "undo" or "remediate" in the intermediate grades. A more reflective approach to primary education would cause less problems in later life. An example which poignantly illustrates this point is the move to destream *high schools*. Many school boards have recently wrestled with ways to destream high schools, a strategy which suggests that the students' problems suddenly occured (or could be rectified) in grade nine. Instead of looking at the elementary school, especially the primary years, to find out why students at fourteen years of age can barely read and find school a painful, alienating experience, it is thought that a solution can be applied half-way through the process. By grade nine, there   have already been many profound twists and turns on the journey — none of which can be overlooked or easily undone.

A third reason for focusing on the primary years has to do not with the students but rather with the teachers. Having done countless workshops with teachers, I have found that primary teachers are the most open and receptive to change. The primary school has often been "the seed-bed of more adventurous practices"[1] which then infiltrate into the education of older students. Change does not come easily, so it would be propitious to begin with a group that demonstrates a willingness to experiment with new practices and can consider alternative approaches.

Approach to Inquiry

This book is both an examination of many aspects of schooling and the construction of a framework for education. In order to complete this project I have had to use a particular inquiry approach. There are many different ways to study education: for example, there is the statistical method which quantifies and analyzes frequencies, ethnography which stresses the distinctiveness of each situation and the importance of participant observation, the traditional humanities approach which critically analyzes the work of one or more figures (or movements) in the field, or a personal narrative style which relies heavily

---

[1] Donald Jones, "Planning for Progressivism: The Changing Primary School in the Leicestershire Authority During the Mason Era, 1947-1971," in *The Changing Primary School*, ed. Roy Lowe (London: The Falmer Press, 1987), 32.

on one's own story. Each of these approaches has validity, limitations, strengths and weaknesses; therefore, we must be careful in choosing a method. Some methods work better to achieve certain goals; in selecting an approach one must ensure that the method chosen is connected to the content of the project and enables us to reach our intended outcomes. My topic, the development of a framework for primary education, requires both knowledge and analysis of many theories of education and knowledge of the practical aspects of schooling. Of the four inquiry styles mentioned above none is exactly suited to my intended goals.

In selecting my approach I kept five principles in mind: first, I wished to consider the broad picture of education; secondly, I was committed to blending theory and practice; thirdly, I wanted a style of inquiry that was accessible to school-based educators; fourthly, I wanted to be able to draw on my own personal experiences; and fifthly, I wanted to include the work of many experts. Given these five considerations I could not simply adopt a single established research method; I could use elements of various approaches but I had to develop my own method.

The first element of my approach is that I identify many factors in the schooling process. Surveying the field requires me to demonstrate its breadth, which at first glance may appear to sacrifice depth of discussion; however, I feel that in actual fact, in this case at least, breadth adds to depth. The value of a wide perspective is that it allows me to identify many of the *key* factors in education. Of course, it is impossible to identify *all* of the factors in education. However, to compensate for this limitation, I often choose to discuss specific issues that are representative of the omitted topics. In other cases I simply mention, in a list format, some of the additional factors which need to be considered. In one way or another, then, the reader begins to sense the big picture of education, a critical step in coming to understand schooling.

A second element of the process is that I draw on my own story as a school student, teacher of children, curriculum consultant, student of education, and professor of education. My twenty years of work in schools constitutes much of the field-work upon which I draw. Using my personal experiences has many advantages. First, I am able to provide many examples of each issue. At times I use an illustration to clarify a point while at other times I present a story and then show the theory underlying it. This method has the benefit of moving the discussion easily between theory and practice. Secondly, the use of personal examples places the framework within the context of schools as they actually exist. I am committed to developing an approach that is feasible and this can only be accomplished by working with a realistic picture of the cultures, histories, traditions, mechanisms, limitations and strengths of ordinary schools. For too long discussions of educational issues have not been placed within the reality of school. To tell the whole story the discussion must include both the academic perspective and facts of day to day schooling. Unless this occurs theory and practice will remain two distinct entities. And finally, my book must be accessible not just to academics but also to classroom teachers. If school-based practitioners were unable to follow my argument and recognize the examples, I would feel that I had betrayed my roots.

A third element of my inquiry approach is the inclusion of references to many other writers; at times I use them to re-enforce my position and in other cases I draw on their expertise in their given field. I do not feel that this latter use diminishes my credibility; in academe, as in life generally, a degree of appeal to carefully selected authorities is often appropriate. It is impossible to check everything independently oneself. Many theses make more extensive use of other writers than I have done; indeed, many are primarily an in-depth analysis of particular works and authors. I did not choose this route, because I wanted to construct an original framework, and it would have been impossible in the space available to present both an in-depth analysis of authors and the construction of a framework for schooling. However, as the references indicate, I have read widely in the field and formed careful assessments of the relative contributions of various authors. This in turn has enabled me to develop a stronger and more comprehensive theory of schooling.

Fourthly, my approach merges theory and practice. Clive Beck refers to my research methodology as "theorizing the practical" which I feel is an apt description. This phrase suggests that I respect both theory and practice; feel that there should be a dialectical relationship between them; value a type of theory that can be applied; and recognize that there is frequently valuable theory underlying practice. This method requires both academic rigour and an extensive knowledge of the field of practice. Although this is an unusual approach for a philosophy of education book, I feel it is a highly appropriate one given the topic, my background, my strengths and the goals of the work. Throughout the book I will refer to Loris Malaguzzi, founder of the Reggio Emilia approach to primary education. He believes that "a theory is legitimate only if it deals with problems that emerge from the practice of education and that can be solved by educators. The task of theory is to help teachers understand better the nature of their problems."[1]

In selecting the issues to be discussed I have had to make choices; another writer would have elected to consider different trends and themes. Who would be "right?" Postmodernism has shown us that many positions can be valid, each representing a different perspective. Having various stances adds richness to the dialogue. As long as one recognizes that one's position is not the definitive answer the conversation will continue. From my view as an educator and theoretician, these are the points that I consider to be crucially important in understanding the present status of schools and charting directions for the future.

Outline of the Book

The book consists of eight chapters. In Chapter One I discuss our changing society. I argue that the upheaval in society, and especially the changing structure of the family, impacts on both the individual and on schools. In response to the demands placed on them, schools have added many duties to their mandate. These many additional duties have obscured their direction.

In Chapter Two I develop further my holistic framework for education introduced above; I propose conceptualizing school as a three dimensional shape, with points interconnecting. I also set some ground-rules for establishing aims, such as the need to include many theories and voices, the importance of connecting the school to the community and the necessity of using a common language for educational goals.

Building on the foundation of Chapters One and Two, in Chapter Three I first discuss the. issue of the possibility of specifying the purpose of schooling. Secondly, I outline my vision of the educated person which emphasizes well-being and a positive attitude towards self, others, learning and the environment. And finally, I present and discuss my five intermediate goals — autonomy/control, reflectiveness, integration, responsibility/care and mutuality.

The first three chapters present the theoretical framework, with many examples provided. The second part of the book extends the theory by placing it in the context of the school. In Chapter Four, I address the importance of the class as a learning community. By examining the

---

[1] Loris Malaguzzi, "History, Ideas, and Philosophy," in *The Hundred Languages of Children: The Reggio Emilia Approach to Early Childhood Education*, eds. Carolyn Edwards, Lella Gandini and George Forman (Norwood, NJ: Ablex, 1993), 82.

way the class culture affects learning, I show that this community is a powerful force, the fibre that connects the many points of schooling. I suggest that the structures and routines that are implemented and the curriculum choices that the teacher makes should support the development of the community.

Chapter Five is concerned with the teacher. While most discussions focus on the "role" of the teacher I adopt a broader perspective. My argument is based on Nancie Atwell's description of teachers as thoughtful practitioners; they question, observe, reflect and make sense of their classrooms; they change in light of their discoveries and they act as scholars.[1] Sharing some of my own story, I attempt to show that teaching is much more than the transmission of data: it is a relational experience and therefore requires a thoughtful practitioner. Finally, I point out that the five intermediate goals previously outlined for students are also relevant for teachers.

Chapters Six and Seven are devoted to curriculum. I first analyze the current approach to curriculum development, noting that it ignores the teacher and the realities of schools; then I provide a strategy for the future. I suggest that curriculum should be reduced to three broad areas: language arts, mathematics and the arts. This approach allows for more integration because there are not twelve separate subjects; and the development of the class as a community of learners is not overshadowed by an excessively weighty curriculum. In Chapter Seven, to illustrate my general approach, I provide a detailed discussion of a proposed language arts program.

The final chapter looks at the links between home and school. Since schools are part of society, the book would be incomplete without a consideration of the effect of the home on the school and vice versa.

In conclusion, I do not attempt to summarize the general arguments and proposals of the book. Rather I suggest a few key strategies for beginning to move schools in the direction I am recommending.

---

[1] Nancie Atwell, *Side by Side: Essays on Teaching to Learn* (Portsmouth, NH: Heinemann, 1991), 3.

Chapter One

Placing Schools in a Societal Context

... the point of edifying philosophy is to keep the conversation going rather than to find objective truth.[1]

Richard Rorty

Schooling is everyone's concern. Although it is often equated with children's work, schooling is a constant in all of our lives. For students, school is a place to learn and socialize; parents look to schools to provide childcare and a basic education for their children; and as adults, we see formal schooling as helping to prepare youth to participate in society.

Schooling must take place in constant "conversation" with the rest of society; it cannot pursue a narrow intellectual or even vocational agenda of its own. It must respond to the changes and continuities of the larger society. In this chapter I place schools within a broad social context. I argue that schools are not separate from society; rather, they are institutions within a *particular* social context which impacts on their well-being and directs, to a certain degree, their future course.

Although I am not an expert in sociology and anthropology I feel that it is important for novices such as myself to address the social context of education. By always relying on and deferring to experts, our information can easily become compartmentalized, full of technical language and inaccessible. I feel that the postmodern approach of integrating knowledge from different fields and encouraging non-experts to venture into other fields is valid and helps overcome these barriers.

Changes in the Family

A discussion of some of the changes that I consider crucial in the lives of children follows. Society is changing in many ways: for example, increased communication technology, expanded entertainment choices,

---

[1] Richard Rorty, *Philosophy and the Mirror of Nature* (Princeton, NJ: Princeton University Press, 1979), 377.

flexible working conditions, relaxed sexual mores and rapid trans-portation services. I have chosen to examine a particular set of changes, beginning (in this section) with ones involving the family.

i. *The Changing Structure of the Family*

The home is the most influential factor in children's lives. My position in this book is that home and school are partners in education; they are not two separate institutions. Accordingly, as the home life of children changes, the school is affected. Relevant trends over the past twenty years include: decline in real family income, except at the top of the so-cioeconomic pyramid; a tendency toward downward mobility: children cannot assume that they will do as well financially as their parents; increased participation of women and mothers in the paid workforce, in order to make ends meet; general reduction in number of jobs available, especially well-paid jobs; declining return on investment in schooling, i.e. a high school diploma and university degree do not have the job market value they used to have; the erosion (in Canada) of the safety net of social services; and increased numbers of single parent and blended families.

In 1960 in the United States, households with a father as sole breadwinner, mother as homemaker and dependent children was the norm for seventy percent of American families whereas in 1986 only seven percent of families reflected this model.[1] In twenty five years, the "traditional" family norm changed radically. It is not just that the configurations of many families are changing that is remarkable, but also the speed with which the change is occurring. Such a rapid and dramatic change cannot be accomplished in a painless and orderly way; there have been serious repercussions for children, the family and school.

For specific information on the conditions in which children are living, I have used various data sources. Following are some of their findings: almost 25 per cent of Ontario's current population were born outside of Canada;[2] in 1989, Children's Aid Societies received more than 15,000 reports of alleged child abuse and in 85 to 90 percent of the

---

[1] Jane Roland Martin, *The Schoolhome: Rethinking Schools for Changing Families*, (Cambridge, MA: Harvard University Press, 1992), 6.

[2] Ontario, Ministry of Community and Social Services, *Children First: Report of The Advisory Committee on Children's Services* (Toronto: Ministry of Commu-nity and Social Services, 1990), 13.

cases, the abuser was someone known to the child;[1] one million Canadian women are battered each year and 70 percent of women who seek help in shelters bring their children with them;[2] one in four girls and one in ten boys has been or is being sexually assaulted;[3] twenty one percent of children aged eighteen and under are classified as people living in low income situations;[4] in 1986, 14.5 percent of Canadian families were led by single parents;[5] two thirds of Canadian children are not sufficiently physically active for optimal growth and development;[6] and twenty five percent of Canadian children are considered overweight.[7]

These statistics suggest that childhood cannot be painted in rosy hues; for many children it is not an idyllic time. The picture that is emerging is one of fractures and conflicts; many homes are rife with physical and sexual abuse; many children are witnessing violence against their mothers; many children born outside of Canada have the usual problems of immigrants, such as language barriers and discrimination; and many children living with a single parent have problems of absentee fathers and the financial hardship of a broken home. Because the percentages are so substantial many children are experiencing the problems first-hand and other children are seeing the families of neighbours, cousins and school chums break apart. I was surprised at the number of children who were in traditional homes but expressed the fear that their parents might get divorced. These problems of the family touch children either first- or second-hand.

a. Disturbed and Vulnerable Children

Given the nature of childhood, children are dependent on others; as the family structure realigns they become vulnerable. They can easily slip through the cracks of the shifting structure. As children look for security, the search often leads them far away from home and often down some dangerous paths. Lucy McCormick Calkins, who has worked ex-

---

[1] Ibid., 22.

[2] Ibid., 23.

[3] Fran Newman, Children in Crisis: Support for Teachers and Parents (Toronto: Scholastic Canada, 1993), 4.

[4] Canadian Census, 1996 — People in Low Income. www.stacan.ca

[5] Canadian Census, 1996 — Families in Private Households by Family Structure, 1991 and 1996 Censuses. www.stacan.ca

[6] Physical Activity Benchmarks. www.activeliving.ca/cflri/prkids.html

[7] The Research File, reference no 97-07 www.activeliving.ca/cflri/prkids.html

tensively with children through her writing programs, examines the way that children's lives are caught in the upheaval. She warns that:

> These are hard times for children. The rate of child suicide has risen 300 percent in the last decade. Thirty thousand young people in West Virginia alone are alcoholics. In New York City every day, sixty thousand young people roam the streets, preferring the streets and what they offer to classrooms and what they offer. One in twenty infants in New York City is born with AIDS.[1]

Calkins is sketching a very grim scenario for many children's future. For the thousands of individual children who are in difficult straits their physical, emotional and intellectual needs are not met — a sense of hopelessness must pervade their everyday lives. As children live on the streets, there is no one besides the other street children to provide direction and support. They have lost the stability and guidance of the family and turn to substitutes: drugs, alcohol or prostitution. As special schools for children with specific physical and learning disabilities are closed, these children are integrated into the regular classrooms. In these larger classrooms they do not have the individual support they and their families require.

b. "Hurried" Children

The rapid increase in after-school programs that children attend is an example of the change in the family approach to leisure and the availability of parents to be with their children. Instead of playing ball hockey in the street, building snowmen in the front yard or helping prepare dinner, children are shuffled off for yet more direct instruction. The impact of these programs is twofold: children are pressured to perform yet again and families revolve around the children's programs. These after-school programs change the set-up and dynamics of the family. It is not just that children are not "home" that is altering childhood, it is also the increased pressure on children to attend and excel at programs such as ballet, hockey, swimming, math preparation and drama. David Elkind in *The Hurried Child* and *Miseducation: Preschoolers at Risk* suggests that children are being pushed to perform and excel at an early age; they are being forced to grow up quicker. He offers some reasons for these changes and notes some of the repercussions of attempts to accelerate development.

---

[1] Lucy McCormick Calkins, *Living Between the Lines*, (Portsmouth, NH: Heinemann, 1991), 23.

In many ways, hurrying was a direct result of the fact that, after adapting to such enormous social changes, parents had few resources left to cope with the unending needs of children. Expecting, indeed demanding, that children grow up fast was one way of avoiding the expenditure of energy that goes along with parenthood. The media both reflected and encouraged this "hurrying" with its abundant images of "adultified" children. And the schools cooperated by downward extensions of the curriculum and test-driven instruction.[1]

Many of the programs that children attend are not destructive in themselves, but combined with other factors they put tremendous pressure on children. And I wonder about the place of the family in the children's lives. Many mothers sadly lament, "I feel like a chauffeur," and this is not an appropriate role for our parents. When one considers the price, participation in these programs seems too high.

When parents justify their busy work schedules by suggesting that they spend "quality" time with their children, they are trying to apply a business model to a relational setting. They do not realize that the whole structure of the home is tremendously important; the values, love and stability cannot be neatly parcelled. Childhood is one continuous, large experience. A business model cannot be applied to the family — children are not debits and credits on a ledger sheet which can be shifted around to fit the timetable. Their needs cannot be reduced to a schedule which has slots for parent-child time. There must be more constancy in the relationship and the security of knowing that their parents are there for them.

c. *Childhood Poverty*

At the other end of the spectrum, childhood poverty persists and some would argue that it is on the increase as more single mothers head households. A shaky economy and single income families are causing many children to depend on the school for meals and adequate clothing. In Metropolitan Toronto, it is estimated that one in six children have used a food bank at least once in the past year and that twenty percent of the children in the Toronto Board of Education (junior kindergarten to grade eight) are undernourished.[2] The extreme contrasts between the hurried children and children wallowing in poverty is one cause for concern but even more importantly the fact that children are malnourished is alarming. When families cannot provide the basic of food, education

---

[1] David Elkind, *Miseducation: Preschoolers at Risk*, (New York: Alfred A. Knopf, 1987), xii.

[2] Al Sokol, "Food for Thought" *The Toronto Star*, Monday, December 6, 1993, C1.

becomes a secondary priority for children. "Lone-parent families with at least one child under 25" spend 26% less on food per person than all other households.[1]Society may have to reconsider its priorities. The question should not be "How can I teach hungry children?" but rather "Why do we have hungry children?". The latter question requires a societal response but the school has to be involved in developing a solution.

d. *The Daycare Situation*

Children in general are subjected to different pressures which previous generations did not have to face. One of the matters with which they must deal is attendance in daycare. Most young, single women join the workforce after completing their formal schooling and subsequently combine work and motherhood. In Canada, seventy four percent of mothers with children aged six to fifteen are in the paid labour force.[2] Since many women either cannot afford to or choose not to stay home with their children, they have to rely on outside programs for child-care. Daycare has presented both a solution and a problem.[3] Many daycare programs are caring, wonderful, stimulating, fun and informative for the children and they allow both parents to work outside of the home. However, some childcare programs are totally unsuitable for children because they are too regimented, poorly run or understaffed. To complicate the matter even further there are not nearly enough daycare spaces to meet the current and growing needs.

Not only must parents juggle workloads, then, they are also faced with the additional burden of finding good quality daycare, at reasonable rates in close proximity to their homes. For many parents, it is virtually impossible to meet these three criteria; they have to settle for what they can afford, regardless of the quality. And for single mothers the challenge is almost overwhelming. Finding care is a strenuous task, and then worrying about the quality creates additional tension for families already stressed to the limit. Regardless of the quality of the program, slotting daycare into an already overloaded timetable presents additional problem for children, families and schools.

---

[1] Statistics Canada, 1996 Census. Family Food Expenditure. www.statcan.ca

[2] Statistics Canada, "The Labour Force", December 1988, Table 10A,36-37, cited in *Children First: Report of the Advisory Committee on Children's Services*, 17.

[3] For a discussion of daycare see Max van Manen and Bas Levering, *Childhood's Secrets: Intimacy, Privacy and the Self Reconsidered* (New York: Teachers College, 1996), 153-159.

Older children often have to sacrifice their own childhood to care for younger siblings. I was astounded at the responsibility placed on primary students who had to care for younger siblings. They often perform many duties before they get to school and are then required to continue that care after school. Other children who attend daycare have a different set of problems. Some youngsters must leave their homes before seven o'clock because they have to travel to the centre — many children are starting their day at six o'clock and they most likely will not be home before seven in the evening. By the time the school bell rings at nine o'clock, these children have already been on the go for three hours. I recall many students falling asleep in class because they were exhausted. The family routines are often frenetic and certainly do not allow for adequate quiet time or opportunities for relational living. Having both parents in the workforce has many advantages but it is a mixed blessing. Both families and schools are feeling the effects of working parents.

e. Media in Children's Lives

Another factor that is changing the home arrangement is the increased role the mass media play in the life of families. The unrelenting barrage of images and values presented by the media makes "television ... the single most powerful communication tool in our world. It has profound effects on all of us, adults and children alike ...".[1] From pushing children to be consumers at an early age to demonstrating many violent acts, the media are influencing our children and the way the home functions.[2] For example, as children watch television or play video games endlessly this becomes almost their sole source of entertainment. It is not just that children are influenced by television; if they are watching TV they are not reading, talking to their parents, playing a game or learning a craft. Television and video games are changing the ways families interact and operate. Childhood is changing rapidly and the media are shaping family structures.

ii. Implications for Schools

When teachers walk into their classes and gather their students, they know that many children are hurting. As they survey their twenty five

---

[1] Jack Livesley and Frank Trotz, *The Penguin Guide to Children's TV and Video* (Toronto: Penguin Books, 1993), xiii.
[2] Max van Manen and Bas Levering, *Childhood's Secrets*, 140-141.

students many teachers wonder who in their class is being sexually abused, is living in an alcoholic home, has seen family members killed or tortured in a former homeland, has suffered discrimination based on skin colour or is living in poverty. Teachers cannot ignore the children's family backgrounds nor can they disregard the larger social context because these factors are part of their class structure and culture. They are dealing with students who are trying to cope with the changing family structure.

Children bring their lives into the class. The changes in the home structure affect the school. There were children from unstable and difficult homes in the past; but I would suggest that many children today are hurting in ways not previously seen. And even if the situation is the same, schools should not continue to disregard the needs of children! Certainly not all children are living in violent, poor, dysfunctional families, but many are. Teachers and society have often taken for granted the children's lives outside of school. I ask the question, "Who will care for the children?" not to be melodramatic but to raise the issue that many children need support, care and understanding. The impact on the school (and society) is great — what role will schools play?

The facts we have been considering about children's lives are frightening but I have not presented them for "shock" value; rather, I want to use them to gain a better understanding of the school population. They help us to see that there are no simple answers to questions such as why can't Johnny read and why is Sally dropping out of school. In order to understand the situation, one must probe beyond the surface. For schools to respond swiftly to demands placed on them and rethink their role in the lives of children, they must first understand where children are coming from.

a. *Highly Disruptive Behaviour*

First, because many children's home lives are not stable, they bring their problems to school; as a result many children are acting out in very disruptive, violent ways. Fran Newman, who has studied the changing lives of children, provides overwhelming evidence in her book *Children in Crisis* that many children are exhibiting inappropriate behaviour. She uses the example of increased angry outbursts to suggest that many more children are in distress.

> The evidence of anger has been around for as long as I have been teaching, but I am noticing it more. For some time, I have been noticing anger expressed in the playground and in the office discipline binder that con-

tains reports of children who have been sent in for fighting. I also hear it in teachers' voices as I walk by some classrooms.[1]

Newman notes that many of the children turn their anger, confusion, distrust, emptiness, and unhappiness inward but then it explodes in violent outbursts, often in the school. In my own primary classes I have seen children pull knives on other students, fight violently, form gangs, torment fellow students and threaten others. (And my class had fewer of these violent incidents than other classes!) These actions are far more than childhood pranks, they are indications that something is wrong. In addition to in-school disruptive behaviour, children are subjected to harassment by gangs. The Metropolitan Toronto Police Force has identified more than 180 youth gangs in the Toronto area: many carry guns and knives.[2]

Many of the children's needs have very little to do with the traditional role of school — academic achievement. Having taught refugee children I know that providing a safe environment and food were two top priorities. In a summer program with twenty children, eighteen were recent immigrants (or refugees) from the Far East (mainly Vietnam, Cambodia and Thailand). The children's behaviour was extreme — either they played very violent war games or they were very withdrawn. Quickly I realized that the proposed curriculum did not match their needs; these children needed lots of activity time, outdoor play, food, stories, music, group games and so on. At the end of the program, the children were calmer. They had learned a great deal about life in Canada, the joy of school and the comfort of the class; but they may not have learned the prescribed curriculum. Children with different needs place a tremendous stress on the system: financial support, additional personnel, flexible hours, additional extra-curricular activities, liaison with community services and so on. Schools, school boards and ministries of education have to redefine their role in children's lives and on this basis reallocate funds and personnel to meet these needs.

Even children who come from fairly "stable" homes are being influenced by the children who have trouble coping. As a teacher, I often spent most of my time dealing with "problem" children. (Whether this label is warranted is not the issue.) The concerns are twofold. First, as a teacher faced with a multitude of problems I often wondered about my competency in dealing with problems that far surpassed my meagre teacher training. I am not a trained social worker or counsellor and I often felt that the demands placed on me far outstripped my abilities.

---

[1] Fran Newman, *Children in Crisis: Support for Teachers and Parents,* 12.
[2] *The Toronto Star* Newspaper (Toronto: Oct. 26, 1998), A1.

The burden of reporting child abuse and neglect caused me, and many of my colleagues, a great deal of concern because we worried about the children and whether we were doing the right thing for them. I recall imploring the social worker to confirm that I was doing the "right" thing. The emotional and physical burden of the changed society takes its toll on the teaching force.

Secondly, I felt that many of the children were deprived of my attention because I had to focus time and energy on just a few children — the neediest or most vocal. My teaching suffered because I had to be attentive to many issues such as meetings with social workers or controlling violent behaviour and similarly the children's learning was affected because they either did not have my attention or the class was disrupted by other children acting out. The behaviour and life-style of our troubled youngsters impacts on the well-being of the other children.

b. *A Very Mixed School Community*

Since the home is changing significantly the experiences, values and mindset that children bring to school are no longer "traditional." Children are coming to school with diverse needs and values. Society has never been totally homogeneous but it seems more multicultural and mixed than ever before. Schools are being asked to make sense of such a wide range of values that it is probably impossible to have a common base from which to work.

Canada has always been a country of immigrants but the majority of newcomers in the past were from Western European countries, and many of their cultural ways could be integrated and absorbed more easily than the ways of the current influx of immigrants. For example, the thousands of Somalis who live in a suburb of Toronto come from a land that has a tribal culture and does not have a written language. The concept of school and its manifestation in our formal education institutions is "foreign" to this culture. As schools blend and merge many groups, it takes time for parents and schools to work out an inclusive, appropriate style.

An example from my own experience will illustrate the clash between cultures. I taught a young Arab boy whose family had fled their country. Not surprisingly, he had real problems adjusting to Canada; he was terrified to go out for recess because he was afraid that he would be kidnapped (which was commonplace in his homeland). It took months to figure out the reasons for his odd behaviour at recess, but this was only the first part of the problem. It became more complicated when I contacted the family to discuss the youngster's very anxious behaviour. The father would not speak to me because I was a woman, and his wife did not speak English. The school board did not have a translator so I could not speak to her even if she was courageous enough to come to see me. It took many, many meetings with the school principal (who was a male), the guidance counsellor (who was also male), the father and myself before we could identify the child's anxieties and then begin to address them. I knew that we were making "progress" with building a bridge between home and school when one day in the spring the young fellow's mother turned up at school and in very, very soft tones asked if she could talk to me. In halting English, she provided a great deal of background information about the youngster and the family and she expressed a willingness to work with the school. Her son slowly became more relaxed and part of the school culture, but the energy and time required were huge. And this was just one student in my class of thirty five.

At another school thirty six Afghan children turned up on the school doorstep the first day of school. The principal was overwhelmed because he could not communicate with the children (the school board did not have a translator), there was no place in the English As A Second Language classes for the children and their physical needs (food and clothing) were great. The time and energy required to sort out these problems were tremendous; as schools are presently arranged they simply cannot deal with all of these needs. The answer is not to limit or stop immigration, but rather to have partnerships across the various government ministries of health, welfare, skills, training and education. They must be aligned and have a plan of action to help the immigrants and the schools.

Contributing to our very mixed society are the images presented on television. Between action heroes, oversexed adolescents, discredited sports heroes and troubled youth, the role models are often of questionable character. For example, the images of school and children portrayed on television are very anti-establishment; teachers are seen as fools who should be humiliated and the prized students are those who are highly non-conformist. (I once said to a student teacher who was praising the television show *The Simpsons*, "Would you want Bart Simpson in your class?".) *South Park*, the latest example of this genre —sexist, racist, homophobic "comedy"— is shown on late night television yet children videotape it and then watch it at other times. In previous generations, children were seen on television as far more complacent and accommodating (which was also an unreal image). The role models on television influence children's behaviour in the class. I am not necessarily making a value judgment about television; rather, I am suggesting that because of the influence of television teachers are dealing with children who do not behave the way *they* did as children; as a result, they often just do not know how to respond.

c. *Social Agencies in Children's Lives*

Schools have expanded their role in the lives of many youth. Other social agencies are already playing a larger part in the lives of many children: wife and child battering are not twentieth century inventions but women's shelters are; and adolescent experiments with alcohol and drugs are not new but juvenile addiction centres are. These are just two examples of the fact that social intervention, by state agencies, is on the increase. Schools are a recognized institution within society; therefore, they along with the others are forced to play a larger role in social assistance. An example from my personal experience will be helpful. In 1988 in my class of 35 grade one students, there were eight children who were Catholic Children's Aid Society "cases"; their fathers (or stepfathers) had all been charged with child abuse. Social workers, case workers, guidance counsellors and social skills development workers were involved with the children. These workers were from different government ministries but the school seemed to be the agency that coordinated many of their functions. This interventionist/social services coordinating role for schools surpasses the traditional one.

The school, which is really the classroom teacher, was a constant presence in the children's lives and a central location for the organization of social intervention. It was surprising the way parents, usually the mothers, turned to the school for support and guidance. For these parents, the school was a recognized social institution within their community. Over the years I have had many, many parents turn up on the classroom doorstep with problems that were not strictly school-based. I would certainly refer the individuals to the correct social agency but I was the first point of contact. The issues that we, parents and teachers, had to deal with were far removed from traditional academics.

The above discussion is certainly not intended to imply that the situation is hopeless; my purpose is rather to place any consideration of education within a larger social framework. To balance the discussion, we must recognize the many benefits of modern society: decrease in childhood illnesses and mortality; increased options in entertainment — movies, videos, compact disc recordings; high quality medical care; well ventilated, comfortable, equipped and attractive schools; greater flexibility in society's norms; ease of transportation; more equitable treatment of men and women; and ready access to information. However, we must also recognize that society today has many problems; so that in attempting to transform the school system we must confront the difficulties of both school and society.

Additional Aspects of the Larger Societal Context

The earlier discussion of family structure provided a detailed illustration of the ways in which changes in one part of society affect other parts and in particular how such shifts require a new approach to schooling. Whether a completely new paradigm is needed is difficult to say, but the new educational system will require much more than just adding on, deleting or tinkering; a new way to think about schooling is necessary. In this section, I will identify four more issues from the larger social context that are now part of the playing field and are already influencing schools. Society is different; therefore, schools must be different too.

i. Public Scepticism Toward Institutions

Not only are schools required to take on many additional duties, they are also subject to the "sting of criticism" or apathy that is permeating society. We must recognize that the community is very wary of schools. Our credibility has been seriously tarnished. This is the context in which schools must try to regain public support and change their approach.

> The past fifteen years of educational theory and review have been marked by a nearly universal criticism of the effectiveness of schools. Conservatives and radicals alike have condemned public education from different sides, but have drawn the same blood.[1]

Currently, education is the subject of intense and unrelenting criticism. Fellow teachers, students, administrators, media reporters, parents and politicians are using a very harsh light to examine every aspect of the schooling process. I do not believe that schools are totally responsible for this current attitude, though they are certainly part of the problem; rather, we are caught in the tide of a larger movement of scepticism toward all institutions.

---

[1]Stanley Aronowitz and Henry Giroux, *Education Under Siege: The Conservative, Liberal and Radical Debate Over Schooling* (South Hadley, MA: Bergin and Garvery, 1985), x.

Many other institutions —churches, governments, the army, corporations— are also feeling the disapproval of society in general. Given the relatively high quality of most of our lives, this sentiment, on the surface, seems ironic; however, when the outer layer is pulled away, there seems to be some justification for this attitude. Modern technology and institutions were supposed to "improve" society; but the general sentiment expressed by Robert Bellah et al in *Habits of the Heart* and Stanley Aronowitz and Henry Giroux in *Postmodern Education* is that all is not well with our society. William Doll is worth quoting at length on this point because he offers some reasons for this sentiment.

> In many ways, the twentieth century has been a century of disillusionment, an age of uncertainty and anxiety. ... Kurt Godel showed that the foundation of mathematics could not be proven in terms of consistency and completeness ... the holocaust of two world wars has shown us that the sweet dreams of reason have not led us to a better, more just, or more moral society ...Finally, in this decade of the 1990s we are finding ourselves hounded by the economic, personal, political and social decisions made in the 1980s ... We face the twenty-first century, the third millennium, gripped by strong elements of doubt and fear.[1]

A lack of faith and often a sense of hopelessness is corroding our public spirit. Any suggestions for educational reform must be positioned within a disillusioned society. One of the questions that must be addressed is, "How can we restore faith in our school system?". In Chapter Two on setting goals and in Chapter Eight on the link between home and school, I include suggestions for collaborative activities between the school and the community as first steps in reestablishing a positive attitude towards schools.

ii. *Moving Away From Determinacy*

For a long time, there was a belief in a specific end point for which schools (and society) should strive; the list of great books to be read, the moral character to be sought after and the necessary mathematical skills were all delineated. This vision shaped the way schools conducted themselves; the rigid program of the "Gray Book" that guided Ontario education symbolized that attitude.[2] This uncompromising, in-

---

[1] William Doll, *A Post-Modern Perspective on Curriculum* (New York: Teachers College Press, 1993), 60.

[2] Ontario Ministry of Education, *Programme of Studies for Grades 1 to 6 of the Public and Separate Schools* (Toronto: Ministry of Education, 1960).

flexible, narrow approach to personhood made schooling for many students a hated experience and limited in value. As the earlier discussion of our changing society revealed, fixed goals and a fixed content no longer exist (if they ever did), and both school and society must accommodate constant change. Our postmodernism society is moving away from the notion of determinacy thus allowing schools to do the same. This in turn may lead to the abandonment of the authoritarian structure that was the hallmark of "good" schooling. The system of schooling that is required will be one that is negotiated not predetermined, generative not static.

A complex changing society requires a school system that is responsive and adaptable. What is needed in schools cannot be worked out in academic halls — the trickle down approach to educational reform has a way of stunting instead of nourishing. Nor can goals of education be established by a group of bureaucrats in government using funding formulas and a bottom-line mentality. Postmodern thought has taken an anti-theory stance, which I think leaves a void; theory can and must have a place in school. As an alternative I would suggest that theory should be developed from practice, thus making theory more accessible, local, useful and dynamic.

> This shift in emphasis in the relationship between theory and practice, where theory no longer precedes practice and where practice is no longer the handmaiden to theory, is not to negate theory or to drive an inseparable wedge between the two. Nor is it to "practicalize" theory. Rather, it is to ground theory in and develop it from practice. It is to assume, as Dewey did, that "ises" can be transformed into "oughts."[1]

To have this type of relationship between theory and practice it is essential to have practitioners study theory and write about schools. And in these writings there must be more than "tight" arguments; there must be narrative, examples, critical analysis, dialogue with others, a sharing of personal experiences and insights which all lead to an articulation of the theory. This kind of theorizing does not have a predetermined end point because the story is still being developed; however, some structure is established. In Chapter Three I will outline goals for education that are complex and inclusive, goals that include both individual development and social responsibility. These goals are flexible, but offer some direction.

---

[1] William Doll, *A Post-Modern Perspective on Curriculum*, 162.

iii. *Caring for More than the Mind*

When I ask who will care for the children, I mean not only their intellectual development but also their physical and emotional well-being. In order for schools to provide and offer this kind of care and support, I see them changing in numerous respects. They have to be humane places where children feel safe; the institutional attitude that prizes efficiency does not allow or encourage a caring attitude.

Throughout society, the harshness of institutions is now seen as detrimental whereas before it was thought to build character. For example, hospitals are no longer so austere, prisons include counselling and education programs, factories value preventive medicine and ergonomic practices and churches are more inclusive and inviting. Schools have moved along in this direction too; buildings are carpeted, brightly painted and so on. Nevertheless, the changes must be even more substantial because of the societal developments. Some of the changes that I see are a larger place for the arts in the curriculum, accepting different ways of knowing and doing, increased opportunities for relational living and an integration of the body and mind in learning. In Chapters Four, Six and Seven I will propose a curriculum that allows for many different approaches to growth; I will emphasize that children must feel part of the community and the curriculum must be flexible, interactive and meaningful.

iv. *Increased Grassroots Involvement*

As society looked to schools to provide the truth, institutions, in general, were seen to be the road to enlightenment. But as William Doll has pointed out, this has not happened. To move beyond our present phase of disillusionment, the next step must be an increase in local and individual efforts. There are many examples of individuals or small groups taking control of their own future. For example, in the last Canadian election there was an increase in the number of smaller, more personal political parties; groups such as MADD (Mothers Against Drunk Driving) have lobbied the government for new legislation; and the United Church has gone through a consultative process with its members on the issue of homosexual and lesbian ministers.

These groups represent a new way of thinking about power and politics. Individuals are not so inclined to relinquish their power or voice to an inaccessible, distant institution — they want to raise their concerns and have them addressed. Schools are seeing parent groups and student organizations crop up which want to be involved in decision making. For example, every school in Ontario has established a School Advisory Council. On the whole, such groups will help to make the school system less authoritarian and distant. People are less willing today to trust blindly either an institution or a leader — they want to be part of the process. In Chapter Eight I will discuss ways for the school and the community to form partnerships; there must be a mechanism to accommodate and address individual and community needs.

While it is clear that there are changes in society, it is often quite difficult to determine which ones are profound and whether they are beneficial or problematic. Richard Rorty's discussion of the contingency of community is helpful in this regard. He says that the early Christians, or Isaac Newton or the Romantic poets did not know at the time the full impact of their discoveries and contributions. "...[B]ut *we* now know these things, for we latecomers can tell the kind of story of progress which those who are actually making progress cannot. ... we have a clear sense of the product which the use of those tools produced. The product is *us* — our conscience, our culture, our form of life..."[1] Although we cannot judge the exact effects of changes in society, we can recognize that the changing world has a strong influence on children's value system and life style; and so we must cease to approach schooling as if it were a self-contained enterprise, without societal connections.

The Current Societal Conception of Schooling

Before looking at goals and strategies for schools, it is necessary to examine the current status of our schools in our society. A significant part of the societal context of schools is the conception of schooling that social members share. We cannot pretend that we will have the opportunity to "erase the past" and start off with a fresh canvas to paint the portrait of our schools. Even if such a chance should present itself, there would be significant similarities between the present and the proposed direction for schooling because there are "enduring interests" (John Dewey) and "tentative frameworks" (Charles Taylor). We have inherited an institution and by examining its currently accepted role we will understand it more fully, which will help in considering its direction.

i. *Schooling as Synonymous with Education*

Modern society is very complex! John Dewey recognized that as society became more complex, it was impossible for the young to learn all they

---

[1] Richard Rorty, *Contingency, Irony and Solidarity*, (Cambridge, MA: Cambridge University Press, 1989), 55, 56.

needed to know just by watching their parents or "by direct sharing in the pursuits of grown-ups ... except in the case of the less advanced occupations."[1] As parents and the public perceived the need for children to have formal instruction, the number of schools increased rapidly. In the nineteenth century there was a great variety of schools; from small schools for young women in private homes to community funded schools, the diversity was immense. "The anarchy had become proverbial: virtually no two schools were alike; facilities were haphazard at best; the teachers untrained, pupils of all ages (and both sexes) generally were jumbled together and, worse still, each attended according to necessity or whim."[2] When Egerton Ryerson in one stroke standardized the curriculum by prescribing the Irish school readers in 1844 and later in 1871 "when the first compulsory attendance clause appeared in the Ontario School Act,"[3] a long chain of events that led to school becoming equated with education was set in motion.

One of the consequences of standardizing the curriculum by government edict was that certain attitudes towards education slowly took root: as Ivan Illich has pointed out, education and schooling became synonymous. The education that parents could provide was not recognized as the official curriculum. Jane Roland Martin notes that "it is a fact too seldom remembered that school and home are partners in the education of a nation's young."[4] As children moved into schools, learning became more institutionalized. And once it was institutionalized, conformity set in and from there it was only a small step for the institution to develop a strong sense of ownership of that product — education. Parents prepare the students for school and help with homework, but schools are the site of knowledge; the knowledge that is valuable is *school-based*. As a result of this attitude, there is a gulf between the school and its surrounding community; families for the most part are excluded from the actual school; textbooks become the source of knowledge; and children are expected to behave in an unnatural style. Alternative ways of doing things and materials other than the official textbooks are unacceptable. Many examples of this institutionalization of knowledge exist: many children know a great deal about crafts, computers, hockey and cooking but there is no place in the school for that

---

[1] John Dewey, *Democracy and Education: An Introduction to the Philosophy of Education* (New York: The Free Press, 1916), 8.

[2] Susan Houston and Alison Prentice, *Schooling and Scholars in Nineteenth-Century Ontario* (Toronto: University of Toronto Press, 1988), 237.

[3] Bruce Curtis, *Building the Educational State: Canada West, 1836-1871* (London: The Althouse Press, 1988), 184.

[4] Jane Roland Martin, *The Schoolhome: Rethinking Schools for Changing Families*, 6.

knowledge; young children's natural curiosity is seen as a problem because it disrupts the official curriculum; children are often confined to uncomfortable desks for long periods of time; and children's reading material is prescribed. As the school's influence spread, it became the only place to acquire knowledge and, quite subtly, the attitude took hold that once students emerge from school, they are fully formed and educated.

This first characteristic of modern schooling illustrates the way that education is reduced to school knowledge. On many levels, I endorse having a somewhat standard approach to schooling, but I feel that there are two problems with this situation. First, conformity leads to schools having exclusive ownership of children's education, whereas everyone in the community should feel responsible for children's education. As a result the link between home and school is weakened. Secondly, when education is institutionalized what is defined as knowledge is narrow. Many of the qualities and skills that are part of the home are not seen as education. In the next section I will examine this attitude towards knowledge in more detail.

ii. *A Narrow Concept of Education*

Once schools take ownership of education (or are given it or a combination of the two), this entitles them to dictate what is considered knowledge. Given this tremendous authority, there should be a great deal of thoughtfulness about this responsibility and power. Because the process has been fairly gradual, I am not sure that many educators recognize the control in their hands. From my viewpoint, the whole conception of what constitutes education is narrow — efficiency of operation seems to take precedence over diversity and individual interests. For example, a child who is a wonderful story teller could be a great addition to the class but this skill of oral story telling is not prized by our school system. The curriculum and daily activities are reduced to a prescribed series of objectives. Lessons are supposed to be straightforward transmission of knowledge which in itself can be mechanistic. School days are highly regimented, curriculum topics are limited and most learning is expected to occur within the class. The official curriculum which is a testable quantity equals education. The move towards so-called experiential teaching/ learning, which is seen as a hallmark in education, is not really far removed from traditional lecture style; often teachers pretend that children are discovering and constructing their knowledge but they have pre-set the materials and experiences so the learning is still controlled by them. William Doll notes that "in such a methodology, ends are external to the process; there is not a dynamic between theory and fact, imagination and practicality; whatever is true, factual, or real is discovered, not created."[1] A cursory glance through primary readers, spellers, and math textbooks clearly illustrates this epistemological framework for curriculum. For example, math textbooks and workbooks do not strive to work with children in discovering the beauty of math, its coherence and logic or its connections to the real world; they are usually page after page of skill and drill.

David Elkind succinctly sums up the attitude of the modern school when he observes that schooling or education is seen as a race with "a starting point and a finishing line"[2] — a self-contained, definable quantity. Even the word curriculum comes from the verb currere and literally means "the course to be run."[3] The consequences of this philosophy of education are: knowledge is viewed as a definite quantity to be acquired through reason; teachers are the controlling force in the class; and student behaviour has to be passive. Modern schools have a particular view of knowledge which is consistent with the current scientific paradigm; once again, schools reflect the surrounding culture.

Recognizing this second characteristic of modern schooling suggests that the need for wider goals for school. They must relate to head, heart and hand and cannot be limited to testable items. As I will argue at length later, schools must help children develop a way of life. School curriculum must include a greater emphasis on personal development and social responsibility — knowledge of certain facts and cognitive skills is not enough.

iii. *Healers of Society's Woes*

Not only are schools seen as the "fountain of knowledge," they have also acquired the unenviable task of being viewed as the "healers of society's woes." A headline in the *Globe and Mail* newspaper, "Schools Must Respond To Additional Needs,"[4] is typical of the attitude towards schools. They are expected to solve many of society's problems by establishing or re-enforcing certain attitudes. Although schools are part of society, grow out of and reflect the given culture, a certain mystique has grown up around the capacity of schools to resolve inequities. As an experienced teacher and avid reader of newspapers and magazines, I note that the public regularly turns to the schools to

---

[1] William Doll, *A Post-Modern Perspective on Curriculum*, 30.

[2] David Elkind, *Miseducation: Preschoolers At Risk*, 83.

[3] William Doll, *A Post-Modern Perspective on Curriculum*, 126.

[4] *Globe and Mail Newspaper* (Toronto: November 3, 1993), A24.

solve its problems. It is naive to think of schools as an oasis amid society's problems but there are such high hopes that schools alone can solve problems of racism, sexism, prejudice and all other societal problems. For example, adding curriculum courses on multiculturalism is seen to be a crucially important step in the making our society more inclusive. An individual course will not root out discrimination in society; it may help to ease the collective conscience and be one step but it will not solve the problem. "[S]ociety is one of the major realities that schools must take into account, and ... school and societal reform must go hand in hand if significant improvement is to be achieved."[1] I certainly feel that schools can make a difference but they cannot do it all, on their own.

A consequence of this hopeful attitude is that a very heavy burden has been placed on schools; they are supposed to level the playing field. The expectations for schools are tremendous; for example, business leaders regularly complain about the skills and attitudes of their employees, failing to realize that they may have a measure of responsibility in helping their workers learn and grow. The approach to social problems is consistent with the school's view of knowledge; both are seen as items that can be parcelled out and universally acquired through a particular method.

This final characteristic illustrates the belief in our society that schools have tremendous power. We should capitalize on this but must also recognize that it is an inflated impression of the school's capabilities. Schools cannot do it all; they cannot forge a course that is far removed from society nor can they solve the problems that society is unwilling to tackle. Partnership within the school and without is key to the school system.

In short, the three features that I have identified are: schooling has become synonymous with education; the view of knowledge espoused by schools is narrow, scientistic and rationalistic; and schools are seen as the mechanism for reducing the inequities in society. As a result of these perceptions, schools are seen as important institutions within society with a very large mandate. In some instances, schools have set out consciously to develop this particular role and in other cases they have been a victim of their own success. Society came to expect more and more from them because they were seen to be doing a "good job."

---

[1] Clive Beck, *Better Schools: A Values Perspective* (New York: The Falmer Press, 1990), vii.

Conclusion

The preceding discussion has set the stage for the development of my approach to primary education. Some of the themes that will be developed in later chapters have been identified. First, by recognizing some major factors such as the shifting family structure and public scepticism toward institutions I have shown that society is changing, requiring a much more comprehensive and flexible approach to schooling. Secondly, the extremely broad mandate of the schools is one which they cannot possibly fulfil on their own, and accordingly they must be in partnership with other groups. Finally, my intention throughout this book, which is already becoming apparent, is to emphasize the need for care and concern for students as individual people. The study of childhood is not a "descriptive science"[1] that can be charted, objectified and universalized — we are dealing with individual people, on their journey through life. Against this background, we can now turn to the framework and goals of education.

---

1 Robert Dearden, *The Philosophy of Primary Education: An Introduction* (London: Routledge and Kegan Paul, 1968), 27.

Chapter Two

A Model for Schooling

Significant educational improvement of schooling, not mere tinkering, requires that we focus on entire schools, not just teachers or principals or curriculum or organization or school-community relations but all of these and more.[1]

John Goodlad

Having been an educator for many years, I can readily identify many strengths of the school system. Unfortunately, I can also rapidly point out many of its shortcomings. We must resist the temptation to list the strengths and weaknesses on a chart with a view to "fixing-up" the problem areas. Although problems such as poor attitudes of some teachers, mathematics instruction often unrelated to children's lives, inferior language arts programs and the unequal distribution of resources are all valid concerns, the problem is more basic. The overriding problem is lack of a comprehensive philosophy and framework for schooling, including a clear definition of the goals for education and a conception of how the "bits and pieces" fit together. The absence of a theory that is understood, accessible and agreed upon by students, parents and teachers, the absence of a clear, well thought out direction, frustrates and sidetracks even the most promising efforts to reform the system.

In this chapter, I describe a general model for education. I argue that the proposed approach in Ontario is fractured and contradictory. I offer as an alternative a holistic model for schooling, one that provides direction and coherence. In presenting a "three dimensional" model, I show how the many facets of the education process are interconnected. In the second part of the chapter, I show that the depth and breadth of my model can accommodate many theories, practices and groups. I also suggest the need for the various groups of society to have a common language, common experiences and shared hope and trust in the institution of schooling.

---

[1] John Goodlad, *A Place Called School: Prospects for the Future* (New York: McGraw- Hill, 1984), xvi.

Outlining a Model for Schooling

Any proposal for educational reform must take into account the societal context outlined in Chapter One. Any attempt to return to previous systems foolishly ignores current realities. The alternative of trying to predict the skills students will need for the twenty first century is also inadequate because it focuses exclusively on curriculum, overlooks other contextual factors and disregards the fact that we cannot accurately predict what children will need. Nel Noddings argues against the return to the emphasis on methods and objectives, stating that our aims must be larger and more inclusive.

> But if the school has one main goal, a goal that guides the establishment and priority of all others, it should be to promote the growth of students as healthy, competent, moral people. This is a huge task to which all others are properly subordinated. We cannot ignore our children —their purposes, anxieties, and relationships— in the service of making them more competent in academic skills. My position is not anti-intellectual. It is a matter of setting priorities. Intellectual development is important, but it cannot be the first priority of schools.[1]

The challenge is to break out of the traditional mode by thinking about education in a different way. The first step is to develop a "model" or framework.

i. Why a Model for Schooling?

A model for education provides both a foundation and a framework for schooling. As a foundation, it anchors the structure to "weather the storms," provides a solid base upon which to build and offers direction. The framework helps the "bits and pieces" fit together, allows the process to remain focused and helps students, parents and teachers understand the purpose of schools. When the various agendas and goals do not mesh, the framework becomes wobbly, unstable and can be unduly influenced by the latest fad or gimmick.

Schools have taken on so many responsibilities that present philosophy and practice embrace a diverse and confusing "hodgepodge" of goals, including traditional ones from nineteenth century schools such as fluent oral reading and neat handwriting, as well as highly current goals such as drug and AIDS awareness and on-site daycare. What is

---

[1] Nel Noddings, *The Challenge to Care in Schools: An Alternative Approach to Education* (New York: Teachers College Press, 1992), 10.

needed is a framework for education which defines the whole so we can determine which tasks should be included, and how more can be accomplished through synergy between various school activities. "Over the years, we have assumed small, discrete additions to our responsibilities ... not one of those responsibilities is backbreaking in itself, but collectively they present an enormous burden that is perhaps many times greater than we are designed for or are capable of sustaining."[1]

Several models of education have been proposed in Ontario in recent years, but in my view they have all been inadequate. For example, while *The Formative Years*, an Ontario Ministry of Education statement for primary education, offered a philosophy that was child-centered and recognized how children learn, it did not address ways to translate its philosophy into practice. Its companion document, *Education in the Primary and Junior Division*, did not provide adequate detail for the curriculum or consider contextual factors such as the learning environment of the class. In an attempt to overcome these problems, a new working document appeared: *The Common Curriculum*. However, it did exactly what I caution against; it tried to "fix-up" the problem areas without seeing how the bits and pieces fit together. It presented a highly fractured philosophy. Jane Roland Martin calls this approach "curriculum restoration."[2]

The Introduction and Rationale of *The Common Curriculum* outlined a philosophy of schooling that was a tangle of conflicting theories, assumptions and goals. The proposed philosophy included a concern for "outcomes" which were "observable/measurable knowledge, skills, and values";[3] a plea to adopt a holistic approach which emphasized connections and relationships; a commitment to collaborative planning for local needs; and a demand for accountability.[4] It was impossible to reconcile outcomes, holism, local needs and accountability in one philosophy when there was no recognition that only *degrees* of holism, *degrees* of local planning and so on can be accommodated. Holism and outcomes based education are two very different philosophies; they involve two different views of the role of schooling and two different conceptions of the person. It is impossible to emphasize the individual's needs and

---

[1] Roland Barth, *Improving Schools from Within: Teachers, Parents, and Principals Can Make the Difference* (San Francisco: Jossey-Bass, 1990), 7.

[2] Jane Roland Martin, *The Schoolhome: Rethinking Schools for Changing Families* (Cambridge, MA: Harvard University Press, 1992), 60.

[3] Ontario, Ministry of Education, *The Common Curriculum* (Toronto, 1993), 1.

[4] *Ibid.*, 1-3.

still have the goal of excellence as defined and measured by an external standard. The second objective undermines the first.

The latest "reform" curriculum documents, in Ontario, the *Ontario Curriculum, Grades 1-8* (subject specific), outline expectations for each grade. Although it is much briefer than the *Common Curriculum*, and appears to be simpler, it is vague. The intent was to make the curriculum more rigorous; themes/topics/skills have been pushed downward creating a domino effect. For example, topics that were previously included in the middle grades are suddenly part of the primary curriculum. Young children are expected to know mapping skills and directions. The lack of resource materials and the difficulty of some of the concepts have created havoc in the schools. In addition, teachers are required to complete a standard provincial report card. Most are not opposed to a standard form of reporting yet the categories and rubrics are not appropriate.

A solid philosophy or model of education must be well thought out; it must recognize the complexity of the schooling process and the symbiotic relationship between schools and society. The authors of the *Common Curriculum* and the *Ontario Curriculum, Grades 1-8* took radically different approaches, the former simply listed everyone's agenda while the later focused heavily on skills. Neither recognized the complexity of the school process. A philosophy of education must start with a great deal of soul searching — what do we want for our children, how do children learn, what do children need, what role should schools play, how has society changed, what are our traditions and how can we best meet our needs. The answers to these challenging questions begin to shape our philosophy and direct our efforts. Simply recognizing that these questions exist is a critical step.

ii. *A Three Dimensional Model for Schooling*

Central to my philosophy of education is the belief that all parts of the theory and practice of schooling are interconnected; I often refer to my theory of education as "holistic." In my view, John Miller's definition of holism identifies the essence of the concept, recognizing connections on many levels.

> The focus of holistic education is on relationships — the relationship between linear thinking and intuition, the relationship between mind and body, the relationships between various domains of knowledge, the relationship between the individual and community, and the relationship between self and Self. In the holistic curriculum the student examines these

> relationships so that he/she gains both an awareness of them and the
> skills necessary to transform the relationships where it is appropriate.[1]

From Miller's definition, we begin to sense the inter-connectedness of
the entire process; his understanding suggests a move from subject integration to conceptualizing the connectedness within life. The system of
education that I visualize is one that is interconnected, within itself
and with the larger society.

Most theories of education are closed; they tend to use either a defined two dimensional matrix or a hierarchical model. In a matrix
model, one axis is usually assigned to curriculum and the other to the
teacher's role. For example, in mathematics instruction one point on the
curriculum line would be computation and one point on the teacher's line
would be effective strategies to increase speed and accuracy in number
skills.[2] Although this theory is not explicit it is implied in the
teacher's manual by headings such as "review," "quick tips," or "the
daily challenge." Jane Roland Martin refers to John Goodlad who noted
that "our schools teach addition, subtraction, multiplication, division,
fractions, decimals, percentages, money measurement year after year ...
[and] the common bonds relating each topic to the preceding ones [are]
rarely revealed."[3] The teacher defines his or her role in terms of curriculum objectives, ignoring other factors such as the children's interests
and needs, contextual factors of the community, the teacher's special
talents and so on. In this model, "mistakes, disruptions, perturbations ...
[are] disruptive qualities"[4] rather than issues that must be addressed.

The common alternative is a hierarchical model where the process
is outlined in a sequential and lock-step manner. Each subject has a hierarchy of skills. This system is often referred to as the "shopping
mall" approach.[5] Each subject area focuses on its content and skills in
isolation. For example, in language arts instruction readiness skills are

---

[1] John Miller, *The Holistic Curriculum* (Toronto, OISE Press, 1988),3.

[2] For an example of this approach to curriculum see *Holt Mathematics System,
Book 1* (Toronto: Holt, Rinehart and Winston, 1980).

[3] Jane Roland Martin, *The Schoolhome: Rethinking Schools for Changing Families*,
59.

[4] William Doll, *A Post-Modern Perspective on Curriculum* (New York: Teachers
College Press, 1993), 14.

[5] Although Sara Lawrence Lightfoot, *The Good High School* (New York: Basic
Books, 1983) was writing about high schools her critique of the typical high
school has relevance for elementary education because many schools have ro-
tary systems, timetable driven schooling and ability grouping.

seen to be a critical preliminary step to learning to read and therefore must be mastered first; the students (and teacher) then move from decoding simple words, to reading simple sentences and so on. The basal reading approach to language learning is a good example of this hierarchical model.[1] Students would proceed through a similar format for mathematics, social studies and so on. At some point all of the subjects or building blocks are supposed to come together. This model ignores the children's interests, the connections between subject areas and the learning environment of the class.

In both of the above models there tends to be a focus on a single aspect of education, with the neglect of crucial components of learning situations. As a result, even the best efforts of both teachers and students often have little positive result, and all the potential advantages of a more holistic, synergistic educational approach are lost. For example, if children do not experience the satisfaction of reading simple stories on a regular basis, they may lack the motivation and understanding required to be successful readers. Furthermore, the failure of these models often passes unnoticed: "educators have been so busy 'teaching' and 'remediating' children according to their preconceived theories and notions that they have not paused to document how and what children actually learn ...". [2]

For effective education, a three dimensional model of schooling is needed. It is useful to be able to visualize such a model in concrete terms. The object that perhaps most resembles my system is a cube — along the six faces there are "points," each representing a different aspect of education.[3] This model recognizes the multiplicity of elements within schooling; acknowledges the interconnections among the various factors; and suggests that there must be a unity to the whole process. The three dimensional model requires all parts to fit together; since one aspect cannot take precedence, we must continuously examine the way each part meshes with and strengthens the whole. The key word for the model is coherence. It stresses unity of purpose and process. Unlike our present system, which is a patchwork of goals and processes, this model represents education as a complex, interwoven process.

---

[1] For a good description and critique of the basal reading approach to language learning see Constance Weaver, *Understanding Whole Language: From Principles to Practice* (Portsmouth, NH: Heinemann, 1990), 54-62.

[2] Constance Weaver, *Understanding Whole Language*, 55.

[3] Some readers may wonder why I chose a cube shape rather than a ball. The danger in a ball shape is that many lines would converge at the poles. These two points would then become "special" and have an elevated status. Granted some points/factors are more influential, I do not think it wise to choose a shape predisposed to this tendency.

Along the lines and faces of the cube there are many points. Some points connect to many others and some to just a few. There are no separate compartments in schooling. For example, the prescribed curriculum affects the role of the teacher which affects student well-being which affects the community's view of the school and so on. In a three dimensional model of schooling many factors are recognized as being influential, and the "big picture" of schooling is the background for specific suggestions.

In a two dimensional model there is not enough potential to accommodate the many factors of school; however, a three dimensional model has much more latitude, depth and breadth. "The primary challenge ... is not to bring process to closure (to produce a 'perfect' product) but to direct the transformations in such a manner that the becomingness of process is maintained."[1] Some of the points which will be part of my model are: children's well-being, language arts skills, the children's interest in literature, mathematics skills, the relevance of mathematics in the children's lives, the texts and materials available, the place of values education, the impact of computers, evaluation procedures, accommodation of special needs students, the interests of minority students, access to family and student counselling programs, the teachers' well-being, the quality and availability of professional development programs, the role of administrators, the relationship between teachers and administrators, the degree of site-based management, the physical lay-out of the class and school, the financial status of the school and community, the community's relationship with the school, the history and culture of the neighbouring community, the impact of organized daycare, links with community agencies and services, dialogue with the business community, partnerships with universities and the sense of community in the class and school. This model recognizes that one component cannot be changed without affecting other components.

> Turning our gaze from the 'big' economic picture to the local level, it brings into sharp relief individual classrooms. Once the quality of life in school commands the foreground, questions arise about the classroom climate, school routines and rituals, relationships between teachers and children and among the children themselves, the teacher's modes of teaching and the children's ways of learning. And with this refocusing of attention comes a reorienting of practice.[2]

---

[1] William Doll, *A Post-Modern Perspective on Curriculum*, 15.

[2] Jane Roland Martin, *The Schoolhome: Rethinking Schools for Changing Families*, 42.

A three dimensional model has many advantages: each issue can be seen from many perspectives; many issues can be accommodated; there is a place for both general and specific issues; it allows for partnerships; it is not static, two points previously not connected can be connected in the future; it is not lock-step; and it clearly illustrates that simplistic answers concerning schools are wholly inadequate. It encourages all parties to *keep the conversation going* because there are endless possibilities for connections. This model does not discard all of the positive features of schooling but rather tries to capitalize on them by placing them in a position to make connections with other needy areas and recognizing their place in the larger context.

A three dimensional model is not as neat and tidy as others; it is very challenging to keep in mind the big picture of education. Under this model change requires collaboration, which traditionally has not been the approach to education. New processes and procedures must be established. (Some would see this as problematic whereas I believe it is a strength of the model.) Because suggestions for change require a great deal of attention to implications, change will come about slowly. Quick fixes, fads, and a little tinkering here and there have no place in this system. (Again, I perceive this as a benefit whereas other might see it as a deficiency.)

The following example will illustrate the complexity of my model and the interconnections within it. Evaluation is often seen as serving just one narrow purpose, namely providing exact information on children's progress in the program. However, using the three dimensional model, evaluation would be seen from the following perspectives: it must be connected to content and pedagogy (curriculum); it must improve student learning (child); it must be consistent with overall school aims (philosophy); it must give parents useful information (parents); and it must provide teachers and administrators with data for reflection (educators). This example, simple as it may be, illustrates the notion that no aspect can stand on its own. And this sense of connection can be applied to every aspect of education.

When conceptualizing the structure of schools I visualize a system that is strong yet flexible, a system that does not break easily but is not so strong that it becomes impenetrable. In concrete terms, we might think of it as a natural fibre, something from the earth; a material that can take different shapes but does not lose its own properties. It can be entwined with other substances; it is self-generating, not restricted to a finite amount. Being built with natural fibres, I see the structure as alive, not petrified or dead; it has a capacity for continuous renewal, not just self-perpetuation.

The notion of coherence and unity immediately triggers fears that a particular model will be exclusive, eliminating certain ideas or groups. However, the model is able to accommodate many different opinions (but not all); there will not be unanimity on all issues but rather diversity and healthy dialogue. It is unfortunate that much philosophical discussion revolves around analyses of dichotomies and arguments for or against one or the other exclusive position. In life we do not follow one path exclusively, but tend to borrow a little from many positions; and given that education is rooted in society, it must draw on a range of positions within society. My model of education draws on Michael Walzer's insight that "we must agree on a deeper level on the rough contours of a way of life and a view of the world."[1] At the core of my model is a broad vision of human well-being and the educated person (which is discussed in detail in Chapter Three). However, many factors and opinions can be accommodated within that vision.

Further General Features of the Model

Conceptualizing schooling as a three dimensional object, with points interconnecting, is central to my philosophy of education; making connections between the various components is essential to my vision of schooling. However, this does not simply happen. I have identified four general principles which will help implement the model. In later chapters I will present more specific implementation principles and procedures.

i. Inclusion of Many Theories, Practices and People

The approach to education for our present society cannot be narrow in focus because communities, as illustrated in Chapter One, are highly mixed and have varying needs. For any philosophy of education to be viable it must be attentive to this situation. In the previous chapter I noted three characteristics of modern schooling: a narrow concept of knowledge, schooling equated with education and schools as healers of society's woes. My model is intended to help the philosophy move beyond these limitations by including other theories, people and practices.

The overarching philosophy that has guided society is being questioned, to a certain degree, under postmodern influences. As William

---

[1] Michael Walzer, "A Critique of Philosophical Conversation," in *Hermeneutics and Critical Theory in Ethics and Politics*, ed. Michael Kelly (Cambridge, MA: The MIT Press, 1989), 191.

Doll notes, the changes are evident in "art, literature, mathematics, philosophy, political theory, science, and theology."[1] In education the impact is seen in the inclusion of whole language theory and practice, media literacy programs and co-operative learning techniques. Even though I find some postmodern thought too negative and pessimistic, it contains many insights and is certainly influencing present society. The "changes [are] questioning ... the basic epistemological and metaphysical assumptions."[2] How these changes will affect schooling is not entirely clear but any new model for schooling must not be built on traditional, that is "modernist," views. As Doll puts it, "the linear, sequential, easily quantifiable ordering system dominating education today —one focusing on clear beginnings and definite endings— could give way to a more complex, pluralistic, unpredictable system or network."[3] Hence, my approach to schooling does not duplicate previous systems, but rather carves out a new direction in light of these changes in culture and society.

When I was a student the model for schooling was highly linear. The scientific method, learning by rote and the teacher as expert were the three principles of that model. There was a consistent, uncompromising message from schools. Like many others I did not question the demand for duty, obedience, respect and worldview conformity that was expected of us. Schools have certainly evolved from that narrow mindset but the change has not gone far enough. Even at the highest levels of educational research there is still a tendency to look for a single theory as the answer to all problems. To make schooling consistent with changes in thought and society other theories must be included. Conversation is a cornerstone of my proposed philosophy, and the inclusion of others in the dialogue will lead to a richer, more complex theory. A three dimensional model can accommodate diverging views because it has breadth and depth; it allows for connections between various theories. Theories such as David Hunt's theory of personal renewal, which emphasizes "rejuvenation," introspection and following one's personal beliefs and encourages every teacher to be an "expert"[4] can be accommodated alongside Dewey's theory which emphasizes experimentation, social life and child-centered strategies. In a two dimensional model there is not enough latitude for these connections because a

---

[1] William Doll, *A Post-Modern Perspective on Curriculum*, 3.

[2] *Ibid.*, 3.

[3] *Ibid.*, 3.

[4] See David Hunt, *Beginning With Ourselves: In Practice, Theory and Human Affairs* (Toronto: OISE Press, 1987), 37-52.

polarity between positions forms; in a three dimensional model, although there is a tension between positions, there is possibility for some connection between them.

In a closed or narrow model the curriculum is highly regimented, there is only one way of working which implies there is only one way of knowing. For a long time the metatheory of reason and its accompanying scientific procedures governed schooling. For example, basal readers outlined a highly "scientific" approach to reading and this became the way of knowing and doing. As adults we do not all learn and act in the same way; and this is true of children too. A colleague of mine was taking a graduate course in education; part of the course requirement was keeping a journal. Rather than write the mandatory page in response to the readings, she drew a sketch. Unfortunately, the professor was locked into a very narrow conception of knowing and doing and deemed her approach unacceptable. The moral of this tale is that students at all levels, including graduate school, should be given the chance to know and do in various ways. Granted there is not unlimited choice: there are standard English forms, rules of mathematics, basic geography facts which must be accepted at least to a degree; however, varied responses to texts, use of math in real life and connecting geography to family history provide an opportunity to open up the curriculum.

The principle of inclusion extends also to the community. My model recognizes the power and importance of the community and tries to forge links with it. One aspect of the model is that many people will be involved in educating our young. Donald Graves likes to draw the community into the formal curriculum process in an unusual way. "In almost every community, someone has travelled to the very country the class may be studying. You can make the subject live by having people share their stories and their own personal reaction in the countries in which they have travelled."[1] Teachers are not the only ones who "teach." For example, there are many talented artists and musicians who could work with children but in our present system only select, wealthy schools have access to them. We must move beyond the position that schools are the only place for education. A student teacher who had been assigned to my class had been a professional flautist. I encouraged her to play for the children. Once she realized I was open to others, she invited some of her artist friends to the class and my students and I were treated to the most wonderful art, music and drama activities. Long after she finished her placement, we continued to "connect" with the artists. Other teachers were shocked that I would spend precious school

---

[1] Donald Graves, *Investigate Nonfiction* (Portsmouth, NH: Heinemann, 1989), 74.

time on these activities but I knew the children were benefitting from the experiences. The attitude of making connections with other people in schools is beginning but it is still in formation partly because our present model of education is not dynamic and does not encourage us to see others as teachers. "Once it is known that a local school wants to learn from and build on community resources, all manner of persons come forward to recommend others who can contribute to children's learning."[1]

ii. *A Common Language and Common Experiences*

Educational theory is written by academics; teaching is the work of practitioners. A two track system for theorists and practitioners creates a whole array of problems. First, most educational theory is incomprehensible to the average teacher or parent because it is written in very dense language. Although academics may be writing about schools, practitioners cannot understand the work. Even ministry of education documents are written in an obscure language. In order to have many groups working together there must be a *common language*; dialogue, an essential part of the process, requires all members to use and understand the same terms. If each group has its own language, its own journals and its own agenda, opportunities to learn from each other will be few. With separate languages it is impossible to have a conversation, let alone keep it going. The dialogue will be very rich when members from many groups are able to exchange insights on similar issues. If theory is inaccessible to practitioners, the uncomfortable question "what is its value?" must be considered. It may lack value both because practitioners have been unable to check and correct it and because, whatever its validity, practitioners cannot utilize it.

The issues that are addressed by theoreticians are often not the ones classroom teachers and parents are confronting; theory and practice, then, proceed on parallel tracks and do not meet. "Researchers rarely ask the questions which teachers want answered ... and educators rarely work to implement the implications of particular research findings."[2] Philosophers consider truth, practitioners techniques, and parents accountability, each in their own specialized language. It would be imprudent to disregard the long heritage and insights of specialized groups, but we must work out a way for groups to cultivate a shared space. An entry point or technique for bringing about a "meeting

---

[1] *Ibid.*, 74.

[2] Marie Clay, *Becoming Literate: The Construction of Inner Control* (Portsmouth, NH: Heinemann, 1991), 16.

of the minds" would be to have individuals share their stories. Philosophers of education would learn a great deal about teachers' lives from their stories and vice versa. Stories tell of possibilities and problems; with additional knowledge and understanding the connections between groups would strengthen. We would still have specialized fields in a sense, but there would be cross-over and collaboration between special interest groups. When I started graduate school I was a first grade teacher; once I gained some confidence I began to participate in discussions. However, I quickly realized that many academics had little interest in stories about the real world of teaching. Lectures on Kohlberg's theory of moral development, for example, seemed to be more valued: there did not seem to be a way (or an inclination) to accommodate both.

Just as important as a common language are common experiences which connect people from different locations. Thus, for example, academics might connect with practitioners through discussion of their common experiences of teaching: helping students, meeting demands for evaluation and so on. There must also be some shared experiences, such as working on curriculum development together (as outlined in Chapters Six and Seven). Joint projects will provide a better understanding of other perspectives and a base for conversation.

iii. *Taking the School Context Seriously*

Accessible language is a key requirement in establishing aims; another extremely important element is the ability of the aim to be translated into practice. Every teacher has examined a ministry of education guideline and uttered, with great despair, "How can I do that?" or looked at a moral education program and wondered how any student discussion group could possibly follow the suggested techniques. When aims are established externally, they do not consider the difficulty of day to day life in the schools nor can they capitalize on the wealth of talents that individual teachers bring to their classes. Roland Barth says that we have fallen into the habit of having external sources create "lists" for educational reform.

> Lists tend to be prescriptions for other people and for other people's children. Most external lists constitute a suffocating description of a teacher's job, a principal's job or a pupil's job. They create roles that few

of the list makers are apt to want for themselves or for their own children.[1]

Lists ignore the reality of schooling, question teacher competence and often cannot be translated into practice because they are unrealistic. For example, at the 1993 meeting of the Philosophy of Education Society, Jean Anyon, the keynote speaker, discussed the unwelcome feeling many minority students experience in schools. She demanded that "schools" address the systemic barriers of racism. She listed many practices and procedures "schools" should implement.[2] As I listened to her suggestions I realized that all of her suggestions for change would fall on the backs of the classroom teacher. She did not delete any jobs from the classroom teacher's already bulging portfolio, she simply heaped on a great many more. Although many of her proposals were valuable, the chance of their being implemented was minimal. It was obvious that she was unaware of the reality of schools. To overcome this fragmented system where change is imposed externally, it is necessary to have educators in school districts involved in working out the framework and setting specific aims. The key question, "How can this be implemented in our current system?" must be posed repeatedly. This is yet another aspect of thinking about schools in a different way — suggestions must be in the context of the present conditions of schools.

Since everyone has a stake in education everyone should have a voice. Richard Rorty takes a rather modest view of his own insights and abilities when he suggests that philosophers are just one voice among many.[3] He reminds us that one group cannot monopolize the proceedings and each group has something valuable to contribute. By including all groups —students, theoreticians, practitioners and parents— we minimize the possibility of one group being overlooked or the aims being univocal. All of these groups are the context of schooling. The conversations cannot take place always on an abstract or remote level. Action research provides an excellent context for collaboration among various groups.[4] For example, in a few recent articles on standardized tests written by established academics there was almost no mention of children, the emphasis was on teacher accountability. The whole issue

---

[1] Roland Barth, *Improving Schools From Within: Teachers, Parents, and Principals Can Make the Difference*, 40.

[2] Jean Anyon, keynote address at the Philosophy of Education Society meeting, New Orleans, March 21, 1993.

[3] Richard Rorty, *Contingency, Irony and Solidarity* (Cambridge: Cambridge University Press, 1989), 37.

[4] See Sandra Hollingsworth, ed., *International Action Research: A Casebook for Educational Reform* (London: Falmer Press, 1997).

of testing is removed from the context of schooling, thus greatly weakening the argument.

iv. *Providing a Basis for Hope and Trust*

When individuals or groups feel they have lost their way, a sense of insecurity follows. I recall once when I was working on a language arts program with an excellent, experienced primary teacher, she suddenly blurted out, "I just don't know if I am doing a good job any more." Rapid change in expectations by the public and an unclear direction by the school board had caused her to feel uncertain. As a consultant I was constantly confronted with teachers and parents who felt that the system was floundering; they felt that there was no direction to schooling. It is an understandable feeling because schools have taken on so many additional duties that their mandate has become unclear. A recent informal survey of students, teachers and parents regarding the aim of schooling produced such widely varying responses that it was obvious our present aims are muddled.

> Schools are of great concern to most of us, whether as parents, ordinary citizens or educators. We are often unsure, however, just what their role is and to what extent they are fulfilling it. We do not know whether to complain about them, or gratefully accept them as they are.[1]

When we have an established direction, we have a firm basis from which to work, a way of modifying the system, a sense of control and a feeling of hope.

Hope in the schools can only be restored through enlightened leadership, clear statements of direction and involvement of our grass roots members in both working out the philosophy and setting specific objectives; trust cannot be mandated. As Rorty astutely observes, common vocabularies and common hopes bind society.[2] As we exchange stories, in a common vocabulary, we will start to form common hopes for our schools and society. As we break through the walls of silence, the special interest groups, the specialized languages, the posturing and the stereotypes there will be a chance for a shared ground and direction.

---

[1] Clive Beck, *Better Schools: A Values Perspective* (New York: The Falmer Press, 1990), vii.

[2] Richard Rorty, *Contingency, Irony and Solidarity*, 89.

Conclusion

I have argued that a model for schooling must be holistic and comprehensive, accommodating a great many factors. Given our rapidly changing society, school must be much more than a place to acquire skills for a job or a ticket to university. It must provide the tools for adapting to new challenges, including attitudes towards learning, self and others. For schools to provide an experience whereby children can gain these tools, they must break down the barriers of individual subjects and cease to see specific curriculum skills as the end point. They must be more comprehensive and unified in their approach to students: they must recognize the connections that exist between the many factors of schooling.

When we understand children, we "know" the specific goals that we must set. "We need to understand the beings and the moments in order to create the curriculum."[1] We must help children acquire academic skills, but this is not the only objective. William Doll quotes Alfred North Whitehead who suggests that the traditional approach to education is seriously flawed. "One could understand all about the sun and all about the atmosphere and all about the rotation of the earth and still miss the radiance of the sunset."[2] When we get lost in the particularities of the process, we miss the beauty of the individual. My holistic model hopes to overcome this shortcoming.

---

[1] William Doll, *A Post-Modern Perspective on Curriculum*, 136.
[2] *Ibid.*, 146.

Chapter Three

Goals for Education

> *... excellent as much of this work has been in detail, it cannot stand alone without some overall picture of how the various bits and pieces should fit together, of what they are all for*[1]
>
> John White

In response to the major changes in the "landscape" of society, my approach to education departs from traditional methods. A little tinkering with curriculum content, extending teacher training or implementing formal tests are inadequate solutions because they still advocate "more of the same," they do not alter the role and practices of schools significantly. To meet children's needs, the school experience must change radically so schools play a different role in their lives. This requires that we think about schooling in a different way, incorporating new factors into the education equation.

My philosophy of education has three general steps: establishing the ultimate aim for schooling; considering intermediate steps between this ultimate goal and more specific practices; and arriving at actual school practices. This chapter considers the first two parts of my philosophy and the subsequent five chapters show how these goals and steps would be implemented. In order to discuss goals for education I have divided this chapter into three sections. The first poses the question, what is the purpose of school and I suggest that schools must see their purpose as more inclusive. The second section of the chapter outlines my ultimate aim for education — well-being. And in the last part of the chapter I suggest five intermediate goals, for education: autonomy/control, reflectiveness, integration, responsibility/care and mutuality.

---

[1] John White, *The Aims of Education Restated* (London: Routledge and Kegan Paul, 1982), ix.

What is the Purpose of Schools?
Is There a Definitive Answer?

At first glance, outlining the purpose of schools appears to be a very straightforward activity; however, the simplicity of the question masks the complexity of the answer. Ada Schermann, professor of early childhood education, started off each school year with her preservice education students by asking, "Why do we bring five year old children to school?". Once the shock of the question wears off, the students generate a long list of reasons why young children attend school. The reasons range from childcare to learning to read and write to socialization to developing creativity. Given the openendedness of the responses, the various interpretations of each term and the breadth of topics, it quickly becomes apparent that there is no easy answer to this question. As they compile their list, the depth and intricacy of their discussion reveal that there are many reasons for five year olds to be at school.

If Schermann's question was rephrased slightly to ask "Why do we have children at school?" and presented to teachers in different school divisions, their answers would also vary markedly. A very brave junior kindergarten teacher, reflecting the sentiments of many early primary educators, once handed in her long-range plan for the year to her principal. On a single sheet of paper was written the one word, "socialization." Many early childhood educators believe that giving children a strong sense of self is the best gift of all. By contrast, many grade eight teachers feel that their mission is to prepare children for the rigours of high school by working methodically through language and mathematics texts; while most secondary school teachers are very concerned with covering the content of their subject to prepare students for university; and university professors often try to undo what has been done to students in the previous fifteen years. In short, experienced educators' reasons are as complicated and extensive as those of preservice education students, while differing from them in many ways.

Without a shared understanding of the purpose of school there is the risk that each educator will become disconnected from the whole, and the further danger that teachers will work at cross purposes. In my experience, educators tend to limit their vision and scope of interest to the group of students at hand. Given the variety of teaching subjects and personalities involved, an answer to the question "Can there be an underlying goal that unites all of school?" becomes elusive. Perhaps philosophers could help answer our question because they traditionally consider the larger questions of life. Some may suggest that knowledge acquisition is the purpose of schools; pursuit of truth has been a consuming passion throughout history. Education, which is often seen as a means to truth, has been the centre of many controversies about the nature of truth and ways to acquire it. As a result, educational issues of both a theoretical and practical nature have been hotly debated within philosophical circles for many centuries. However, many of the debates about knowledge have not really helped determine the purpose of schools because they have been too narrow in focus and have tried to entrench a particular position.

Richard Rorty is a philosopher who takes an approach to schooling very different from the traditional one; his suggestion is that the purpose of school is to *keep the conversation going*. He asserts that the search for the one, ultimate, definitive truth is fruitless. Schooling will not help find that "something," it does not exist; rather, he says that the purpose of our search should be to engage in debates, a free flow of ideas, which in turn enriches our being. A conversation where we learn from others and are engaged in a meaningful dialogue will be repeated and continued. Is Rorty's justification for schooling an adequate foundation? I will now explore this notion of conversation more fully.

In order to *keep the conversation going* a narrow stance must be avoided; it is impossible to learn with a closed mind or a constricted attitude. Educational theorists and practitioners have often fallen into the trap of searching for the ultimate answer or the best method or the correct program; the one right way. As a result, each search becomes defensive and exclusionary, thus ending the possibility for conversation. An approach which hopes to keep the dialogue going may not result in finding objective "truth," but the search will be rich and worthwhile. Conversation implies that there is an openness to what others have to say, and a willingness to consider other options or meanings, it also implies an attitude of hopefulness and the possibility of change. Conversation leads to learning.

A conversation requires more than one voice; there must be participation by others. Education, like conversation, is not a solitary exercise. Students learn with and through others. Basing education on conversation encourages discussions, group projects, responses to texts, analysis of illustrations, debates, jointly determined goals and collaborative teacher-student relationships. Because learning is highly interactive and formal school takes place in a class with many other students and teachers, conversation seems a natural part of the process. Extending the link further, what is learned in schools is used in social settings, it shapes who we are and how we act in society. From my perspective education is a social experience like conversation. Conversation recognizes the social aspect of learning.

In order to have a true conversation everyone must feel that they are heard; the agenda cannot be preset or dominated by only a few. Not only must there be shared access to the agenda but there must also be a climate that is encouraging and safe. Individuals must feel secure in their ability to express themselves and confident that others will respond appropriately.

> In conversation, I must know how to listen, I must know how to understand your point of view, I must learn to represent to myself the world and the other as you see them. If I cannot listen, if I cannot understand, and if I cannot represent, the conversation stops, develops into an argument, or maybe never gets started.[1]

Conversation requires a respect for others and an effort to understand other points of view.

Conversation is an intellectual experience too; the participants must have shared knowledge —it is not just an emotional interchange. Ideas are exchanged, matters are discussed, facts are considered. In order to understand the other and participate in the conversation both parties must be growing in knowledge— a conversation requires some common understanding of facts and a willingness to expand that understanding. There certainly will not be universal agreement and many conversations will end inconclusively but they will close in such a way that they can begin again. Life-long learning is continuing the conversation of learning.

On the other hand, Rorty's phrase *keep the conversation going* implies a somewhat relativistic stance: a position with which I am uncomfortable. If there is just conversation, the participants may get locked into an eternal debate or the direction finally agreed upon may not be child-centered or supportive of the good of society. There is a danger that Rorty's approach may lead to inappropriate practices or an ideology that is unhealthy for society. Does the spectre of relativism disqualify Rorty's position? Not totally. I feel that Rorty's insights into the importance of conversation are valuable and I endorse his belief that the search for an objective truth is a misleading goal for education. Nevertheless, I feel that education requires more structure. "... [C]onversation is only one among many features of the complex

---

[1] Seyla Benhabib, "In the Shadow of Aristotle and Hegel: Communicative Ethics and Current Controversies in Practical Philosophy," in *Hermeneutics and Critical Theory in Ethics and Politics,* ed. Michael Kelly (Cambridge, MA: The MIT Press, 1989), 23.

social process that produces consent and shared understanding."[1] Conversation, even ideal conversation, is not a strong enough foundation for education. We need some goals for education which nudge the conversation in a particular direction. Goals and direction, however, do not have to be totally prescriptive and constricting; there is a way to provide general direction and still leave many areas open for discussion within the framework. The trick or the genius is to find goals that provide some "scaffolding" for the structure without creating a closed system. These goals and the framework must be of a different nature from what has been traditionally adopted in education. The goals will not be specific "exit outcomes" or behaviourial objectives, they will consider broadly the student's attitudes and well-being. Rorty's stance can be married, to a certain extent, to a more structured approach without undermining the strength of his insights. The goals I advocate are open-ended and not nearly as restrictive as the ones Rorty rails against; but they still do suggest a course for schools.

The basic question about the purpose of school still remains, "Does participation in conversation justify schooling?". The answer is a yes and a no. On the one hand, being part of a conversation, in the broadest sense of the word, which includes both the oral and written forms, is an authentic, affirming activity which promotes mutual respect and helps the individual thrive. However, this justification for schools seems quite ethereal — one could have conversations in the park or the local community centre. Why do we need schools? In my view schools allow certain *types* of conversations, some academically rigorous, some friendly and ordinary, some emotionally supportive and some very challenging. Schools are places for a wealth of conversations. Further, the purpose of school goes beyond conversation, even of these varied types. We must return to Schermann's preservice teachers and my more experienced colleagues who provided *many* reasons for schooling. Their rationales cannot be dismissed; each has merit. What emerges is a complex answer; there are many purposes for schools, some basic and some more tangential — schools have a complex set of purposes. Conversation is an essential part of the complex answer. It is one of the cornerstones of the framework and as such it is critical to the structure. Having conversation as a critical purpose will influence the types of goals proposed, the curriculum choices and the place of the teacher within the school.

---

[1] Michael Walzer, "A Critique of Philosophical Conversations," in *Hermeneutics and Critical Theory in Ethics and Politics*, ed. Michael Kelly (Cambridge, MA: The MIT Press, 1989), 192.

The Ultimate Aim: Well-Being

One way to think differently about schools and to see the possibilities of schooling is to start with the end point — the educated person and the goals for education. Portraits of the educated person abound and lists of goals are plentiful, but they are often too focused on curriculum skills, books to be read or projects to be completed. My vision of an educated person does not focus solely on skills; it includes attitudes and a way of life. If I were simply to outline curriculum objectives, I would be locked into replicating the traditional role for schools. The previously described holistic model discussed in Chapter Two allows me to have broader goals for schools.

Our vision of the educated person must permeate the entire schooling process. Every choice teachers, principals and administrators make must be in light of this vision; they must regularly ask themselves, "Are my decisions supporting the development of educated persons?". This constant would reduce both the fragmentation of schooling and the cross purposes at which people often work.

i. Problems with Traditional Approaches to Ultimate Aims

Traditionally, there have been two approaches to determining the concept of the educated person. One is to list the skills to be acquired and books to be studied. Theorists such as Cubberly and Tyler[1] have itemized curriculum skills in excruciating detail. Recently, E.D. Hirsch has developed an education program which lists every book to be read, lesson to be covered and activity to be completed from grade one onward.[2] However, this approach reduces individuals to the lowest common denominator and relegates teachers to the role of technicians. A further problem with this approach is it leads to the scientific management of schools rather than addressing the human beings within the schools. It ignores the larger societal changes which are impacting on schools and disregards the contextual factors of the community. This contrasts with, for example, the wider perspective which guides the Reggio Emilia

---

[1] See Ralph Tyler, *Basic Principles of Curriculum and Instruction* (Chicago: University of Chicago Press, 1949) and for a more detailed critique of Cubberly see William Doll, *A Post-Modern Perspective on Curriculum* (New York: Teachers College Press, 1993), 42, 47.

[2] An example of this type of program is, E.D. Hirsch, *What Your First Grader Needs to Know: Fundamentals of a Good First Grade Education* (Chicago, Delta, 1993). There are similar books for grades two to six.

schools: "we must, however, state right away that we are also emerged out of a complex cultural background. We are immersed in history, surrounded by doctrines, politics, economic forces, scientific change, and human dramas...".[1]

A second approach to describing the educated person is to isolate characteristics to be acquired such as commitment to justice in the sixth stage of moral development as described by Lawrence Kohlberg[2] or "good character" as outlined by Thomas Lickona.[3] John White's discussion of moral education identifies the problem with such approaches; he suggests that focusing solely on one objective such as justice misses the point of ethics because a singular concern cannot encompass all of the issues of life.[4] These narrow approaches overlook the individual's total way of life, the individual's well-being; they ignore the way the "bits and pieces" fit together.[5]

ii. *Well-Being*
A Broader Concept of the Educated Person

To think about the educated person or the ultimate aims of schooling, a broad lens must be used. As Michael Walzer advocates, we need to consider the "shape of a human life."[6] One dimension —cognitive, affective, social or physical— should not take precedence and one characteristic, say within the cognitive field, should not be *the* end point. When our concern is the overall quality of a person's life, specific skills are not the starting or ending point.

Central to my philosophy of education is the ultimate goal —*well-being*. People should live well and education must be a means to well-

---

[1] Loris Malaguzzi, "History, Ideas and Philosophy," in *The Hundred Languages of Children: The Reggio Emilia Approach to Early Childhood Education,* eds. Carolyn Edwards, Lella Gandini and George Forman, (Norwood, NJ: Ablex, 1993), 51.

[2] For a thorough discussion of Kohlberg's work see Joseph Reimer, Diana Pritchard Paolitto and Richard Hersh, *Promoting Moral Growth: From Piaget to Kohlberg* (New York: Longman, 1979).

[3] Thomas Lickona, *Raising Good Children: Helping Your Children Through the Stages of Moral Development* (Toronto: Bantam Books, 1983).

[4] John White, *Education and the Good Life: Autonomy, Altruism and The National Curriculum,* (New York: Teachers College Press, 1991), 40.

[5] For a discussion of the impact of schooling on females see Carol Gilligan, *In a Different Voice: Psychological Theory and Women's Development* (Cambridge, MA: Harvard University Press, 1982), 5-23.

[6] Michael Walzer, " A Critique of Philosophical Conversation," 192.

being.   Clive Beck's description of well-being captures the breadth, depth and interconnectedness of the concept.

> Human well being, in turn, may be defined in terms of basic values such as survival, health, happiness, friendship, helping others (to an extent), insight, awareness, fulfilment, freedom, a sense of meaning in life and so on. This is an interconnected, open-ended set of values which are largely ends in themselves. They arise out of basic human needs and tendencies: they are inherent in human nature and the human condition. They are what ultimately makes life seem good and worthwhile.[1]

I recognize that this ultimate aim is broad and open to interpretation. Just as education has been defined narrowly so too has the educated person. In order to change the role and practices of schools, the concept of the educated person must be rethought. By defining an educated person as someone who has achieved a good way of life which includes certain attitudes and relationships, I am rejecting the typical school focus on cognitive development. I am proposing that schools expand to recognize there is more to the person; the many domains, cognitive, affective, social, aesthetic, spiritual and physical, are highly interconnected and all important. Further, since well-being cannot be taught formally, children will have to experience well-being in their schooling years, be able to discuss well-being and be able to identify ways of maintaining well-being for themselves and the group.

The following description illustrates how different my concept of educated persons is from traditional ones. (I recognize that it is somewhat idealistic. Although no one person could embody all of these characteristics in complete form, this description sets the direction toward which schooling should strive.) I see our educated persons as having a positive attitude towards schooling and education; they are able to look back on the years in formal school with great fondness because schooling contributed to their well-being. It is not just nostalgia but a recognition that schooling helped them to gain useful knowledge, skills and self-confidence for living and for adapting to new situations; it encouraged a joy of living; it inspired them to be open to others and new ideas; and it promoted a willingness to be involved. My educated persons have the skills and courage to face new challenges with the confidence that they can meet the demands made on them. From their schooling, they have developed a sense of accomplishment and are able to recall many successful projects and endeavours. (Many adults cannot identify these bright spots, they recall school as drudgery and humili-

---

1 Clive Beck, *Better Schools: A Values Perspective* (New York: The Falmer Press, 1990), 2.

ation.) They are reflective and realistic about their strengths and weaknesses. (Far too many children can recite a litany of their deficiencies, pointed out by teachers, and can rarely identify their talents). They know what they can do well and what they need to know. Our educated persons are able to look back on school as a time when they belonged. They felt part of the community; the community supported them; they felt responsible for the group; their learning was enhanced by the group; they learned how to belong to a community; and they learned about life in general. Through participation in their community they learned to respect and appreciate others. They feel confident about themselves in relation to others, their jobs and their community. An attitude that education is life-long is a cherished value. The curiosity they brought to school at four years of age was not stamped out of them; rather, they still feel a sense of wonder about the world.

The way the individual leads life is crucial. It is not enough that the student completed the program, scored 4.0 on the standardized test or obtained a job at a prestigious law firm. What is more important is the way that person approaches life, fulfils tasks and sees himself or herself in the grand scheme of life. Obviously, my focus is on attitudes more than specific skills. My ideal educated persons live positive, healthy lives.

Of course, terms such as a positive, healthy way of life can mean many different things. White contrasts the lives of a Mafia boss and an Oxfam worker, each of whom claims to achieve "the good life."[1] He seems to suggest that it is almost futile to propose a singular vision of the educated person. However, instead of abandoning hope, we must push the argument to the next step and suggest that each person's aims must fit into a larger framework. All humans need some kind of community links and support, a *degree* of self-esteem, some sense of fulfilment, and so on. Within these general goals —both communal and personal— there will be individual differences, but the general goals are crucial. They give direction to schooling and to people's lives.

An educated person cannot be defined in terms of having certain academic skills or knowing specific texts. Since there will be great variance in each person's well-being, it is impossible to try to compile a definitive syllabus. There is no universal list. The taxonomy approach to aims tries to mandate a personality by determining specific academic ends and this is clearly a mistake. However, there are broad, enduring values within which individual variation occurs. I see our educated person as someone who has cultivated a sound approach towards self,

---

[1] John White, *Education and the Good Life: Autonomy, Altruism and The National Curriculum*, 2.

others, the environment and learning, whatever form this takes for a particular individual.

An Approach to Setting School Goals: Five Intermediate Steps

Holistic education has an immense mandate which seems overwhelming. It is a tremendous challenge not only to define holistic education but also to work out its implications. It would be very easy to revert to the old standby —a taxonomy of specific skills— but this would undermine the foundation of holistic education. Nevertheless, the "educational task" must be broken down into more manageable segments because it is impossible for educators to work solely from a broad perspective. Moving back and forth between the more specific (role of the teacher, approaches to curriculum and so on) and the general (goals of education) is the only approach possible.

As noted earlier, Clive Beck suggests that human values form a network," an interconnected, open-ended set."[1] Our task is to develop a set of values that are interrelated, broad and consistent with society's goals. As Piaget noted, the "various activities of man form an indissoluble whole;"[2] it becomes important, from the outset, to have *connections* as a major consideration for these goals. My five intermediate goals recognize this connectedness and the necessity of developing the whole person.

Most discussions of school values and aims follow a typical format: one or more ultimate goals are listed followed by many specific curriculum objectives which are supposed to be the way to realize the goals. This sets the process on a course which itemizes and carves education into many separate spheres. To avoid this pitfall, an intermediate "step" between the broad and the specific is necessary. I suggest five intermediate goals which steer a middle course between the ultimate goals approach that only works in the abstract and the detailed, itemized lists of curriculum objectives which often overlook more general considerations.

The five intermediate steps are a combination of values, skills and attitudes which give form to my holistic model. The word "step" suggests that they are part of an ongoing process rather than the finished product. *I use the words "step" and "goal" interchangeably; and it*

---

[1] Clive Beck, *Better Schools: A Values Perspective*, 2.

[2] Jean Piaget, *To Understand is to Invent: The Future of Education* (New York: Grossman Publishers, 1973), 69.

should be noted that they are both being used in an unusual sense. They establish both the experiences and directions for: the community; the life of the school; the children's activities; and the children's learning and development. They are not the external end points; rather, they provide both *direction for* and *description of* the process. They help us to think about schools differently, giving recognition to the fact that the life of the school must already embody the outcomes we have in mind for schooling, otherwise those outcomes will simply not be achieved, now or in the future. The intermediate goals serve a twofold purpose: they further specify both the nature of well-being and the conditions for achieving well-being.

The five intermediate goals described below are closely tied to the vision I have for future schools and society; these qualities are from my viewpoint crucial to life and learning. However, they do not exhaust all the possibilities. They are a starting point for discussion and are open to modification; for flexibility is necessary if we hope to *keep the conversation going.* Beck's description of well-being includes other goals as well, which are equally important. These five goals are illustrative of the kind of intermediate goals we need in education and how we must incorporate them into all aspects of schooling. I will keep coming back to these goals throughout the book. A similar approach could be taken with other intermediate range values.

i. *Autonomy/Control*

The first intermediate step, autonomy/control, involves freedom to learn and live, an independence of spirit and opportunity to plan one's life. The focus of this goal is "inward": personal development of skills and talents; control of one's own learning; and a sense of hope about life. Describing autonomy/control as inward directed is a somewhat arbitrary decision: a particular goal cannot be totally inward or outward. However, later goals focus more on "outward" concerns: the difference is one of degree.

Total freedom is an illusion because we are all somewhat culture bound and limited by biological functions; however, within these confines there are many opportunities to create oneself and to have some control over one's life. Autonomy and education are connected because *genuine* learning cannot take place in a strictly controlled environment. If individuals are totally dependent upon the teacher for direction and the content of lessons is strictly controlled, learning is greatly restricted. Part of the challenge for teachers is to help children "become aware of what could be."[1] Studying in the stifling environment of many traditional classrooms merely promotes imitation of the teacher's acts, fosters a superficial knowledge of the subject and provokes certain children to devise ways to subvert the system.[2] Further, each person's individual talents cannot be developed in a pre-set school system. In contrast, respect for the children's autonomy encourages both the development of skills and strengths and the devising of alternative ways to do and know.

Young children are often shuffled from one activity to another, carried along like little corks bobbing on the sea. A sense of control comforts and empowers; it encourages children to feel that the present and the future are within their grasp, an essential part of learning. Children often do not feel a sense of power because they have such limited control over their lives. Control of one's own learning is an essential part of being an educated person and it should begin in primary school. An attitude of control helps one be a life-long learner because learning is not dependent upon the teacher's initiative.

As young children take some control of their learning, their understanding of the learning process increases, another of the seeds of life-long learning.[3] For example, most youngsters in grade one identify their goal for the year as "learning how to read" but educators take control of the learning situation, break the process into a "thousand steps" and do not explain the connections between the steps to the students. Children do not see how the lessons and worksheets connect to learning how to read and feel that their goal is not being taken seriously. When this pattern is repeated throughout elementary school, it is not surprising that adolescents often feel very alienated from the school. As a result, the "independence of spirit" and "opportunities to plan" get lost in the timetable and the child loses the chance to develop attitudes and skills of autonomous living. In arguing for a more open-ended play-based program Otto Weininger shows the value of children having more autonomy and control in their school experience.

> So essentially, when children are playing, they are elaborating for themselves the whole business of what a problem is, how you solve a prob-

---

[1] Ralph Peterson, *Life in a Crowded Place: Making a Learning Community* (Richmond Hill, Ontario: Scholastic, 1992), 94.

[2] For a discussion of the negative implications of a teacher controlled environment see Philip Jackson, *Life in Classrooms* (New York: Teachers College Press, 1990), 31-33.

[3] See Robert Dearden, *Problems in Primary Education* (London: Routledge and Kegan Paul, 1976) Chapter vi for a discussion of the concept of learning how to learn.

lem, and then once you've solved a problem and reached some kind of conclusion, how you then go about formulating other problems to solve. If we can tap into this process, then we can have the most effective educational system available.[1]

I am not suggesting that all drudgery, such as learning standard spelling or teacher directed lessons, should be purged from schooling; rather, I am recommending that the reasons for their inclusion should be explained and that they be kept to a minimum.

Donald Graves notes one of the problems which arises when children are highly dependent upon the teacher: "[a]ny time a student waits for me to start the class or the day is time wasted ... I want children to use time effectively, and they don't if I have to tell them what to do fifteen times a day."[2] Time is too precious to waste. A further critical consequence, which Graves does not emphasize sufficiently, is that this typical classroom behaviour projects a certain attitude to the whole learning process. It suggests that experts (teachers) and texts are the only "legitimate" sources of knowledge, a counterproductive message to be sending in our "information age." Teachers are not the source of all knowledge.[3]

To develop a sense of autonomy and control there must be a move away from the "education = schooling" attitude outlined in Chapter One. This perspective undervalues young children who bring all sorts of knowledge to school which is not acknowledged because it was not acquired in the formal school. Children's knowledge and comments should be taken seriously because this encourages individuals to value their own insights and instincts and draw on real-life experiences. Rather than wait for the experts to tell them what to do, children should be encouraged to trust themselves and see that they can learn from peers, family, friends, television, books and so on. For example, many children have independently acquired a great deal of knowledge about computers, hockey players and dinosaurs and they freely discuss this with enthusiasm. They were very efficient learners without the help of a lesson plan; part of the success of their learning is that the impetus came from within them. This example of enthusiastic learning should become our model.

---

[1] Otto Weininger, "Understanding Educational Play," *Orbit* 25, May 1994, 4.

[2] Donald Graves, *Build a Literate Classroom* (Portsmouth, NH: Heinemann, 1991), 15,16.

[3] For a detailed breakdown of how children actually spend their time in school see John Goodlad, *A Place Called School: Prospects for the Future* (New York: McGraw Hill, 1984), 107.

Autonomy and control are either encouraged or hindered through the structures —routines, rules, traditions and processes— of the class. There are a multitude of rules in school: in many ways it is a complicated game; but unlike a game the rules are not clearly identified and each year they change. This set-up inhibits children from being autonomous learners because the playing field shifts too frequently. In *Education and Social Control*, Rachel Sharp and Anthony Green report their study of progressive education classrooms, observing that the many unstated "rules" placed constraints on learning which in turn penalized both the more free thinking and the less able students. Although I disagree with the authors' final conclusions, which are highly critical of teachers and indicate the authors' insensitivity to many aspects of the reality of working in a school, I found their recounting of conversations within the school and their observations of the dynamics within the class revealing. The conclusion that emerges for me is that the organization and "rules" of many classrooms prevent children from controlling their own learning and developing an independence of spirit. Autonomy and personal control are penalized not cherished.[1] Students cannot learn control, responsibility, loyalty or autonomy in the abstract or in teacher controlled settings; rather, they learn such values experientially. The organization of the class sets the limit and tone for the children's involvement. In Chapter Four I describe a type of learning community which would promote autonomy and control; in response to Sharp and Green, one alternative is to have explicit rules and routines which may be open to negotiation.

Since young children's experience of school is initially limited they are fairly dependent on their teachers. Teachers become significant others and often in children's minds they are the experts. It is difficult to encourage a sense of autonomy when youngsters cling to the teacher. Educators can compensate for this situation by adopting an attitude that values student independence while providing activities that promote the skills of autonomous living and learning. White refers to Joseph Raz who concludes that we need an "autonomy supporting environment"[2]: the structures of the class should be ones that encourage independence of spirit and the opportunity to plan. Simple classroom activities that promote this growth are: letting children do individual projects on an interest or hobby (with the assistance of the librarian, student teacher or parent volunteer); encouraging children to partici-

[1] For a discussion of the strategies that children use to show that they are conforming see Philip Jackson, *Life in Classrooms*, 34.
[2] John White, *Education and the Good Life: Autonomy, Altruism and the National Curriculum*, 99.

pate in all stages when planning a class outing (from identifying on-site activities to duplicating permission forms); and planning regular class meetings (with teachers sharing their authority and being open to student suggestions). Respect for the children and willingness to share control are essential. Children will make mistakes, but that too is part of the learning process.

ii. *Reflectiveness*

The second intermediate step, reflectiveness, is an integral part of the individual's quest to be a healthy, autonomous, integrated person with a vision of the future. I am using reflectiveness in the sense of thinking about actions, choices, consequences and possibilities; pausing to look around at life; and listening to one's inner voice. It is an opportunity to ponder and plan and a necessary part of development; as a young child once said, "you have to be slow to grow." Reflectiveness does not just happen, like acquiring facts from a book, it is a gradual process; as in our metaphor of the journey there are many steps on the road to self-knowledge and primary education is an important part of that journey. As Bruno Bettelheim notes:

> If we hope to live not just from moment to moment, but in true consciousness of our existence, then our greatest need and most difficult achievement is to find meaning in our lives. It is well known how many have lost the will to live, and have stopped trying, because such meaning has evaded them. An understanding of the meaning of one's life is not suddenly acquired at a particular age, not even when one has reached chronological maturity. On the contrary, gaining a secure understanding of what the meaning of one's life may or ought to be —this is what constitutes having attained psychological maturity.[1]

Reflection makes life-long learning a possibility because it helps us identify personal needs and goals — much of the impetus for controlling our own learning. Simply telling students what their "needs" are and how to meet them is not an adequate approach because students are not involved in the process. For example, until students see a place for reading in their lives, teachers will have to nag, implore or resort to rewards to have students participate. Learning is not something "done" to you, it requires both physical and emotional involvement; and such involvement is dependent upon reflection.

---

[1] Bruno Bettelheim, *The Uses of Enchantment: The Meaning and Importance of Fairy Tales* (New York: Alfred A. Knopf, 1975), 3.

As children are given many opportunities to initiate and explore, the learning cycle must be completed by providing the children with an opportunity to reflect. Often, teachers provide wonderful activities but the process ends before the children have a chance to think about their experiences. One year my primary students made Thanksgiving Day posters to brighten up a food bank/soup kitchen for the needy. What could have been a simple art lesson was extended to mean much more because the children and I thought and talked about the situation.

Granted, young children often do not appear to be very reflective; but I would suggest that part of the reason for this is the attitude of adults. Clive Beck argues that given the limited responsibility, contact with others and opportunity for close friendship, young children's behaviour and relationships "quite appropriately reflect their life situation."[1] Youngsters are not given the opportunity to slow down and reflect nor do the teachers (or adults generally) model thoughtfulness. Many times I have been surprised by the cleverness and thoughtfulness of children's suggestions. I have learned that children are much more aware of their surroundings than they are often given credit for. (However, we must also recognize the limitations of children and be realistic in our expectations.) I found that children need time to think; they are not forthcoming when pressed for an immediate response. My students and I often joked because I assigned "thinking homework," which meant that the children had to think about a current problem or situation in the class and the following day we would discuss it. This strategy gave children time to consider the possibilities, recognized that they had opinions and showed that I valued their suggestions.

Encouraging (or nudging) children to be thoughtful requires much more than scolding them "to think about what they are doing" when they have acted inappropriately. Reflectiveness requires time, patience, a safe environment, an open-ended program, a variety of experiences and other individuals with whom to share. Teacher must not be so totally absorbed in managing the curriculum or student behaviour that they do not have time to participate in thoughtful discussions. Opportunity to talk to others and reflect on experiences should be combined with a curriculum that helps children develop personal interests and expand their knowledge.

Following is a poem written by a junior division student. Although the writer is older than the age group being discussed here, I am including the poem for a few reasons. First, it is touching; secondly, it shows that curriculum, the writing program, can assist in the process of reflec-

---

[1] Clive Beck, "Is There Really Development? An Alternative Interpretation," *Journal of Moral Education* 18, October 1989, 177.

tion (in this case it was a vehicle to work through some painful feelings); and finally, the poem shows that reflection does not just "occur." Learning to be reflective is a life-long process that begins very early on and involves other people, in this instance a caring teacher who valued reflection and a supportive sister.

My Sweater

by

Gene Blackmond

Dedication:

To the memory of my brother, Mickey,
and my sister who helped me put it into words.

It's red and warm.
I feel good and warm when I wear it.
I love my sweater.
When I don't have my sweater on ...
I really miss it!
It was my brother's
He gave it to me.
And that's why I love it!
I had it for a long time.
He died.
That was ...
Eight years ago.
All I have left to remember him by
Is my red sweater.[1]

Paradoxically, although reflectiveness is very personal we cannot acquire it on our own; it requires us to be in relation. The teacher, the curriculum, the peer group and the school community must all be partners, and through these relationships a greater reflectiveness grows with respect to self, others and life in general.

---

[1] Lucy McCormick Calkins, *Living Between Lines* (Portsmouth, NH: Heinemann, 1991), 75.

iii. *Integration*

In Chapter Two, a highly interconnected model of education was presented. Integration is the process of bringing separate parts together but it is also a goal for schooling. I consider two types of integration: first, I argue for integration between home and school experiences; and secondly, I advocate a unified curriculum. At present, school is often an "impediment they must endure along the way to what really matters"[1] because the whole process is so fragmented. My goal of integration hopes to change this present situation.

For young children it is important to bridge home and school so that the learning at school becomes as natural as the learning that takes place at home. Since the home experience should be the foundation upon which children will build, it must be incorporated into schooling. Home and school are two different worlds and it would be impossible (and inappropriate) to try to duplicate the home in the school; however, there should be stronger links than at present. A steady flow of information between the two would strengthen the connections. Integration of home and school is an important step to help parents and teachers see that both groups are responsible for children's learning.

Most children are given many responsibilities at home but in school they are often not viewed as very capable individuals. As a teacher, I was often surprised by the home responsibilities some of my youngsters had which they seemed to handle with ease. From babysitting to helping with dinner preparation, they were able to deal with much more responsibility than I was giving them. Just as it is very difficult for adults to change demeanour between home and work, so it is difficult for children to change "hats" between home and school.

With respect to curriculum, at present the school experience is carved into many separate spheres; and while each has some value on its own, however, this approach is inconsistent with how children learn. Children do not separate reading into "grammar" and "phonics" but just see reading as reading. The goal should be to connect the various subject areas so "learning" becomes the goal rather than reading, grammar or phonics. Furthermore, learning can and should include interests from elsewhere. Often children's hobbies are not acknowledged (or capitalized on) by the classroom teacher. This creates a tension within the child and a schism between the school and non-school worlds in the child's mind. It is also a lost opportunity for learning.

---

[1] Constance Weaver, *Understanding Whole Language: From Principles to Practice* (Portsmouth, NH: Heinemann, 1990), 63.

Integration also means learning skills because they fill a present need. This helps children integrate content and skills into their present activities which in turn will change their perception of learning. When parents of grade one students suggest that children should concentrate on the 3R's so they will be accepted into a good university, they are asking children to have a goal that is at least twelve years away and beyond their comprehension. No one would ask adults to wait over a decade before their skills became meaningful; skills should be for a need now, not just somewhere off in the future.

iv. *Responsibility/Care*

The fourth intermediate step or goal is responsibility/care, an important part of personal development. This goal should be viewed as more outward directed, providing a balance to autonomy/control which has an inward focus. By responsibility I mean being accountable, reliable, trustworthy and willing to fulfil obligations. It is much more than duty or something done to avoid punishment; it is a commitment to others. Since responsibility is not particularly emotional in its connotations I have combined it with care. Nel Noddings suggests that care is "the very Being of human life,"[1] not a specific behaviour. The responsibility/care step places the individual in a larger social, ecological context.

A sense of responsibility and caring provides the opportunity to "give back and share." The first intermediate step focused on schools supporting and assisting the individual's development. However, the mandate of the school must be broad enough to foster a reciprocal relationship between the individual and society.

Learning and living are done in relationship. Schools are rooted within society, schools are communities and learning is done with others. "The reasons for seeking the well-being of others are many. In the first place, concern for others comes naturally to human beings ...."[2] Schooling has a long tradition of promoting self-actualization or rugged individualism but these goals often ignore the social aspect of learning and living. Robert Bellah et al note:

> Perhaps the crucial change in American life has been that we have moved from the local life of the nineteenth century —in which economic and so-

---

[1] Nel Noddings, *The Challenge to Care in Schools: An Alternative Approach to Education* (New York: Teachers College Press, 1992), 15.

[2] Clive Beck, *Learning to Live the Good Life: Values in Adulthood* (Toronto: OISE Press, 1993), 62.

cial relationships were visible and, however imperfectly, morally interpreted as parts of a larger common life— to a society vastly more interrelated and integrated economically, technically, and functionally. Yet this
is a society in which the individual can only rarely and with difficulty
understand himself and his activities as interrelated in morally meaningful ways with those of other, different Americans.[1]

In balancing our goals for schooling, we must recognize the relational
part of living.

Responsibility/care can be seen from at least two perspectives: in
terms of the inner self there must be a responsibility to the Self for personal development; on a broader scale, there must be a commitment to
the group; a responsibility for attaining and maintaining (or procuring)
its well-being. My educated person is an individual within a community; the group supports the individual, but the individual in turn
contributes to the group's well-being. Both spheres are part of the person and both must be given opportunity to develop; the individual's inner world and the individual within the world are deeply connected.

Noddings is correct when she suggests that everyone needs someone
or something for which to care and her proposed model —school
divided into basic skills instruction for half a day and centres of care
for the remaining time— has the right intent. However, I do not feel
that precisely this approach would work with young children: it is too
compartmentalized. Caring and responsibility should be part of all
aspects of school, not restricted to certain activities or times of the day.

Responsibility and care are often viewed on a grand scale, as having to do with restoring the ozone layer or helping third world countries
solve their economic problems; however, on the whole, these goals are
too big for primary children (or anyone else). Projects should be concrete,
simple and manageable so that responsibility/care becomes part of
their way of life. It should be recognized that young children cannot
dash off and perform community service work but they can develop the
skills and attitudes of responsible living through classroom activities
which in turn will influence their way of life. As previously established, children learn by doing; and they can only learn care and responsibility through personal involvement. As Piaget noted,
"education, founded on authority and only unilateral respect, has the
same handicaps from the ethical standpoint as from the intellectual
standpoint. Instead of leading the individual to work out the rules and
the discipline that will obligate him to work with others to alter

[1] Robert Bellah, Richard Madsen, William Sullivan, Ann Swidler and Steven Tip-
ton, *Habits of the Heart: Individualism and Commitment in American Life* (New
York: Harper and Row, 1985), 50.

them, it imposes a system of ready-made and immediately categorical imperatives on him."[1] In two ways schools should foster this growth: first, they should provide genuine opportunities for students to get involved with projects; and secondly, an attitude of care and responsibility should pervade the whole school experience. Caring and responsibility as general goals emphasize the need to humanize institutions; if we want our students to be more caring and responsible we must adopt such an attitude towards them.

As a practitioner I was continually dismayed by students' lack of regard for school property; library books, textbooks, gym equipment, audio visual material and so on were treated carelessly, lost or vandalized. Students justified their behaviour by saying "it's only school property," failing to connect themselves to the school. And one would assume that they would have the same thoughtless attitude in the larger society. Similarly, many students take limited responsibility for their own education or the well-being of the class: they say that "it is the teacher's job to teach me." In some classes student behaviour is so disorderly that teaching and learning cannot occur — many students simply "do not care" about the class. Their highly disruptive behaviour suggests much more than just poor manners; it is apparent that many students lack a sense of responsibility to themselves, the class or school. There could be endless discussions as to which came first, alienating school practices or unhealthy student attitudes; but the important thing is to recognize that many students, at present, do not feel responsible *for* or *to* themselves or school. Placed within the larger social context, the long term consequences for society are frightening.

v. *Mutuality*

Mutuality is my fifth intermediate step and in many ways is part of care; Nel Noddings points out that for genuine "caring" to occur the cared for must respond to the caregiver since caring is a mutual activity.[2] However, while the above discussion included many points related to mutuality, I feel that responsibility/care does not adequately illustrate the connectedness between individuals that is crucial for well-being; and Noddings' treatment in particular does not capture sufficiently the reciprocity needed in caring. This final section re-emphasizes the need to shift away from the individualism that has guided

---

[1] Jean Piaget, *To Understand is to Invent: The Future of Education*, 118.
[2] Nel Noddings, *The Challenge to Care in Schools: An Alternative Approach to Education*, 15-27.

many of our schooling practices and suggests a more relational focus for living and learning.

The term "mutuality" has become common in feminist writings; Judith Jordan in her work uses the *Oxford English Dictionary* definition "possessed, entertained, or performed by each toward or with regard to the other; reciprocal regard".[1] However, this definition does not bring out sufficiently the intent that I am seeking, which is *affecting and being affected by the other(s)*. The former definition does not capture the connectedness, the give and take, the reciprocity which I want to stress. Lacking another suitable word, I will use the term mutuality in this broader sense.

Many primary teachers believe that one of the goals of early schooling is to socialize children; since youngsters come from very different backgrounds, the school's job is to inculcate "appropriate" behaviour. Mutuality does include an element of this type of socialization but I would like to focus on *social growth*. Mutuality includes: learning how to build and sustain relationships; being committed; and receiving from and responding to others. "The importance of friendship and other personal relationships was recognized by classical Greek philosophers. Aristotle, for example, saw friendship as a *virtue* and emphasized the need for special attachment to a relatively small community, the *polis*, without which (as Socrates had said) life would not be worth living."[2] Since the current approach to relational "skills" is haphazard and the emotional context of the class is often ignored, it is not surprising that many primary aged children find the relational part of living and learning confusing. By the time peer pressure becomes an almost irresistible force, around grade four, children have not sorted out relational living. A focus on mutuality in primary education is critical. (I recognize that the peer group has an iron grip on the life of many adolescents but I would suggest that we should once again consider some of the practices in primary education as contributing to this current situation.)

Vivian Paley recognizes the importance of mutuality; in her kindergarten class she instituted the rule, "you can't say you can't play" and has tried to make this a school-wide policy.

> Being told you can't play is a serious matter. It hurts more than anything else that happens in school, and distraction no longer works very well. Everyone knows the sounds of rejection: You can't play; don't sit by me;

---

[1] Judith Jordan, "The Meaning of Mutuality" in *Work in Progress* No 23 (Wellesley MA: Stone Center Working Paper Series, 1985), 1.

[2] Clive Beck, *Learning to Live the Good Life: Values in Adulthood*, 66.

stop following us; I don't want you for a partner; go away. These would
be unforgivable insults if spoken at a faculty meeting, but our responses
are uncertain in the classroom.[1]

When friendship breaks down in the class, there is a ripple effect
through the whole school experience.

We have tended to think of relationships as something we have
when we are not "doing," "acting," or "working" because "relationships
are seen as meeting needs for support, affection, and contact, not as opportunities for action or growth."[2] Because of a narrow view of how
growth occurs, namely, through cognitive activities only, and the dis-
missal of the importance of relationships to learning, the possibilities
for relational living and learning have been limited. To move beyond
the narrow conception of learning criticized in Chapter One, schools
must value friendships and recognize their importance to learning and
living. Through curriculum activities, the structure of the class, the
adults' model and sufficient unscheduled time mutuality can be developed.

As twenty to thirty five students are assembled together for ten
months of the year, the group is a powerful force in their lives. I have
found that the classes where students are committed to each other tend
to be joyful places — the children and teacher want to be part of the
community. Schools have the potential to be places where strong,
healthy relationships can grow because there are ample opportunities
for connections. "[A]lthough we all begin school as strangers, some children never learn to feel at home, to feel they really belong."[3] Our goal
for school will only be realized when everyone feels that they belong.

In one school where I was a teacher, a school trustee lobbied to
have Heritage Language (Italian) included in the daytime schedule.
Because of bus routes, the school day could not be lengthened to accommodate the extra half-hour of instruction. The principal decided to
shorten the recess and lunch periods because the thirty minutes could
not be tacked on the end of the day. The primary teachers argued passionately against this move: children need the outdoor play; they need
ample time to get their games organized; they need unstructured time to
develop friendships; and they do not need another subject crammed into
the day. Unfortunately, this story does not have a happy ending, from
my perspective; the timetable was revised and Italian instruction was

[1] Vivian Gussin Paley, *You Can't Say You Can't Play* (Cambridge, MA: Harvard
University Press, 1992), 14,15.

[2] Janet Surrey, "Relationship and Empowerment" *Work in Progress*, No. 30
(Wellesley MA: Stone Centre Working Paper Series, 1987), 1.

[3] Vivian Gussin Paley, *You Can't Say You Can't Play*, 103.

included. All of the primary teachers noticed a deterioration in most children's behaviour but our concerns continued to be ignored. The timetable made mutuality a difficult goal to achieve and it was apparent that mutuality was not one of this principal's goals.

Not only do we grow socially and spiritually through relationship, but also our learning of school subjects is enhanced through our relationships. I have found that children's difficulties with the academic program lessen once they have a "good" friend in the class. It is not a coincidence that the more popular students in the class usually tend to handle the academic program with a fair degree of ease. Mem Fox noted the benefits of a student drama performance.

> Much has occurred in the half-hour performance: hearts have been given emotional nourishment arising from the curriculum; children have been enthraled; literature with its possibilities of words, structures, and rhythms has been heard and stored in the marrow of memories from where it might be borrowed later for writing or speaking; a sweetness of spirit has uplifted my students and their pen pals as they share the feast, chatting shyly ...[1]

Because relationships are so important to personal and academic growth, schools should make relational living a priority. It is not enough that the teacher care, the students must care about each other and feel cared about; there should be a network of friendships within the class. In the Reggio Emila system "relationship is the primary dimension of our system, however, understood not merely as a warm, protective envelope, but rather as a dynamic conjunction of forces and elements interacting toward a common purpose."[2] A recurring theme in parent-teacher interviews is friendship. Most times when a child does not want to come to school it is because he or she does not have any friends with whom to play or is being picked on in the school yard.

The growth that occurs through friendship is plentiful; for example, when a small group does a project on whales they pool their knowledge while learning about group dynamics; or when a novice joins a soccer team she acquires physical skills while learning about team spirit; or when two youngsters must handle one of them moving away, they learn to console and cope. These relationships provide tremendous opportunities for growth which is what school is all about; these experiences of friendship stay with you for life. In each of these three instances the child is affecting the other group members while being af-

---

[1] Mem Fox, *Radical Reflections: Passionate Opinions on Teaching, Learning and Living* (San Diego: Harcourt Brace, 1993), 93.
[2] Loris Malaguzzi, "History, Ideas, and Philosophy," 62.

fected by them. This give and take between members, based on respect and affection, is mutuality.

As stated earlier, many adolescents feel alienated from schools; our goal for primary education, then, is to help children stay connected (or become connected). In most cases it is easier and more fulfilling to connect to fellow students than to a mathematics or science program. Friends "give back" while encouraging the child to grow in many ways. When children or adults are in a positive, healthy, relationship there is a "spring in their step" because they have connected to another person. My vision of educated persons suggests that they should be able to look back on their schooling and recall, with fondness, a sense of belonging which can only come about through friendships and other reciprocal relationships: through mutuality.

Conclusion

By exploring the question, "Is there a definitive purpose for schools," I have shown that schooling is a complex process. Accordingly, the goals of schooling must have breadth and depth. Through my description of the ultimate aim, well-being, and my vision of the educated person, I have established a general direction for education and further emphasized the complexity of the situation. Schools must address all aspects of personhood — skills, values, attitudes, physical well-being and personal interests. Central to my position is the claim that these factors must be in harmony and supportive of one another. For too long, we have had educational practices that work at cross purposes and hence are often detrimental to well-being.

To provide balance and to halt further fragmentation of schools, I have proposed five intermediate steps which provide a unity to the process, recognize the need to address both skills and attitudes, have an inward and outward focus, and include both the individual and the community. The steps are a new way to think about schooling because they are both goals and processes. I have chosen to ignore "end point" or "exit outcomes" approaches because they lead to a fractured process and only promote "more of the same." I have argued for a balanced and comprehensive approach to schooling, identifying goals which are inclusive and connected. Autonomy/control cannot develop without reflection; mutuality extends responsibility/care; and autonomy/ control is linked with responsibility/care.

Such a broad account of the goals of schooling may be discouraging to teachers: how can we achieve all this? I would like to close this chapter, then, by saying that *schools cannot do it all;* they must be *in partnership* with other institutions and groups. For example, schools and industry are *both* responsible for job preparation; schools and social service institutions are *both* responsible for childcare; and schools and families are *both* responsible for educating the young. To achieve such partnerships, schools must become the hub of the community, forging links with many groups and being a respected, vital part of people's lives. Schools should not be the dumping ground for issues and problems that no one else wants, nor should they feel that they can operate separately from society. Life does not unfold like a domino wave, first family, then school, then job and so on, each having a specific agenda. All aspects of living and learning are connected; like the centre of a venn diagram, the areas overlap. The "conversation" and "partnerships" must become inherent in the way both schools and society are constituted.

Chapter Four

The Learning Community

The ecology of the school is at least as inter-connected as the ecology of the planet.[1]

Lucy McCormick Calkins

Schools are distinctive communities: they are not families but they share some similar characteristics; they are places of employment for adults but not for children; and although they must be fiscally responsible they are not businesses. There is no model in society which schools can duplicate. However, like all communities they are a highly interconnected network of relationships, practices, processes, traditions and goals.

Recent educational reform has focused on trying to make schools into cost effective, business-like, productive enterprises. For example, one of the latest catch enthusiasms in educational administration is "Total Quality Management"[2] which focuses on the end product, overlooks the general school experience and fails to recognize the interconnections within. Many current reform efforts emphasize "correcting" highly visible, specific elements such as spelling and mathematics instruction, because they are seen to be the crux of schooling. By ignoring the deeper structures of the school process and failing to recognize that schools are communities, the complexity of the school process is overlooked. Although the sense of community, the vision of an educated person and the intermediate steps are highly elusive, they are the essential infrastructure for the whole process. They provide direction and support development. Taking account of these factors requires a complex, sophisticated approach, unlike efficiency oriented outcomes based approaches.

In this chapter I will examine the concept of the class as a learning community and the practices which support its growth. There are two main sections to the chapter. First, I define community of learners and explore this concept through a discussion of the class culture. Secondly,

---

[1] Lucy McCormick Calkins, *Living Between the Lines* (Portsmouth, NH: Heinemann, 1991), 14.

[2] See Leo H. Bradley, *Total Quality Management for Schools* (Lancaster, PA: Technomic, 1992), 167-193.

I show that community cannot be developed in isolation; it is linked to the academic programs, the structures and the relationships in the class.

The Class as a Community of Learners

Traditionally, schools have had two approaches to the individual within the class: either the competitive one, where the goal for the student is "I win and you lose"; or individual self-realization, which is still very inward looking but less competitive. A third alternative which I wish to advocate, is an interactive process — the individual and the group are both enriched as the class becomes a "community of learners." "Community can help teachers and students be transformed from a collection of 'I's' to a collective 'we,' thus providing them with a unique and enduring sense of identity, belonging, and place."[1] In this approach, students know that their presence and contributions make a difference to the group and their growth is supported by the community.

The interest in schools/classes as communities is steadily rising. The range of groups interested in community is vast: Vivian Paley who instituted the rule in her class "You can't say you can't play" examines how rules shape her class. Jane Roland Martin suggests the model of the "schoolhome" for schools. Roland Barth says we can only improve schools from within. Thomas Sergiovanni offers a model of schooling based on community. Nel Noddings advocates schools as caring communities. Kathy Gnagey Short looks at the link between community and language arts programs.

There has also been a renewed interest among educators in the work of German sociologist Ferdinand Tonnies who delineated two types of communities: gemeinschaft and gesellschaft. In gemeinschaft, the community is bound by ties of kinship, of place and of mind whereas gesellschaft is bound by contractual ties. Our goal should be more like the former. Sergiovanni notes the following qualities of communities of this type.

> Relationships within a community of mind are based not on contracts but on understanding about what is shared and on the emerging web of obligations to embody that which is shared. Relationships within a community of kinship are based not on contracts but on understandings similar to those found within the family. Relationships within communities of

---

[1] Thomas Sergiovanni, *Building Community in Schools* (San Francisco: Jossey-Bass, 1994), xiii.

place are based not on contracts but on understanding about how members will live their lives together as neighbours.[1]

All organizations and communities have elements of both gemeinschaft and gesellschaft. Schools, however, have come to place too much emphasis on formal structure, picturing "young children as raw material,[and] teachers as workers who process their students before sending them on to the next station on the assembly line."[2] We have lost the sense of kinship, togetherness, commitment, responsibility and friendship which are central to genuine communities.

i. *Linking Community and the Intermediate Steps*

A recurring theme throughout my discussion of well-being, the educated person and the intermediate steps has been "community." Although it may seem an obvious part of the process, the question, "Why is community important?" must be considered. The following reasons for emphasizing community not only show its importance but also illustrate the connectedness within my schooling model.

First, given the precarious situation of many families, schools must provide children with stability, caring and more "family" or community type activities. In her Casa Dei Bambini, Montessori compensated for the difficult family lives of many children by giving them "a double sense of belonging: they would feel that they belonged to this home and also that it belonged to them."[3]

Secondly, as we saw earlier, an educated person must have certain attitudes towards living and learning as well as skills. Attitudes and habits are developed through personal experiences within the general environment of the class; the type of community in which the children work shapes their values and practices.

> Authentic community requires us to do more than pepper our language with the word "community," label ourselves as a community in our mission statement, and organize teachers into teams and schools into families. It requires us to think community, believe in community, and practice community — to change the basic metaphor for school itself into community.[4]

---

[1] *Ibid.*, 7.

[2] Jane Roland Martin, *Schoolhome: Rethinking Schools For Changing Families* (Cambridge, MA: Harvard University Press, 1992), 41.

[3] *Ibid.*, 13.

[4] Thomas Sergiovanni, *Building Community in Schools*, xiii.

Because being an educated person includes having a sense of responsibility for the well-being of the group and learning to care and be connected with others, we must have a class community that is supportive, considers the whole person and emphasizes relational living.

Thirdly, learning of all kinds, including academic learning, can be enhanced through the class environment; a vibrant community which encourages participation provides many learning opportunities. Children can learn a great deal about relational living through active participation in the community. Knowledge of traditional academic subjects is enhanced through group work and joint projects, pairing with older students, and partnerships with experts from beyond the school.

> The kind of social setting within which learners form relationships and dialogues with others has a major impact on the potentials and constraints those learners perceive for their own learning. Vygotsky (1978) has argued that the way we talk and interact with others becomes internalized and determines the way we think and learn. In classrooms, then, the kinds of social relationships and conversations that are encouraged will greatly impact the thinking processes of learners.[1]

Further, Vivian Paley notes "I am certain the children who are told they can't play don't learn as well. They might become too sad to pay attention."[2] The class community is more than just a single point on the three dimensional model; it permeates the whole structure. Often attempted curriculum reform efforts precede any discussion (or recognition) of the group's influence on learning.

Community is essential to the five intermediate goals. "Mutuality" can only thrive in an atmosphere that supports relational living; the community requires its members to be "responsible" and "care" for the group's well-being; an emphasis on the learning community is essential in an "integrated" approach to education; the children must be "reflective" about the group's values and their place in the community; and children are not to lose their identity or "autonomy" to support the community's goals, as it becomes part of their goals.

---

[1] Kathy Gnagey Short, "Creating a Community of Learners," in *Talking About Books: Creating Literate Communities*, eds. Kathy Gnagey Short and Kathryn Mitchell Pierce (Portsmouth: Heinemann, 1990), 33.

[2] Vivian Gussin Paley, *You Can't Say You Can't Play* (Cambridge, MA: Harvard University Press, 1992), 28.

ii. *Defining the Term "Community of Learners"*

Comments from experienced teachers such as "This group just isn't the same as last year's class," or "This class is so easy," or "I could never do that activity with this class" indicate that the collective group has its own personality and values: it is a community. Because of the increased attention to co-operative learning methods and the role of peer conferencing in process writing programs, the term "learning community" is becoming more common in school literature. There is a danger, however, that the "group" will be seen merely as a pedagogical instrument useful in achieving certain specific ends; in fact, the learning community plays a critical role in all aspects of the schooling process. It influences, among other things, interactions within literature groups, the level of discourse in moral education programs and more generally, the students' self-esteem and friendship patterns.

As the term "community of learners" has become more common in the literature, it has come to mean many different things. In order both to clarify the term and broaden its meaning, I have developed the following definition. A community of learners is a cohesive group which has a common focus and shared values, and encourages the individual to make connections. There is a dual purpose to the community: *individual growth* and *group development*. The relationship between the individual and the community is mutually supportive — both are strengthened through the relationship. The individuals in the community have three different types of responsibilities: first, a caring for the community's smooth functioning and for the group's well-being as a whole; secondly, an obligation toward their own personal education and happiness; and finally a duty toward the individual well-being of the other members. Within the community students learn about life, experience the joy of relational living and increase their knowledge of more traditional academic subjects: these goals are complementary.[1]

In a sense, as I have noted, every class is a community; however, some are highly fractured and competitive while others are supportive and positive. Becoming a community of learners in the sense described above is not a natural consequence of being in a school class; it requires

---

[1] Sergiovanni offers the following definition: communities are collections of individuals who are bonded together by natural will and who are together binded to a set of shared ideas and ideals. This bonding and binding is tight enough to transform them form a collection of "I's" into a collective "we." As a "we," members are part of a tightly knit web of meaningful relationships. This "we" usually shares a common place and over time comes to share common sentiments and traditions that are sustaining. Thomas Sergiovanni, *Building Community in Schools*, xvi.

certain attitudes and activities on the part of teachers, administrators, students and parents. Gnagey Short in her writings on whole language identifies six elements which help the class become a genuine learning community:

> ... a community of learners is formed as learners (1) come to know each other; (2) value what each has to offer; (3) focus on problem solving and inquiry; (4) share responsibility and control; (5) learn through action, reflection, and demonstration; and (6) establish a learning atmosphere that is predictable and yet full of real choices.[1]

In Gnagey Short's view, then, knowing, valuing, sharing and working together in a supportive environment are basic to the learning community.

In *Democracy and Education* John Dewey explores the concept of community and argues that communication and common values are part of community building. He concludes that "men live in a community in virtue of the things which they have in common; and communication is the way in which they come to possess things in common."[2] A community is more than a collection of individuals, it is a cohesive group with shared values which are   discussed with all members. The aspects Dewey identifies are also points on the cube which must be connected; if the connections are weak the community will falter.

iii. *The Culture of the Class*

In many ways the class is typical of larger communities; the elements of any society are present within this tiny microcosm. When children enter their first school class, dramatic changes occur in their lives: the teacher and fellow students become "significant others"; and they are now a member of another community. This new community is much larger than the family unit or daycare group. For children, their class is not merely a collection of strangers; rather, it is an important part of their world. As adults, we often forget the significance of school in the life of children because we are involved with so many groups. We have our immediate family, our health club, our arts and crafts group, friends from university, childhood friends, our fellow workers and on and on. Children, on the other hand, do not have all these groups with which to interact. As a result, what goes on in the class takes on a great deal

---

[1] Kathy Gnagey Short, "Creating a Community of Learners," 35.

[2] John Dewey, *Democracy and Education: An Introduction to the Philosophy of Education* (New York: The Free Press, 1916), 4.

of importance. Ralph Peterson, who has written on class communities, notes: "[l]ife in classrooms is an intense social experience. For six hours a day, week after week, month after month, one teacher and anywhere from twenty-two to thirty-four students (sometimes more) live together in a space the size of a large living room."[1] For both the teacher and the children this group is important; as such, its goals and processes should be taken seriously.

Each class comes to have its own distinctive "culture"; the students are well aware of the rules and customs of their group even though they may have difficulty articulating or identifying them precisely. "There is no recipe for community building — no correlates, no workshop agenda, no training package. Community cannot be borrowed or bought."[2] Community cannot be "taught" in a specific program for it is embedded in the relationships and activities of the classroom. Through repeated practices the community develops certain attitudes and traditions; the class in general adopts a stance towards learning, authority, new-comers, altruism and so on. Granted, there are exceptions, but for the most part there are pervasive outlooks and practices in the class. To the dismay of many moral philosophers, most values are "taught" indirectly through these common attitudes, traditions and practices and not through formal programs. For example, when a teacher sets up a "committee" whose function is to welcome new students to the class by giving them a class tour, showing them the class photo albums, playing with them at recess and so on, the activity "tells" students that the teacher wants the community to be welcoming and inclusive and that friendship is important. She orchestrates the resources and develops the structures to help this goal become a reality. This simple practice contains many messages which influence the values of the students and sets the tone for the class. The traditions and rules established by the teacher affect the attitudes the students develop and shape the culture of the class.

> Tying the inhabitants together with invisible threads spun by shared emotions that derive from common experiences, they can thus weave young people of different races, classes, ethnicities, religions, physical abilities, sexual orientations into their own web of connections.[3]

Another factor which cannot be overlooked is that the group of children in the class share a history. They are together for ten months

---

[1] *Ibid.*, 2.

[2] Thomas Sergiovanni, *Building Community in Schools*, 5.

[3] Jane Roland Martin, *The Schoolhome; Rethinking Schools for Changing Families*, 98.

of the year and often socialize together after school; many remain with
the same group for a number of years. Teachers come and go but the
group stays together. Many times I have overheard children discussing
an experience from previous years, perhaps involving a supply teacher
who made a strong impression or a class outing that was memorable.
This history of shared experiences shapes them individually and as a
group. By encouraging dialogue and reflection on their previous experiences together and their present "history in the making," the bonds
within the group are reinforced. As a classroom teacher, I used to take
many photographs of my students, at play, at work, on field trips and
so on and these were kept together in photo albums. I noticed that these
books were the students' favourites. They became a record of our shared
history.

Whether we use the analogy of the class as an ecosystem or that of
a three dimensional shape, the many elements of the learning experience interconnect. For example, since children live together in the same
space for ten months of the year, serious attention should be given to
that space to ensure that the physical conditions are conducive to
learning and community development. Although at first glance the
physical conditions of the classroom may not seem relevant in a philosophical discussion, I cannot over-emphasize the importance of this
factor in developing the class as a community. I once taught in what
was supposed to be a classroom but was really an oversized closet; it
was swelteringly hot in warm weather and cold in the winter, had only
one tiny window, and contained uncomfortable furniture with desks and
chairs bolted together. To complicate matters even further, it was impossible to arrange the furniture so that everyone could see the black-
board and supplies of books and consumable materials were very, very
limited. With thirty five students jammed into this tiny space, many of
our problems were directly related to the cramped physical conditions.
(The mind-body problem can be very real even to five year olds!) The
unsuitable physical conditions of many classrooms hinder the growth
of the class as a community.

Fortunately, many newer schools have common spaces, large windows and circular designs; but even under favourable circumstances we
need to be constantly looking for new ways to ensure that the class lay-
out supports community life. In the Reggio Emilia school system the variety of rooms and room configurations —a large piazza, small work-
rooms, large common spaces and a special atelier (art room)— are conducive to community building. "These spaces tend to be pleasant and
welcoming, telling a great deal about the projects and activities, the

daily routines, and the people large and small who make the complex interaction that takes place there significant and joyful."[1]

Three Elements of the Learning Community

The preceding discussion identified the class as a major factor in the schooling process; each class is a unique and influential community. Although communities can take many forms, the class should be a community of learners where children value each other, feel responsible for others, learn with others and develop the skills of relational living. Each class will have its own "look" and "feel," but there are certain components common to all good classrooms. The following discussion identifies three key elements of the learning community.

i. *Linking Academic Learning and Community*

Since curriculum is a central aspect of the school experience, the class as a learning community must be seen in relation to it. The choice of activities, the structure of the lessons and the methods of evaluation all influence the formation of the community. Since the formal curriculum is value laden and a major component of schooling, it should reflect the broader goals of the community and help to realize them. For example, when teachers complete report cards with A,B,C,D,F grades, determined by comparing students and only considering particular qualities, the community becomes competitive and narrowly focused on certain types of academic achievements. This evaluation method suggests that less able students do not have a place in the community; this aspect of the formal curriculum hinders the growth of the community.

On the other hand, the quality of the community affects the academic program. When the class is not a cohesive group certain teaching/learning methods which rely on co-operation cannot be used successfully. It is impossible to have a dynamic, academic program in a highly regimented classroom. For example, as a consultant I have seen teachers try to implement process writing programs in highly teacher-directed, competitive classes. Not surprisingly the program failed miserably because the students and teacher did not have the social skills or attitudes to support it.

---

[1] Lella Gandini, "Educational and Caring Spaces," in *The Hundred Language of Children: The Reggio Emilia Approach to Early Childhood Education*, eds. Carolyn Edwards, Lella Gandini and George Forman (Norwood, NJ: Ablex, 1993), 137.

Learning is social: through interactions with others the students move to a new level of knowledge and a better understanding of self and others. For example, "[p]upil talk in a lesson has many functions. It increases the understanding of concepts, enables pupils to learn how to communicate clearly with others, makes them active learners, gives them a diversity of viewpoints and a critical tolerance of others."[1] As children engage in discussion, work collaboratively on a project or participate in organizing a class event, they are clarifying meaning, developing arguments, articulating a position and readjusting their thinking.

Genuine learning results from taking risks; it involves taking a chance with what is unknown, flirting with failure. To take risks, children must have a comfort level with the task: taking "big steps" on their own and meeting new challenges is a formidable challenge for most children. However, the anxiety of the new gamble can be lessened in a supportive community. Sara, a child in my grade one class, used a very novel approach to her paintings and stories about our trip to the zoo. Instead of doing the typical "follow-up," she painted pictures of some of the animals and accompanied them with animal jokes. The glee on Sara's face when she showed the pictures to the class and told the jokes was matched by the enthusiasm of her fellow students. The spontaneous applause she received at the end of her comedic/literary routine showed that the class appreciated her individual approach; the community supported her learning. Sara knew that it was acceptable to be an individual within the class because the program was open-ended; I encouraged children to take risks and the children were used to "doing" in different ways. Sara's growth as a writer was enhanced and the class also benefitted because they saw another model of story writing.

The connection between community and academic learning is seen particularly clearly in the twofold role which dialogue has in the classroom. As Dewey noted, communication within a community is a necessity; dialogue is essential to the formation and growth of community. However, dialogue is also essential for academic learning. Since children come to school already speaking, we assume that they already understand the dialogue process; teachers focus on building up their oral vocabulary and writing skills rather than helping them develop their dialogue skills. For youngsters oral discussion is often a more accessible medium for academic study; it also has the benefit of including all of the children, not just the able readers. The curriculum must not focus ex-

---

[1] Carol Thornly-Hall, *Let's Talk About Talk* (Mississauga, Ontario: Peel Board of Education), 9.

clusively on reading and writing: dialogue is an essential aspect of all schooling.

> Dialogue and democracy go hand in hand. Without a democratic sharing of power, true dialogue doesn't take place because people don't listen to each other. And without dialogue, democracy doesn't work because there is no way of arriving at good decisions. Dialogue enables us to find out what each of us needs, learn from each other, reach reasonable compromises, and commit ourselves to those compromises because we see the point of them.[1]

We see, then, the extent to which the process of community building and academic learning overlap.

ii. *Structures in the Community*

Classroom teachers are critical to the learning community: their behaviour is a model for interactions; they choose curriculum; and they implement classroom management strategies. This last point is the one I wish to concentrate on in this section. Too often our focus is simply on curriculum objectives and standard teaching strategies. However, the way the teacher organizes the class has a significant impact on the way the community coalesces and on the learning that follows.

Teachers organize the children through classroom management routines or "structures." Much more than just "discipline" techniques, these shape the community; they are powerful tools. Structures are many things: they are guidelines, routines, rules, traditions and processes. A structure can be described orally as "This class works well together"; or be posted as a rule such as "Do Not Push In Line"; or be a class slogan such as "Everyone Is An Expert"; or sometimes simply be understood by the students: "Ms. Smith believes in us." The structures are *organizing principles* and *processes for the class*. Structures form the backbone of the class: the way the activities flow from one to another, the organization of the children, the choices the children have, and the limits and boundaries for their behaviour.

One of the structures by which the whole school operates is the bell: when it rings, recess time is over. This rule governs student behaviour and organizes the school experience. I found it interesting that some kindergarten children in September often disregarded the bell and continued playing — they did not yet recognize its significance. Some structures that I used in my class were: opening exercises included a re-

---

[1] Clive Beck, *Dialogue and Democracy*, unpublished manuscript, 1993, 1.

flection on the previous day; every Friday, five students were chosen to read to the class the following week; every Friday, we did something special; the "student of the day" was encouraged to bring in something of interest from home; and every week, we worked with our grade eight buddy class. Every structure has a dual purpose: it conveys a message about the class values and it organizes the students. All of the structures listed above are value laden: they send messages that thoughtfulness is to be encouraged, that others are to be seen as resources, that the community must be joyful, that there should be links between home and school and that learning is not limited to the activities in our class.

Structures affect the formation of relationships and the quality of the children's learning. For example, one common structure is grouping children by ability. John Goodlad has found that the difference between high and low ability students starts to emerge in grade one and as each year passes the gap becomes larger. "The work of upper and lower groups becomes more sharply differentiated with each passing day. Since those comprising each group are taught as a group most of the time, it becomes exceedingly difficult for any one child to move ahead and catch up with children in a more advanced group ..."[1] Goodlad identifies one problem of ability grouping, namely that academic differentiation between students becomes insurmountable. Another serious consequence of this practice is that the formation of the whole class as a community is undermined. This structure carries many messages to the children about the goals of the class and their place in the community. Ability grouping emphasizes the academics and not the community. As children become splintered into ability groups it becomes exceedingly difficult to feel a sense of community and for the large group to support everyone's learning. Certain students who are not strong in the designated subjects are largely excluded from the community. Structures, then, not only provide the vehicle for the community to grow, they can also hinder it.

Before teachers teach their first lesson of the year, they must have an overall vision for the class. They must ask themselves, "What kind of community do I want?". By reflecting on this question and discussing the larger school community with colleagues, a direction is established. In the Newton School District teachers make "decisions about how they will treat each other and work together, decide what to teach and how to teach, and plan for evaluation."[2] Given the way schooling unfolds, with the intense pressure in September to get chil-

---

[1] John Goodlad, *A Place Called School: Prospects for the Future* (New York: McGraw Hill Book Company, 1984), 141.
[2] Thomas Sergiovanni, *Building Community in Schools*, 73.

dren into routines, teachers often do not have time to reflect on the implications of their decisions. With a well defined direction for the community flowing from the vision of the educated person, teachers will be able to make thoughtful choices about structures and appropriate curriculum materials. The same attention given to long range curriculum plans should be given to the routines, rules, traditions and processes of the class.

Ralph Peterson in *Life in a Crowded Place* outlines the underlying structures or elements that are used to build communities. "Just as painters work with the elements of point, line, tone, and plane, teachers and students use ceremony, ritual, rite, celebration, play and critique when they make a learning community. These elements are as old as humankind."[1] One of Peterson's techniques is the use of celebrations. Achievement "celebrations whose purpose is to recognize success cannot be truly appreciated by outsiders. Only members of a community who live closely together can weigh the significance of such an event."[2] He cites the example of an achievement celebration where a child who has moved ahead in her writing is given the chance to sit in the "author's chair" and share her work with others. The chair, in that class, is a symbol of having achieved. Each class must develop a whole array of celebrations, rites and rituals that are special to them; these structures are a way of developing the common values necessary for the community.

A high level of consistency between the direction for the community, the classroom structures and the curriculum materials is one of the strengths of the Montessori model. It provides a clear concept of the type of community to be developed and the classroom structures and chosen curriculum support this goal. For example, in Montessori classes one of the goals is respect for others' learning. The structures that are implemented help to realize this goal: one child per activity; a quiet atmosphere in the class; highly individualized programs; emphasis on manners; and materials returned to specific places. The Montessori routines and processes "direct" the formation of a particular type of community. Although I find the Montessori program too prescriptive and closed, we can learn from its consistency of purpose and coherence of structures.

Teachers must analyze and critique the structures in their classes; they must look at them from the children's viewpoint and try to determine the messages they are sending. Structures are powerful tools that have far reaching implications. The structures are points of the cube

---

[1] Ralph Peterson, *Life in a Crowded Place: Making a Learning Community*, 13.
[2] *Ibid.*, 42.

connecting with many other parts of the school program; they simply cannot be disregarded.

iii. *Seeing Others as Partners in Learning*

A third element of the community is that *all* others are viewed as resources or partners in the learning process. When relationships and connectedness are valued, there is a place for the bright, the artistic, the scientific, the athletic and the playful; everyone can and must be part of the community. The opportunity to participate in the community is not limited just to the "good" academic students. Everyone is valued for what they can contribute. For example, in my primary class we used to play a game called, "Who is it?". We would take turns describing the special characteristics of a particular student, and the others would have to guess who was being described. The children became very skilful at looking for positive qualities in each other and began to see that everyone had an expertise.

Jane Roland Martin's description of her ideal Schoolhome supports the view that the class community must be built on and around the talents of its members, not on the formal curriculum or a remote vision statement.

> I give thanks too that the Schoolhome is not relying on a common body of knowledge or information to establish kinship bonds among its inhabitants. These inestimable goods will be manufactured in other ways: by the inclusion of diverse voices and viewpoints; by the insistence that everyone take seriously the experiences and points of view of people unlike themselves; by the explicit rejection of stereotyping; by working through racial, ethnic, and religious as well as gender antagonisms ...[1]

The attitude that we are a community of experts (or partners in learning) and an inclusive community provides a space for everyone and draws on the family-like structure of the model. In (most) families participation in daily life is not dependent upon excelling in certain skills; there are accommodations so that all can contribute.

Seeing others as resources has many functions: it strengthens the students' sense of self, helps them connect to others, validates their efforts, supports learning and adds beauty, humour and majesty to the class. Recognition of others is not simply window dressing, a response to the demands of political correctness. Rather, it is deeply embedded in

---

[1] Jane Roland Martin, *The Schoolhome: Rethinking Schools for Changing Families*, 84.

the internal structure of the class; it is an essential dimension of a community that is learning and experiencing well-being.

The environment of the class community must encourage collaboration and the structures must support this style of learning and teaching. The teacher's genuine recognition of the students' abilities is an essential first step. As a primary school teacher I realized that there were students in my class who were far more accomplished in certain areas than I was or ever will be. For example, Fabian was an incredibly talented artist, Dorian had an endless supply of basketball stats and strategies, Christina was a natural athlete and Giovanni was a whiz with computers. I valued these students and it set the tone for us to be a class of resources. Students followed my lead and consulted with the class experts on all sorts of matters.

When we pool our talents, the whole becomes greater than the parts and we function as a team. On most teams each person at a given time has a specific job requiring a minimum level of competence in the particular area: each member is not expected to have identical abilities nor perform the same function. A team functions as a unit yet is made up of individual talents. Similarly, each person in the class community would not be expected to have the same interests or abilities, yet each person's abilities would be recognized and appreciated because they contribute to the well-being of the group. This allows children the opportunity to capitalize on their strengths or interests while augmenting the growth of the community.[1] We must safeguard against some children being permanently designated as a particular resource, just as we do not want children to be labelled academically; but viewing the class as a team would give students a chance to try out different roles, participate in the community and value others.

It is exceedingly difficult to have respect for others or see others as resources if no deviation from the standard school view is permitted. Learning from an early age that there are different perspectives is critical for our educated person. Unfortunately, schools have often operated on the mistaken premise that there is only "one right way." Seeing and treating others as resources would prevent a narrow perspective from forming. This is something that cannot be taught in a course; it must be modelled in the class culture. In a class of experts students begin to see and appreciate other approaches and styles.

> Through negotiation, students come to understand how someone else interprets an event, text, or situation: thereby, the basis for their own un-

---

[1] For further discussion of the concept of the class as a team see John Goodlad, *A Place Called School: Prospects for the Future*, 108-109.

derstanding is broadened. Too, they have an opportunity to see how another person goes about thinking through a situation or problem.[1]

When a class is a community of learners there is opportunity to foster an acceptance and understanding of different perspectives. Even though the class is composed of twenty five children roughly the same age, these youngsters are all individuals. The aim should not be to homogenize the group, but rather to discover our commonalities and appreciate our differences. We cannot graft this appreciation of others onto a competitive class; the class must be cooperative and pluralistic in nature. Expanding our concept of education leads to other ways of knowing and doing.

Conclusion

The learning community is a powerful force in the whole school process; we must recognize the role it can play in the lives of children and we must attend to its formation. There are no universal principles, no step by step plan to which we can refer. The community is formed in many ways; however, all members of the community must be involved in the process and all voices must be heard. And as the community is formed, the children and teachers learn the important skills of negotiation, caring, mutuality, responsibility, listening, responding, sharing, compromise and so on. Our learning community must *keep the conversation going* between children, teachers, administrators and the larger community.

Building the class into a community of learners is a complex process: it requires a vision of the educated person, a direction for schooling, intermediate steps and a great deal of collaboration involving everyone. Further, establishing a community of learners cannot be a separate mandate, it is interconnected with the curriculum, the larger school structure, the role of the teacher, parents' expectations and so on. In many ways this chapter is a bridge between the general theory of schooling and its practical application. The idea of the learning community begins to give form to the general goals of schooling and helps to illustrate the connectedness within the process of schooling. As we discuss more specific aspects of schooling we will return again and again to this mediating concept: the class as a community of learners.

---

[1] Ralph Peterson, *Life in a Crowded Place: Making a Learning Community*, 81.

Chapter Five

Teachers as Thoughtful Practitioners

> *The first day of school my teacher said she was going to teach me how to smile ... and she did.*
>
> *My first grade teacher kissed me.*
>
> *The principal remembered my name.*
>
> *She let us do something on our own, she trusted us.*
>
> *I could tell that the counsellor was genuinely interested in me. She listened.*[1]
>
> William Purkey and John Novak

Among the variables in the schooling process, the classroom teacher is one of the most important. Every student has vivid memories of a particular teacher; we have long forgotten the grammar lesson, the mathematics equation and the geography facts but we can recall with accuracy our teacher's mannerisms, quirks and favourite sayings. The impact that particular individual had on our learning and development becomes part of our being. A teacher who turned us on to literature which then opened up new worlds to us, or another who ensured that we would not select a career that required any knowledge of mathematics, has helped to shape who we are. John Goodlad notes, "the intellectual terrain is laid out by the teacher. The paths for walking through it are largely predetermined by the teacher."[2] I would extend this to say that the teacher sets the emotional climate by establishing attitudes towards self, others and learning. Teachers do much more than "teach" curriculum, they influence the school experience.

The teacher's role in the school community is very complex. In order to understand this, many perspectives must be considered. To deal with this complexity I have divided this chapter into five sections: first, a consideration of four problems currently facing teachers; secondly, a description and justification of teachers as thoughtful practitioners; thirdly, an account of my own story as a teacher; fourthly, a considera-

---

[1] William Purkey and John Novak, *Inviting School Success: A Self-Concept Approach to Teaching and Learning.* (Belmont, CA: Wadsworth, 1984), 8.

[2] John Goodlad, *A Place Called School: Prospects for the Future* (New York: McGraw-Hill, 1984), 109.

tion of the larger school community with emphasis on the school culture and school-based governance; and finally, an outline of five intermediate steps for teachers which parallel the goals for students discussed in Chapter Three.

Current Problems Facing Teachers

In order to have a changed role for teachers, many factors must be considered. To complete this analysis I will use my three part research methodology: consider the current situation; draw on personal experiences; and outline a model in the context of schooling. I begin by considering four problems which are strongly affecting the teaching profession. Many problems could have been chosen; the ones I discuss are crucial from my perspective and are related to the larger societal problems discussed in Chapter One.

i. *Teaching: A Multifaceted Job*

Having been a teacher for many years and having worked with many teachers, I know that a common complaint is "people just don't know how hard it is to be a teacher." The demands on teachers are many: they are intimately involved with approximately thirty children, all with differing needs; they must develop a positive class atmosphere, often in a school and community that are fraught with difficulties; they must organize learning often with limited resources; in addition to their regular duties they are expected to be actively involved in the larger staff community; often they must implement a curriculum that is inappropriate for their students; and they must build relationships with parents of all their students. All of this must be done in ten months. For primary teachers there are often additional parenting/ childcare tasks. Lack of public recognition of the many duties makes teachers feel unappreciated and even resentful. Too often teachers' work, like that of mothers, is taken for granted and undervalued.

In Chapter One I noted that schools are expected to be healers of society's woes. This ambitious mandate places teachers in the unenviable position of having to be "experts" on many topics while addressing crushing social problems. Classroom teachers face a monumental challenge each day, and from my work with them I know that the demands on them are unrealistic.

Drawing on Willard Waller's landmark study of teachers Andy Hargreaves and Peter Woods identify nine broad themes as they sketch out the large picture of teaching:

... what strategies they use to maintain their authority; how they cope
with the pressures that bear down on them; how they manage the teacher
role; their treatment of pupils; the implications of these classroom in-
volvements for teachers' relations with their colleagues; what goes on in
staffrooms; how teachers engage in educational debate; what ambitions
teachers have for themselves; and how their perceptions of their careers
are affected by changing socio-economic circumstances and educational
policies.[1]

Their themes focus on the professional duties of teaching, whereas
Andrew Pollard addresses the personal dimension of teaching: maxi-
mizing enjoyment, controlling workload, maintaining health, avoiding
stress, retaining autonomy, obtaining classroom order, and ensuring
children's learning.[2] These two lists illustrate the complexities of the
teacher's role and the wide range of professional and personal issues
which are part of the teacher's portfolio. Because of the breadth of the
issues, teachers must work in a variety of arenas and employ many different strategies.

ii. *Technicians or Superteachers*

In trying to make schools more responsive and efficient in solving society's problems, teachers are considered to have a crucial role; but there
are differing opinions on what that role should be. There are two common views of teachers: technician or superteacher. This dichotomy has
created confusion because teachers do not know what is expected from
them. On the one hand, there is the view that teachers are technicians
who should concentrate on teaching the basic curriculum more effectively. If only teachers were better at teaching phonics, computation
and spelling, the problems of youth unemployment or the competition
from the Japanese would be solved; if teachers were more competent the
solutions devised by experts outside the system could be implemented.
This mindset presupposes that teachers must be told exactly what to
do. In Ontario *Ontario   Curriculum, Grades 1-8* dictates to teachers
what skills are to be taught and learned. Benchmarks, the current label
for standard tests, will be used to see if the teachers have taught
"properly" and the students have learned what they were supposed to
know at each grade level. This assumes a very dim view of the capabil-

---

[1] Andy Hargreaves and Peter Woods eds., *Classrooms and Staffrooms: The Sociology of Teachers and Teaching* (Milton Keynes: Open University Press, 1984), 1.

[2] Andrew Pollard, "Primary School Teachers and Their Colleagues," in *The Primary School Teacher*, ed. Sara Delamont (London: The Falmer Press, 1987), 105.

ities of teachers to think and sort out what is appropriate for their classes. It in turn impacts on teachers' self-esteem and professionalism because they start to see themselves as less than worthy or equal in society.

On the other hand the Ministry of Education continually adds new programs to the curriculum in the belief that teachers are superteachers who can incorporate new program materials, approaches and activities into their already overloaded day. The multitude of programs from computer literacy, to drug awareness, to anti-racist education to environmental studies in addition to reading, writing and mathematics requires teachers to devote countless hours to making sense of the policies and presumes the ability to weave the curriculum together into a coherent program. In addition to this overwhelming content, there is an unstated demand that teachers must provide love and care for children. From the 1960s onwards, the relationship between teacher and child "was increasingly stressed as one of love."[1] Teachers must be a combination curriculum wizard and loving parent. Having been down the path of superteacher I must ask, "Is this a realistic expectation for teachers?".

iii. *Public Scepticism Toward Teachers*

A third problem facing teachers is the increasingly negative public attitude toward schools. In Chapter One I noted the growing public scepticism toward public institutions in general and school in particular. As symbols of the school, teachers are most often the target of this backlash. The title of Stanley Aronowitz and Henry Giroux' recent book, *Education Still Under Siege*, aptly sums up the sentiments of many educators who feel that their professional reputations and personal wellbeing are suffering under the weight of constant carping criticism from parents, politicians and professors reported frequently in newspapers and on television. Every newspaper seems to have its resident teacher bashing education critic.

The public, encouraged by the media, openly criticize teachers. It is much easier to blame a faceless group for society's problems than to reflect on one's own responsibilities. Lucy McCormick Calkins states that these are hard times for children; I would extend her idea to say that these are hard times for teachers as well. Daily attacks by the press on schools, which chiefly means teachers, have eroded much of

---

[1] Peter Cunningham, "Open Plan Schooling: Last Stand of the Progressives?," in *The Changing Primary School* ed. Roy Lowe (London: The Falmer Press, 1987), 57.

the pride that teachers had in their profession and their level of apathy has risen significantly. This attitude undermines teacher's good work and weakens the school community. "It seems, then, that teachers are already in a position of considerable self-sacrifice, offering care in a situation which is draining and often unfulfilling. Any major advance in achievement of the goals of schooling will require improvement in the lot of teachers *as well as* the students."[1] I feel that our journey as teachers has detoured down a very rocky road which has many twists and turns, and at this point there does not seem to be an end in sight.

To complicate the problem further, I find many teachers unwilling to enter into conversations with colleagues, consultants or superintendents about teaching — they are not used to these discussions, feel threatened by the constant criticism and want to return to the days of strong school autonomy. They see advocates of change (parents, administrators, consultants) as enemies; because they are protective of their programs and insecure, it is very difficult to have a productive discussion because they view all suggestions as criticisms or attacks. Teachers are rightly wary of proposals for change which are thrust upon them by outside experts who do not seem to understand what they are facing in the classroom on a daily basis. For many teachers the conversations among themselves and with parents and administrations are limited, thus leading to even more isolation. The "good old days" will not return, yet many teachers are not developing the skills to live in this changed and changing world.

iv. *Special Concerns of Primary Teachers*

Each division and age-group has special concerns. Intermediate division teachers feel they must prepare students for high school, junior division teachers try to consolidate the learning from the previous years and primary teachers have intense pressure to teach children to read and write. Primary teachers have additional pressures; Sara Delamont identifies two myths about primary teachers which have very negative implications. The first is that primary teachers are "'soft', 'permissive' and 'progressive' people who fail to discipline children or teach them anything systematically." The second myth is that "there was once a golden age when primary teachers were strict and children were forced to learn ...". Related to these myths is "a powerful rhetoric of abuse levelled at primary teachers which has little relation to facts

---

[1] Clive Beck, *Better Schools: A Values Perspective* (New York: The Falmer Press, 1990), 45.

or evidence ...".[1] Probably more than any other group, primary teachers face a barrage of criticism about their methods. As a teacher I heard endless complaints from junior and senior division teachers about the children, implying that I had not done my job properly. This constant criticism is unfair and demoralizing. The myths described by Delamont haunt primary teachers and undermine their good work.

Although primary teachers are constantly criticized, they must put aside their frustrations because they are in highly intense relationships with their children. All teachers have close relationships with the students but this is especially so in the primary division because the children are so dependent on them, often as substitute care-givers. Many primary teachers feel a conflict between teaching academics and being in-relation with the children. This was apparent in a dialogue I organized with primary consultants.[2] The topic was the "basics" but the conversation revolved around helping children feel secure, providing a sense of belonging, encouraging a love of school and so on. The moderators, who were fairly knowledgeable about school, expected the consultants to provide a list of academic skills. Primary teachers' perception of their job is very different from the public's expectations, and this creates a tension.

Furthermore, since primary teachers are often the children's advocates they begin to identify with the children's needs. Sara Delamont quotes a headteacher from a British primary school:

> Associating with a group of children continually and with her peers only occasionally, identifying her interests more and more with these children and standing with them against the world, she began to think and act as her pupils did ... So Mrs. Gregory fought for a playground field as if she were ten, not fifty-five. Mrs. Cornhouse and Miss Tuttle regaled the other teachers with first graders' jokes.[3]

As a primary teacher I loved working with children but I often felt isolated from my colleagues. Because primary programs are not very portable —activity centres, big math workbooks, water tables, large chart paper— primary teachers tend to remain in their classrooms which further isolates them from colleagues and causes them to identify more closely with students.

---

[1] Sara Delamont, "The Primary Teacher 1945-1990: Myths and Realities," in *The Primary School Teacher* ed. Sara Delamont 4.

[2] See "Primary Educators in Dialogue," *Orbit* 25, May, 1994 25-27.

[3] Sandra Acker, "Primary School Teaching as an Occupation," in *The Primary School Teacher* ed. Sara Delamont, 85.

The four points outlined above have created a problematic situation for teachers. They are misunderstood, faced with overwhelming demands, feel isolated and are demoralized. Since teachers themselves are frustrated and confused in the face of all this, it is not surprising that the public at large questions their effectiveness. Having identified some of the problems, I will now offer a way out of the maze.

Thoughtful Practitioners

Most books on schools have an obligatory chapter titled "The Role of the Teacher" which outlines techniques for classroom management and delineates many aspects of curriculum implementation. Long lists of terms such as 'facilitate,' 'support,' 'instruct,' 'model' and so on are commonly provided, often in a fancy flowchart. Although these analyses may be neat and tidy and suggest that teachers do more than convey facts to their students, for the most part they only tell part of the story. This view equates the teacher with curriculum implementation; it only sees teachers supporting the student's academic learning, overlooking many of their less formal influences. It also dehumanizes teachers: their needs are not recognized and their role is dealt with in isolation. Any discussion of the teacher should have a dual focus: teachers assisting the students' learning *and* the school supporting the teachers' well-being.

Since I am attempting to redefine the teacher's role, a frame of reference is necessary. My central concept is that of the teacher as "thoughtful practitioner." Nancie Atwell defines thoughtful practitioners as *educators who question, observe, reflect and make sense of their classrooms; they change in light of their discoveries; and they act as scholars.*[1] Her perspective surpasses the typical or traditional view of the teacher as mediator between text and child or organizer of the learning environment. As thoughtful practitioners teachers observe children; plan collaboratively with colleagues; communicate with families; adapt to changed situations; read professional literature; attend conferences; assume leadership roles; participate in meetings; speak thoughtfully to others; and take initiative. Although at first glance this list appears long and onerous, the burden will be lightened because in my model of schooling, teachers work together; are supported by their principal; have access to consultants; have influence over school structures; and have fewer curriculum subjects to address. Other

---

[1] Nancie Atwell, *Side by Side: Essays on Teaching to Learn* (Portsmouth, NH: Heinemann, 1991), 3.

elements of the schooling process support their growth as thoughtful practitioners. It is not a matter of simply adding duties to make teachers into superteachers; rather, it involves a new way of seeing their role in the class and in the larger community.

The value of Atwell's concept is the dynamic role it posits for teachers; it recognizes their power and expands the possibilities. At present, some teachers are thoughtful practitioners but it is not commonplace; many are so caught up in the day to day demands of running their class that there is little time to read, reflect and plan for the future. Because many schools have not adopted the notion of the teacher as a thoughtful practitioner, the system does not encourage teachers to develop the skills to reflect and change. Atwell's concept of the teacher is radically different from that of the flow chart analysts previously mentioned; she advocates a strong role for the teacher in the school and challenges a system which has long induced compliance and complacency in its teachers. Similarly, John Loughran and Tom Russell advocate a researcher role for teachers to move them towards more innovative and thoughtful practice.[1]

Since teachers are central to the schooling process their theories of education, their relationships and their procedures shape the experience. It is not sufficient for a teacher to have "a" single theory of education, it must be modified and changed in collaboration with colleagues as situations change. Neither is it enough to have a few tried and true pedagogical tricks; curriculum theory and its connection to community building must be clearly understood. Loris Malaguzzi, founder of the Reggio Emilia schools in Italy, recognizes both the importance of teachers and the necessity of working out their beliefs and elaborating their practices in a thoughtful way.

> It is well known how we all proceed as if we had one or more theories. The same happens for teachers: Whether they know it or not they think and act according to personal theories. The point is how those personal theories are connected with the education of children, with relationships within the school, and with the organization of work. In general, when colleagues work closely together and share common problems, this facilitates the alignment of behaviour and a modification of personal theories.[2]

---

[1] John Loughran and Tom Russell, eds., *Teaching About Teaching: Purpose, Passion and Pedagogy in Teacher Education* (London: The Falmer Press, 1997), 3-9.

[2] Loris Malaguzzi, "History, Ideas, and Basic Philosophy," in *The Hundred Languages of Children: The Reggio Emilia Approach to Early Childhood Education*

The isolation of teachers has hindered their growth as thoughtful practitioners because it impoverishes their resources and limits their potential for professional growth. Like students, teachers learn a great deal when they collaborate with peers, jointly solve problems, share strategies, modify their approach and take ownership of their work. In *The Hundred Languages of Children* there are countless examples of teachers observing, reflecting, consulting and acting with parents, children, colleagues and administrators; this pattern is repeated so frequently that it has become inherent in the way teachers go about their business. It is obvious that the strength of the Reggio Emilia approach is its strong teaching faculty and their ability to communicate with the public; the schools are partners with the community not scorned by them. One structure of the Reggio Emilia system that helps teachers become collegial partners is the assigning of two teachers to each group of students. (Rather than one teacher per class, there are two teachers for one very large class.) This set-up provides more flexibility in grouping children, encourages partnerships, breaks down the isolation of primary teachers, requires teachers to discuss theory and practice and models collegiality for the children. This system should be given serious consideration for our schools.

George Wood describes Hubbard Woods elementary school in Chicago, whose success is in large part due to the teachers' attitudes and sense of ownership. "While outside wisdom does influence the staff's work, the majority of curriculum development and writing, school organizational changes, and new approaches to teaching come from within. The people closest to the students thus make the crucial decisions about teaching and learning. The community of learners teaches itself."[1] Teachers teaching and learning is the crux, and as they see themselves in these roles apathy and low morale will recede. Through these activities and support from peers, teacher's self-esteem will be restored.

Schools should not only be concerned with the needs of the children but should also be addressing the needs of the adults who work with the children. I believe that school can only be a "worthwhile, rewarding experience" for children if teachers feel that it is a "worthwhile, rewarding experience" for them personally. In many ways the goal for children —enhancement of their lives through the educational process— should be applied to teachers. Because educators and children go

eds. Carolyn Edwards, Lella Gandini, George Forman (Norwood NJ: Ablex, 1993), 85.

[1] George Wood, *Schools That Work: America's Most Innovative Public Education Programs*, 30.

through the schooling experience hand-in-hand, schools must consider teacher well-being. A common phrase in the educational literature is "the whole child" and this commitment to the entire well-being of the child should be extended to teachers too. Teachers' physical, emotional and cognitive states must be considered. Constant criticism has eroded teacher's self-esteem and pride — school is not good for them. Goodlad asserts, "teachers are made of clay like the rest of us."[1] The whole teacher must be a consideration too. For example, by giving primary teachers more opportunities to step outside their class and work with colleagues, the problems of isolation and frustration will be lessened. The working conditions for most teachers is a problem; they do not have offices, often do not have a desk (I had to wait eight years before I got a desk), there is limited opportunity to make a phone call in private, often they have to use the same washroom facilities as the children and so on.

In the following example of four thoughtful practitioners I show that care for the whole teacher is essential; collegiality is indispensable and there are connections between student and teacher well-being. At D'Arcy McGee Catholic School I was part of a genuine learning community. I had the good fortune to work in an open area complex which housed four teachers and approximately one hundred and thirty students. We called our classes "suites" and referred to ourselves as the team; we were a combination of novices and veterans. Our teaching was outstanding because we pooled our ideas and resources, read professional literature, had team meetings at least once a week *during* school time (usually an hour) and most importantly we were mutually supportive. Through a great deal of cajoling we were able to all have our breaks together so that we could work together. Teaching was not just a job; we enjoyed the children, loved the challenge and were proud to be called teachers. We laughed about disastrous lessons and consoled each other when faced with a difficult student. We helped each other with student observations, one of the most critical parts of teaching, and worked together on program modification. We saw our role extending beyond the classroom walls; we regularly contacted parents, consulted with the principal, reviewed the prescribed curriculum, suggested alternatives and worked efficiently. One word that described us was dynamic. Because of the physical layout, we were able to observe each other. As a team we had a great deal of autonomy in planning and because we knew the students and ourselves, we could make wise and appropriate decisions. The students were in grades two and three so they stayed in the suite for two years.

---

[1] John Goodlad, *A Place Called School: Prospects for the Future*, 170.

Although the level of mutual assistance and help from other sources fell short of the ideal of collaboration that Roland Barth[1] discusses or that is found in Malaguzzi's Reggio Emila school system it was an experience that brought to life the notion of the learning community, relational living and collegial teaching. Although we did not have the language or knowledge to discuss our journeys as teachers (the concept had not been named yet) or leadership from the administration, in many ways we were thoughtful practitioners. We shared and practised the belief that schools must be good places for both teachers and children. We modelled the values of autonomy, control, responsibility, care and mutuality and they became inherent in the structures of the class. We supported each other, generally and in curriculum development. The respect from my colleagues and the strength they provided influenced my own journey as a person and a teacher. When it works open area arrangement is wonderful for the adults and children involved, although it takes tremendous effort.

Unfortunately, in the conservative mood of the late nineteen eighties the large open areas were partitioned into the traditional box-like classrooms(incidentally, without our being consulted or even forewarned). It is interesting to note that the strong teams of teachers, instead of being appreciated, were seen as a threat to the administration and the principal encouraged the dismantling of the large open areas. The walls did more than change the configuration of the classrooms, they broke the co-operative and collaborative spirit of the teaching teams. "Open plan schools are the outward sign of inward change,"[2] and obviously some did not like the change that was going on in D'Arcy McGee. Once the walls were in place the whole tone of the school changed to one of more individualism and competition, and from my viewpoint the quality of teaching, learning and living declined.

Students, teachers, curriculum and society are linked; all parts of the whole are important and each part impinges on and influences the others. Although some would say that teachers are *the* key to the process, I support Beck's view that "the fact of the matter is that, in addition to the teachers, the curriculum and a range of other elements are also important."[3] The concept of thoughtful practitioners recognizes these many factors and their interconnections; the focus is not exclu-

---

[1] See Roland Barth, *Improving Schools From Within: Teachers, Parents and Principals Can Make the Difference* (San Francisco: Jossey-Bass, 1990), 30.

[2] Peter Cunningham, "Open Plan Schooling: Last Stand of the Progressives?," in *The Changing Primary School*, ed. Roy Lowe, 50.

[3] Clive Beck, *Better Schools*, 46.

sively on the teacher performing. As I have argued, there are many other aspects to the school process.

Clare's Story

Having had the luxury of being a full-time student, I have been able to reflect on my many years as a classroom teacher. By revisiting many scenes, lessons and activities of my career, I see my growth and development as a teacher and as an individual. By sharing some of this story, I will show my development as a thoughtful practitioner. The narrative tradition that is emerging in the academic world has proven to be very helpful for me (and apparently for others) in understanding teaching. "Narrative inquiry involves the recovery of stories from life texts and personal beliefs which we then reconstruct into new meaningful wholes."[1] My reflections have helped me identify the elements of teaching; link theory and practice; and arrive at a better understanding of teaching. David Hunt who is one of a growing number of writers on the topic of teachers "making sense of their own teaching" makes a strong claim for teachers (re)discovering their voice.

> Your common sense ideas and your unexpressed theories, growing out of your own personal experiences, provide enormously rich sources of knowledge about human affairs. By beginning with yourself, therefore, you are taking advantage of this rich reservoir — tapping what you know about yourself and others to bring out your experienced knowledge on topics that psychologists would call interpersonal relations, self-awareness, individual differences, teaching and learning, and so on.[2]

Teachers do not have to rely on experts to interpret the situation and provide guidance. Thoughtful practitioners use their own wisdom, think about their story, share it and learn from others' stories; stories become their research and part of their teaching style.

When I look back on my teaching career I see that my journey falls into three phases: saviour, disillusionment and consolidation. Like most new teachers, in the saviour period I bubbled with enthusiasm, felt that I knew best and could save the children by offering them a superb program. Working in an inner city area, I believed that the school

---

[1] L. Delores Furlong, *Natural-Ethical Decisions in Caring Relations*, Paper presented at the Learned Societies Conference, Charlottetown, June 1992, 2.

[2] David Hunt, *Beginning With Ourselves: In Practice, Theory, and Human Affairs* (Toronto: OISE Press, 1987), 1.

could do it all, that a solid education would solve the children's problems and society's difficulties. I loved my job, I loved the children and I gave myself to them through hard work and devotion; the children in return gave me their affection. I was living the model of the superteacher — I worked endlessly and often on my own. After about seven years of very long hours and taking the children's problems home with me a degree of disillusionment set in; I was emotionally (and many times physically) exhausted, I felt that the system was not working because other teachers did not care as much as I did and parents did not try hard enough to raise their children. Frustration with the children and the system were common in this period and to add to my dismay I began to have doubts about my effectiveness. My teaching was definitely not as strong in this second phase because of my less than positive attitude. My outlook influenced the class culture because my curriculum choices re-enforced my sense of hopelessness. I tended to be more of a technician; following a boring basal reading program, teaching formal lessons and so on. The school community was fraught with difficulties: the principal was often in a rage; money was limited; parents were frustrated; school board initiatives were numerous and mostly inappropriate; and students felt pressured. In hindsight I realize that the community was not supportive of me personally or professionally.

As I re-live many steps of my journey as a teacher, especially this second phase, I have come to appreciate how lonely it was. Given the large number of people and the constant activity in schools it seems absurd to suggest that teachers can feel a sense of isolation; however, being confined to a class with a group of young children all day, and to conversation with other adults revolving around yard duty schedules, art supplies, dissatisfied parents or naughty children, the school can be a very alienating place in which to work. The school culture undermines a sense of connectedness and opportunities to interact are limited. Even lunch hour is crammed with sports supervision, returning phone calls to parents or scrambling to photocopy worksheets; it is not an opportunity for "quality interaction" with peers. Goodlad notes "the classroom cells in which teachers spend much of their time appear to me to be symbolic and predictive of their relative isolation from one another and from sources of ideas beyond their own background of experiences."[1] Loneliness makes being a thoughtful practitioner almost impossible.

Gradually, through changes in my personal life, a new principal, a change of grade, involvement in professional organizations and outside study, my perspective changed. I moved into the third phase, consoli-

---

[1] John Goodlad, *A Place Called School: Prospects for the Future*, 186.

dation, where I began to have a better understanding of the whole educational process and more realistic expectations for myself and the students. In this stage I became more of a thoughtful practitioner. My enthusiasm for teaching returned but this time I saw education as a partnership between myself, students, colleagues, parents and society in general. I was more realistic about the effectiveness of schools and realized that I must take more responsibility for my well-being. I began to set more reasonable goals for myself and re-established some connections with colleagues. I read widely, attended classes, connected with likeminded teachers and assumed greater control over my personal and professional life. In this phase I now question, reflect, act and share. I still believe that schools can make a tremendous difference, but they cannot do it alone. I now know that I cannot save the children singlehandedly, but I recognize that I am a strong presence in their lives. My journey in the educational world is definitely not over because I plan to stay involved in schooling. I know that there are more phases to come, changes to make, insights to be gained and goals to be redefined. As I look around at my friends and colleagues in education, I would suggest that my experiences are very similar to their stories.

During the first two phases of my career, I knew that something was missing but I did not have the opportunity or words to describe my teaching or what was happening to me. Professional development, which could have been a partial solution to my isolation, was focused solely on improving teaching techniques and did not provide opportunities for me to grow as a thoughtful practitioners. I needed what Judith Warren Little refers to as "collegiality": educators talking about practice; observing each other; working on curriculum; and teaching each other.[1] Teachers need to talk about their teaching; have exemplary models; and be helped to develop as thoughtful practitioners. As George Wood notes, in the schools that work there is the common belief that "a community is only as strong as its weakest link...".[2] Teachers must feel part of the community and feel responsible for its well-being. I see this now, and will work to guide teachers toward being thoughtful practitioners who move out from and beyond their individual classes.

---

[1] Roland Barth, *Improving Schools From Within: Teachers, Parents and Principals Can Make the Difference*, 31.

[2] George Wood, *Schools That Work: America's Most Innovative Public Education Programs*, 85.

The Larger School Community

Until now the discussion has focused on individual teachers in individual classrooms; however, they are part of a larger structure. Having
once worked in a school that was highly regimented I realize that the
overall school culture is pervasive and is crucial in determining
whether or not teachers can be thoughtful practitioners. The general
school environment must be considered as it affects curriculum choices,
behaviour codes, relationships within the community and the teacher's
journey.

The individual school is the place to commence change; outside organizations certainly assist teachers in their journey and general
statements about education from the school district level may be helpful, but the actual school is central to any change.

> Schools will improve slowly, if at all, if reforms are thrust upon them.
> Rather, the approach having most promise, in my judgment, is one that
> will seek to cultivate the capacity of schools to deal with their own
> problems, to become largely self-renewing. [1]

i. The School Culture

As a school board consultant I have had the opportunity to visit many
schools and after a while I developed a "sixth sense" which identified
the school culture. Similar to the individual class, each school has a
way to treat newcomers, an attitude towards professional development,
a discipline style and so on.

In George Wood's affirming, hopeful book, *Schools That Work*, he
profiles many schools that are success stories, "schools and classrooms
... that you know are special the moment you step into them."[2] His observations and conclusions re-enforce my belief that the general school
environment influences everyone; the school culture must *keep the conversation going*. He concludes that teachers, parents and administrators
cannot do it individually, they must work together to develop the
school culture.

> None of the teachers, administrators, or parents we have visited would
> say that they have gone it alone. Many of them, in fact, know one another

[1] John Goodlad, *A Place Called School*, 31.
[2] George Wood, *Schools That Work: America's Most Innovative Public Education Programs*, xiii.

and share ideas, insights, and strategies. Just as important, they have read widely, visited other schools, made use of a multitude of resources.[1]

The schools Wood considers outstanding have a positive school culture; reading "between the lines," communication, community and common values are the bedrock of these success stories. Schools cannot mandate teachers to be thoughtful practitioners but they can provide opportunities and establish structures to help them develop. This changed role for teachers is contingent upon many other factors in the school system.

Rather than list the features of a positive "school culture," an example of a particular school might be more useful. I had the good fortune to work with an outstanding group of teachers at St. John the Baptist/King Edward elementary school in St. John, New Brunswick. The building was old but bright; the classrooms spilled out into the hallways; the corridors were filled with student work and art; at recess and lunch hour the staffroom buzzed with activity; and a special section of the staff bulletin board was filled with notices of professional development opportunities. Just walking through the school I felt invited and a sense of openness among the staff. As I was setting up for the workshop, teachers wandered in to the library to see if I needed anything; the principal asked if he could join in the workshop; and the session was conducted during class time because the principal wanted to show his commitment to on-going professional development.

The dynamics among the participants exemplified a healthy school culture: the teachers' comments and questions always centered around the children's needs; they viewed their peers as resources —they freely consulted each other; and they had identified their particular needs as teachers— they knew what they required. This staff had worked out goals for the school, they were clearly articulated and they were shared by all members of the school community. The atmosphere in the group was one of mutual support and admiration; Colleen was the artist, Sandy was the adventuresome one and so on. The group was a solid community but it was not closed, they had invited the curriculum consultant to be part of the session because they valued her expertise. One of Wood's success stories seems similar and he notes that "it is a family place in the best sense, honouring the diversity of all its members, providing a community where all can flourish. It is the type of community that makes democracy possible ...".[2] St. John the Baptist/King Edward school was a family place in the best sense of the term.

---

[1] *Ibid.*, 267.
[2] *Ibid.*, 31.

The New Brunswick group's hospitable attitude extended beyond the inner group; the school was located in a very needy part of the city but there was never a hint of disrespect for the surrounding community; in the discussions the teachers raised the issue of how to involve parents in the programs. On a lighter note, the workshop was filled with laughter; these were teachers working in a very difficult setting, but they had not lost their sense of humour. For these educators, teaching was not "just a job"; their well-being was enhanced through their activities. Obviously this was not the first time the staff had worked together because they possessed the confidence and skills of thoughtful practitioners. As the workshop progressed I was watching this dynamic, caring group of teachers grow as individuals and as a staff. My presentation was only another step in the development of their school culture and hence the growth and development of the children and adults. It is interesting to note that many of the elements that I identified as being necessary for a positive classroom culture were apparent with this group of adults; it seems that the experiences which are good for children in their individual classes are also necessary for the larger school culture.

One of the first steps in becoming thoughtful practitioners is for everyone, both literally and metaphorically, to step outside their classrooms and offices. At St. John the Baptist/King Edward school, the open doors of the classroom and office signified open minds and attitudes. As Wood writes:

> Doors to these schools and classrooms are open to all, board members, parents and community members are issued invitations to come see the program at work. In all, it is an approach to potential criticism that typifies the healthy community — welcome the critic, listen and learn, take from him/her what we can use, reject that which is inconsistent with our aims and goals. [1]

As teachers and administrators step outside their comfortable and familiar domains, they have a chance to see other perspectives; only then is there a chance for them to start making connections with others and develop as thoughtful practitioners.

ii. *School-Based Governance*

For children to become autonomous, reflective, caring, responsible individuals, we must change our (adult) attitude towards them. Similarly

---

[1] *Ibid.*, 38.

there must be a change in administrators' (which includes principals, bureaucrats and policy makers) view of teachers if teachers are to become thoughtful practitioners. In addition to a more "enlightened" view of teachers there must also be "structures," in the broad sense of the word discussed earlier, that allow teachers to grow and develop. For teachers, a change in attitude accompanied by structures such as forums in which they can participate in school decision-making will help *to keep the conversation going*.

The key to establishing these structures is the school principal; as a consultant I have visited many schools and I know that the principal not only establishes school policies but also sets the tone for the school community. In the following discussion of school-based governance I emphasize the principal because administrators are key to the school culture and hence the teacher's journey.

Many school boards have moved towards school-based governance as an important step in making the school more of a community centre. There are two problems associated with this movement, however. First, the move towards school-based governance may be seen by some as a way to save money and for superintendents at the board level to shift tasks to the school that they no longer want to perform or feel they do not have the budget to carry out. Secondly, teachers who are used to working in the present system may not be ready to assume responsibility for this type of decision-making; nor may they have the skills necessary for these tasks. It is unrealistic to move too quickly to a local school governance policy; some groundwork must be laid. For example, one Metro Toronto school board declared all consultants redundant and assigned all professional development and mentorship programs (for beginning teachers) to the local schools; the schools floundered badly because teachers and administrators were not ready to assume these duties.

Traditionally, principals have had a great deal of the power within the school and have made many of the on-site decisions; in school-based governance, the principal would share this decision making power. (Some principals may have to be encouraged and trained to share their decision making authority.) In my proposed model for schools I see an "education council" being a central force in the life of the school; it would be composed of the principal and representatives of teachers, parents, support staff, students and educational assistants. The council would meet regularly, discuss issues, make presentations to the general staff and the parent community, plan the direction for the school and have real power and responsibilities. The council would represent a wide range of perspectives.

The benefits of participating in the council would be many: members of the council would learn and refine their communicating and negotiating skills; being part of a legitimate body would raise self-esteem; and the individual's connection to the school would be strengthened because there would be a lessened sense of alienation. After teachers had been involved with the council for a year or two, they would have a much better understanding of issues of budgeting, board policy, accountability, the Education Act and Regulations, community concerns and so on: it would be almost impossible for individual teachers to gain this information and insight without participation in council activities. Furthermore, this experience would enhance the individual's personal journey. Most likely after participating in the larger governing body teachers would change their teaching style because they would have gained a better understanding of the big picture of schooling; administrators would have a better grasp of the issues facing teachers; and parents would become aware of the many facets of education that tend to be overlooked by the public. "It is possible to treasure the uniqueness of a whole range of perspectives without losing sight of commonalities."[1] This council would help to keep the school from turning inward and would strengthen the bonds with the wider community. As the larger community got to know the demanding nature of the teacher's job, the myths of teaching would be dispelled.

As council members interacted with the larger school body, they would share the knowledge gained from their experiences; because classroom teachers tend to be more accessible to the general staff than the principal there would be a greater sense of cohesiveness on staff. Being a council member would take time and commitment; however, this could not be a duty in addition to all of the other regular tasks. (The model could not be built on the concept of superteacher.) High schools have a system of release periods for department heads and the elementary school could adopt part of that model for working out ways to give teachers in-class time to work on council duties. This would entail a move away from the one teacher per class system that is currently in operation; there would have to be a greater use of parent volunteers, students from faculties of education, teaching assistants, teaching vice-principals and so on to accomplish this more fluid staffing.

Wood shares the example of La Escuela Fratney, a Milwaukee school where teachers, administrators and parents gained a measure of control over their school. They turned the school around from being a dumping ground for poor teachers to being a vibrant, bilingual commu-

---

[1] Jane Roland Martin, *The Schoolhome: Rethinking Schools for Changing Families,* 56.

nity centre. To do this there was a "team of people [to] direct the school. Parents elected by other parents, teachers and paraprofessionals appointed by the staff, and a principal form a site-based management team that runs the school." And what makes this work is that "they maintain this spirit ... [of] working on something real that they care about."[1] Once again the analogy of the team recurs in Wood's description of the site-based group; he is talking about a team of experts —teachers, administrators and parents— each with special talents working on a real project.

Five Intermediate Steps For Teachers

The previous discussion has moved from the individual teacher to the larger community; now I want to return to the teacher. The five intermediate steps that I am suggesting for teachers parallel the goals for students outlined in Chapter Three. Returning to the premise that values education occurs through the structure of the school, it makes sense that the values for adults are the same as the ones for children. The term "goal" and "step" describe both expectations and experiences. These goals for teachers are a combination of the structure and life of the school; the teacher's experiences; outcomes expected from the teacher in terms of teaching; and outcomes for the teacher within the larger community. The intermediate steps help teachers move from the more abstract concepts of the educated person and the thoughtful practitioner to the realities of the classroom situation.

i. Autonomy/Control

Autonomy/control, the first intermediate step, refers to a sense of freedom to learn about oneself, about others and about teaching; and the opportunity to plan given one's personal teaching style and the needs of the children. Since teaching should support the individual's journey, autonomy must include a freedom of spirit; teachers should not be under constant threat or surveillance from administrators, parents and the press. Thoughtful practitioners can only make wise decisions if they are not encumbered by a host of external constraints. On the other hand, it is unrealistic to propose unlimited freedom for teachers because commitment to the community is a critical aspect of the schooling experience. When teachers feel they have a degree of control over the work-

---

[1] George Wood, *Schools That Work: America's Most Innovative Public Education Programs*, 24.

ings of their class they become deeply connected to the experience. (Teachers as technicians do not have this ownership or connection.) Just as children should have some control over the choice of reading materials and writing projects, teachers must feel ownership of their program. Pride in your work can only come about if it is truly your own work, and pride in a job well done can be the impetus for continued growth and learning. Placing teachers in a "curriculum straitjacket" removes the possibility of ownership.[1]

My schooling model places a heavy emphasis on teacher participation in the life of the school; teachers must feel they can make a difference and that their individuality is appreciated. If children are to take more control of their learning, the atmosphere and structures of the class must support them in this; however, this can only be accomplished if teachers feel empowered. Teachers and students go through the education process side by side and it is tremendously difficult for teachers to encourage ownership, free thinking and active participation in the class when they feel disenfranchised. "Having some say over how I teach makes me feel wonderful. I feel people are trusting me to know what is best for my kids. I am recognized as a professional."[2] In our open area arrangement at D'Arcy McGee we had a great deal of control over our program. The children witnessed us using our initiative and it became an important value that flowed through the life of the community.

Aronowitz and Giroux in *Education Under Siege* make a strong case for teachers having a central role in all school activities. For example, they argue that separating curriculum planning from curriculum implementation will undermine the teacher.

> ... viewing teachers as intellectuals provides a strong critique of those ideologies that legitimate social practices which separate conceptualization, planning, and designing from the processes of implementation and execution. It is important to stress that teachers must take active responsibility for raising serious questions about what they teach, how they are to teach it, and what the larger goals are for which they are striving.

---

[1] Clare Kosnik and Clive Beck, "Does Involvement in Action Research Develop a Sense of Ownership for Student Teachers in Their Preservice Programs?" paper presented at the American Educational Research Association meeting, San Diego, April 14, 1998.

[2] *Ibid.,* 25.

This means that they must take a responsible role in shaping the purposes and conditions of schooling.[1]

In my overall scheme for schooling, I want the people who are directly involved with the children to be directly involved with setting the goals. To have a consistency between goal setting, planning and implementation teachers must be central to the process and have a measure of control over it.

ii. *Reflectiveness*

The notion of reflectiveness is, of course, integral to teachers becoming thoughtful practitioners; throughout this chapter I have been advocating that teachers think about their teaching. By "reflectiveness" I mean looking inward — teachers reflecting on teaching as part of their personal journey. Teachers must pause to look around at life to see how their daily activities fit in with their general well-being. This will require teachers, like all individuals, to stop and listen to their inner voice. In my period of disillusionment I eventually responded to my inner voice when it told me that something was not right. By listening and then acting I grew both personally and professionally.

Reflectiveness has many advantages for a healthy way of life, not all of which can be explored at this point. "Self-knowledge precedes learning from others"[2]; until we have a good understanding of our self, teaching styles, strengths and so on, we will rely on "experts" and prepackaged curriculum materials to dictate the working of our classrooms. (Or we will become duped by the latest fad in the curriculum marketplace.) The teachers at St. John the Baptist/King Edward school had thought about what they needed; they listened to my presentation with open minds; they kept what was appropriate and discarded what did not fit with their present agenda. They could fully benefit from my expertise because they considered themselves experts too. Reflectiveness leads to a greater sense of power over the situation. When you "realize that you own your ideas [it] increases your own agency and control, which creates more choices."[3] This ownership gives teachers a greater control over their class and their personal journey.

---

[1] Stanley Aronowitz and Henry Giroux, *Education Under Siege: The Conservative, Liberal and Radical Debate Over Schooling* (South Hadley, MA: Bergin and Garvey Publishers, 1985), 31.

[2] David Hunt, *Beginning With Ourselves: In Practice, Theory and Human Affairs*, 33.

[3] *Ibid.*, 34.

Teachers in a school cannot rely on others to enhance their journey, they must turn both inward and outward to reap the benefits of life in a school community.

iii. *Integration*

Just as children should feel a continuity between home and school, so too should teachers feel a connectedness between their personal and professional lives. Teaching should enhance the individual's personal life and teachers should bring some of their personal interests and skills into the class. This will lead to a greater integration of these two worlds. Kathy is an example of a teacher who bridges the two worlds; she is an avid and accomplished photographer in her personal life and brings her hobby into the class. She shares some of her photos with her students, does a photography unit with them, begs and borrows a class set of cameras for her students to use and takes students on excursions to photography exhibits. Through these activities the students see the very human side of their teacher as she is pulling back the traditional teacher veil of silence; and her expertise also enhances the school experience for the children.

Given the large urban sprawl, many teachers do not work and live in the same community; some travel long distances to their school. While I am not suggesting a change in this demographic pattern, there is a serious consequence of teachers being split between two communities. They can easily be "out of sync" with the concerns of the school neighbourhood and as a result develop an inappropriate agenda for the children. Schools cannot be a community centre if the staff do not know the local concerns and are not actively involved in the community; we cannot meet community needs if our objectives are determined in isolation. Teachers can help overcome this disconnection by participating in the School Advisory Council or Home and School Council. Occasionally they should take the time to a walk in the community, shop in the local grocery store, or even attend neighbourhood functions such as the local street fair, church service or sports event. Participation in these functions will help teachers get to know parents, students and the community in a way that is not possible by merely gazing out their classroom windows. I know that parents appreciated my efforts when I stepped out of the traditional teacher role and participated in community activities. The goodwill that was developed through my participation went a long way in breaking down the barriers between the community and the school.

iv. *Responsibility/Care*

To balance autonomy/control, teachers must exercise a high level of responsibility and care toward their children and programs. By responsibility I mean being accountable to one's self and others (not in the sense of higher student test scores!); providing for the children's needs; being willing to contribute to both the individual class community and the overall school culture; and being trustworthy in supporting children's needs. Care for children, colleagues and self cannot be reduced to specific behaviours — it is a way of being. When teachers step beyond the limited role of technicians they can meet others as individuals and allow others to meet them as persons. Responsibility/care helps to break down the barriers of isolation.

Responsibility/care addresses two main areas: children and curriculum. Caring for children is often tied to the notion of relational teaching. Nel Noddings, who has written extensively on the relational aspect of education, emphasizes the importance of the relationship between the teacher as care giver and the student as cared for.[1] In emphasizing care she places the social, affective and interpersonal before facts, figures and skills. By proposing a shift from a strong cognitive orientation to an emphasis on the affective, she forces us to rethink our ends and means; the head, heart and hand are all legitimate goals. She dismisses the "one size fits all" model which concentrates on academic adequacy (some would suggest inadequacy) and stresses a less tangible but equally important goal.

Noddings shows that relationships are reciprocal in nature. Both the care giver and the cared for must act in a way that allows the relationship to flourish: in a caring cycle the care giver acts, the cared for receives and responds appropriately and finally the care giver receives the response. Thus a cycle of caring is complete. This is a very different concept of teaching because we have traditionally seen the student-teacher relationship as one way: the teacher dispenses and the student receives. In Noddings' model the student must not only receive but also respond in an appropriate way, and the teacher in turn must receive the response. Both student and teacher receive and respond in a caring way. In my own experience I cared for my students and their responses nurtured me. The reciprocity of the relationship helped everyone to grow.

A second aspect of responsibility/care is curriculum implementation. In Chapter Six I will discuss curriculum in detail, but at this point I simply want to note that teachers have a responsibility to locate and

---

[1] Nel Noddings, *The Challenge to Care in Schools: An Alternative Approach to Education* (New York: Teachers College Press), 53-55.

examine the best quality curriculum materials; to read research on learning/teaching; and to integrate some of the new methods into their work. Attending courses and participating in professional organizations are two ways for teachers to keep abreast of the ever changing knowledge field. The reasons for attending these professional development sessions should not be "give me a new gimmick or teaching trick"; rather, it should be part of ongoing growth as teachers. There should be an element of intellectual rigour in teacher education courses. An example from my own professional development courses illustrates the problem; when I attended the Principals' Certification course my instructor threw up his hands in despair when I asked a question about the links between school and society and accused me of being too academic. Questioning, probing, examining and reflecting, the ways of thoughtful practitioners, must be part of all professional development —supplying strategies, "recipes" and content is not enough. The *Standards of Practice* developed by the Ontario College of Teachers are highly supportive of teachers taking a measure of control of their professional development.[1]

v. *Mutuality*

The fifth intermediate goal for teachers involves inter-personal connectedness, reciprocity, and give and take. Mutuality is a conscious attempt to move away from the individualism that has been the basis for schooling — both teachers and students have suffered under the competitive rule. It is a shift from isolation, a bridging of the "we" and "they" posturing that is commonplace in schools. Teachers are threatened by parents and administrators, parents do not trust teachers, principals are not sure whom to trust. In this general atmosphere it is difficult to develop a sense that we are all in this together; we become hesitant to open ourselves up to others.

Students, new teachers and parents easily pick up the combativeness between members of the school community; this "chilly" environment makes it difficult for children to learn about and practice relational living. It also makes it very difficult for teachers to be collegial, active members of the larger community. When I worked in the open area complex the students witnessed: the give and take of working together; the friendship between the teachers; and the joy we experienced in each other's company. The children learned about friendship

---

[1] Ontario College of Teachers, *Standards of Practice for the Teaching Profession* (Toronto: 1998).

to after school hours, we brought them right into the classes and they became part of the learning environment. Teaching is a demanding, difficult profession and being part of a team eases the burden. Since teaching should be more than just a job, schools must allow for and encourage a relational way of being for all members of the school community (parents, teachers and administrators as well as students).

In my model for schools I see some of the barriers crumbling between the classes because teachers feel part of a supportive environment. When teachers see each other as resources they ask for advice; share success stories; and are willing to be consoled. Mutuality and collegiality are complementary values and as such go hand in hand. These are necessary elements for a school community and are integral to a person's journey.

Conclusion

Throughout this chapter I have argued that teachers are critical to the complex process of schooling. "Teaching well is a difficult art if only because it requires balancing conflicting claims in order to find the best course in a great variety of circumstances."[1] Most would accept Dearden's assumption as valid; I have tried to go beyond the rhetoric to gain a deeper understanding of teaching. By considering four problems that teachers face I have probed beyond the curriculum. By moving away from the notion of teacher as technician, I have argued that teachers have a profound impact on the school experience. I have also shown the inappropriateness of basing schools on superteachers. A corollary of these investigations has been making explicit the human side of teaching. With a more in-depth understanding of the nature of teaching, I have suggested that the model for teaching should be teacher as thoughtful practitioner. Although this role is a radical departure from the present system it includes many familiar elements; the fundamental difference is that thoughtful practitioners are dynamic, powerful and collaborative problem solvers. They see beyond the class, see school in the larger scheme of society, understand other forces and recognize broader issues. They see themselves as part of the change process; they are not just acted upon, they understand, control and act.

---

[1] Robert Dearden, *Problems in Primary Education* (London: Routledge and Kegan Paul, 1976), 59.

Being thoughtful practitioners requires the whole schooling system to be supportive. Other factors or points on the three dimensional shape must connect to make this a possibility. By building on the concept of community, recognizing the factors in society which affect schools and using the same intermediate steps, I am showing that there must be an internal coherence to the whole process of schooling. Teachers cannot be thoughtful practitioners if the school is not a learning community or the values for the children are different from theirs. The values that flow through the process must be the same for all. We can only *keep the conversation going* between children and the school if educators are engaged in discussions and collaborative ventures with students, parents, colleagues, administrators and academics. Through these conversations and subsequent actions the school experience for children and teachers will become more meaningful and fruitful. The conversation must be open-ended, worthwhile, supportive, innovative, humorous, constructive, focused and self-perpetuating.

Chapter Six

Teachers' and Students' Perspectives on Curriculum

[T]he proof of a good [curriculum] is found in the fact that the pupil responds; his response is use. His response to the material shows that the subject functions in his life. It is unsound to urge that, say, Latin has a value per se in the abstract, just as a study, as a sufficient justification for teaching it.[1]

John Dewey

Visiting a number of classrooms at the same grade level and at the same time of year in a city like Taipei gives one an intense feeling of déjà vu. All [students] within the school, within different schools in the city, even within all of Taiwan, are studying the same lesson. Whether it is reading about Iceland, learning new Chinese characters, or finding out how to calculate the volume of a cube, the same material will be covered more or less on the same day of the school year. This uniformity is a result of the central control of the curriculum by the Ministry of Education, which specifies in great detail the order and content of what shall be taught.[2]

Harold Stevenson and James Stigler

The two quotations above illustrate the sharp divisions in approaches to curriculum: Dewey advocates a dynamic, child-centered and flexible style while Stevenson and Stigler, representative of a more conservative position, recommend an authoritarian, rigid and controlled approach. As one reads their works more extensively, it is remarkable that the general goals advocated by both are fairly similar. Both want children to have a high degree of literacy and numeracy, be problem-solvers, love learning and function well in society. However, when the discussion moves to the specific path for attainment of these goals and a more precise interpretation of their aims, the two positions part company. Thus, it is not sufficient simply to describe broad objectives for education, or to delineate general content and teaching/learning strate-

---

[1] John Dewey, *Democracy and Education: An Introduction to the Philosophy of Education* (New York: The Free Press, 1916), 242.

[2] Harold Stevenson and James Stigler, *The Learning Gap: Why Our Schools are Failing and What we can Learn From Japanese and Chinese Education* (New York: Summit Books, 1992), 136.

gies. There must be detailed specification of the form schooling should take. We must trace all the links in the three dimensional phenomenon which is schooling.

In this chapter, I will build on previous chapters by examining curriculum development in relation to teachers as thoughtful practitioners and students as educated persons, making reference again to the intermediate steps. To begin, I will set the discussion in context by outlining current approaches to curriculum development in Ontario, showing how curriculum development is often a separate activity from classroom practice and often excludes teachers. This will illustrate the point that it is not just the content of the curriculum that is crucial, but also *the way that it is developed*. Secondly, I will link curriculum to my vision of the educated person and the five intermediate steps. And thirdly, I will look at curriculum from the students' perspective, to see what would be fulfilling curriculum. I will argue that school as a way of life can give children a reason to learn.

Curriculum Development

On a broad level, curriculum is much more than facts and figures to be memorized and skills to be acquired. The choice of curriculum topics, methods and strategies is controversial because the materials studied are not value neutral. There is a specific intention; although largely unstated, society's values and aims are promoted through the education of its young people. As Decker Walker and Jonas Soltis note, "it hardly seems necessary to remark that curriculum designs and decisions are guided by our ideas of what education should aim at."[1] Similarly, Jane Roland Martin notes that "whatever it is that a culture chooses to call education will comprise the information it takes to be important for young people to know and the activities it considers worthwhile."[2]

But while these writers have correctly observed the significance of the *content* of the curriculum, there are two other highly relevant issues that are often overlooked. First, the way school boards and ministries develop curriculum reflects a particular attitude toward teachers. I will show that most teachers are absent from curriculum development and hence their place in the process and their insights are disregarded. Secondly, most teachers do not look at curriculum in an analytic

---

[1] Decker Walker and Jonas Soltis, *Curriculum and Aims* (New York: Teachers College Press, 1992), 12.

[2] Jane Roland Martin, *The Schoolhome: Rethinking Schools for Changing Families* (Cambridge, MA: Harvard University Press, 1992), 74.

way; they do not seriously consider how curriculum fits into the broader picture of education, nor do they consciously acknowledge or critique the values being promoted. Since teachers are entangled in the day to day running of the class and overwhelmed by the massive amount of content to be covered, they often do not "see" beyond the immediate tasks. These two factors result in teachers acting more as technicians than as thoughtful practitioners, which is less rewarding for both children and adults; curriculum becomes an end in itself, reinforcing the narrow conception of education identified in Chapter One. Since this situation undermines and limits the possibilities for schooling teachers should play a more central role in developing an appropriate curriculum.

As stated in Chapter One, we will not have a chance to wipe the slate clean; a great deal of curriculum content will remain as it was. However, the current approach to curriculum development, which often overlooks the key participants —children and teachers— must be changed radically. It is important to understand the strengths and weaknesses of the current process of curriculum development before an alternative approach can be advocated. As elsewhere, I will use the situation in Ontario as the primary source of illustrative material.

i. A Three Step Process for Curriculum Development

In Ontario, the first part of the curriculum development process begins with the Ministry of Education; in order to realize its goals, society, through the Ministry of Education, provides guidelines containing general goals and specific objectives for schools. The *Ontario Curriculum, Grades 1-8* outlines overall and specific expectations per grade level, for each subject. Traditionally second tier of Ministry documents such as *Science is Happening Here, Antiracism and Ethnocultural Equity in School Boards* and *Computers Across the Curriculum* are released periodically and deal with current topics; they are expected to be incorporated, either in specific subjects or across several areas. The Ministry policy documents, including the second tier ones, offer broad statements about education; few examples of curriculum strategies or activities are provided. There is very little dialogue between ordinary classroom teachers and the bureaucrats who write the documents. This is the first step in teachers and children being excluded from the process of curriculum development.

The second part of the process focuses on school boards where curriculum teams, consultants, principals and curriculum co-ordinators examine the Ministry guidelines and write additional guides; these documents outline specific methods, determine content and suggest techniques. Like most school boards, the Toronto Catholic District School Board (TCDSB), a very large board with approximately 200 schools and 6,000 teachers, provides a formal curriculum for its teachers. At its centre is the "core curriculum," a detailed listing of objectives to be covered; each division —kindergarten, primary, junior and intermediate— has its own "binder" which lists the curriculum objectives to be realized.

The TCDSB core curriculum is fairly standard; it begins with the board mission statement and the Ministry of Education's vision of the learner;[1] from there, each subject is dealt with separately. There are twelve subjects for the primary grades: dramatic arts, family life, French as a second language, guidance, language arts, mathematics, music, physical and health education, religious education, science, social studies and visual arts. The co-ordinator for each subject usually writes a particular section of the guideline. Within each subject there is a detailed listing of goals, skills, strategies, evaluation methods and names of additional TCDSB support documents. Some goals are very vague such as "students will integrate thinking, viewing, listening, speaking, reading and writing activities,"[2] while others are much more specific such as "classify things used by people according to the natural materials from which they are made (e.g., blocks, desks, and toys made from wood)."[3] There are very few specific teaching suggestions or references to actual classroom practice; in essence, the TCDSB core curriculum document is a 243 page listing of curriculum objectives. In addition, for each of the twelve subjects mentioned, there are board resources or documents that further describe specific content and teaching strategies. After a writing team completes a draft version of the document, the board of trustees, the superintendents and other senior administrative staff review it and approve it. Some of the sections may be reviewed by a classroom teacher but in general this step excludes teachers and children.

Following the writing and board approval, curriculum materials are printed and distributed to all TCDSB schools. The third step is

---

[1] The image of the learner is described as a "self-motivated, self-directed problem-solver, aware of both the processes and uses of learning and deriving a sense of self-worth and confidence from a variety of accomplishments. This learner is guided by values consistent with personal religious-ethical beliefs, cultural traditions, and the common welfare of society."
    Metropolitan Separate School Board, *Core Curriculum: Formative Years, Grades 1,2 and 3* (Toronto: 1990), vi.

[2] Metropolitan Separate School Board, *Core Curriculum: Formative Years Grades 1,2 and 3* (Toronto, 1990), LA1.

[3] *Ibid.*, SE13.

passing the curriculum documents to the teachers. There may be some in-servicing for teachers and principals but this step of the process is some-what haphazard. There is neither follow-up to ensure that teachers are implementing the suggested content nor a process to evaluate the document; opportunities to question or to receive additional information are limited. The amount and level of in-service usually depends on the interest or style of the local principal and the availability of school board consultants. This step tends to be one directional, teachers receive the directives and are expected to implement them.

ii. *Problems with the Current Process*

The three step procedure described above is distant from actual class-rooms; documents arrive and teachers are expected to follow them, re-gardless of the quality of their individual programs or the children's needs; there are few opportunities for dialogue. The process contributes to a fragmented schooling system and the top-down approach sets a negative tone toward teachers and students. Two underlying assump-tions of the process are: first, curriculum can be developed outside the context of schools; and secondly, teacher ownership of curriculum is not essential. I would challenge both these assumptions: teachers need to feel part of the process; ownership of the process and product affirms them as professionals; and collaboration draws on many sources of knowledge. This process, in its current form, is demeaning and under-mines teacher confidence. As noted in Chapter Five, teachers who work directly with the children must have substantial in-put into their pro-gram. They only learn the skills of thoughtful practitioners by having opportunities to analyze their practices, read scholarly works and col-laborate with colleagues; the current approach to curriculum develop-ment effectively shuts them out. In the long term, both teachers and children suffer. As a teacher, I was fortunate in being able to work on curriculum development. Through the process I was forced to analyze my practices, rethink my goals for education and consider society's val-ues. I became a wiser and stronger teacher; my program became more child-centered, active and relevant. This participation reduced my sense of alienation as a teacher and increased my self-esteem.

Roland Barth suggests that "parallel play," the term used to de-scribe the play of three and four year olds, applies well to relation-ships within schools. This description is also an appropriate one for current approaches to curriculum development: each sector —the Min-istry, the school board and individual teachers— works quite sepa-rately.

> In schools, like sandboxes, the benefit of parallel play is isolation from others who might take our time, challenge our practice, steal our ideas, or have us do things differently. The price of parallel play, is of course, that we ward off those who might help us to do things better and with whom together we might do grander things than either could do alone. And the price is isolation from other adults.[1]

This fragmentation limits opportunities for conversation between various groups and for teachers to grow as thoughtful practitioners; further, bureaucrats, consultants and teachers often work at cross purposes. The researchers and bureaucrats have "tended to be good at description but poorer at model building";[2] the research and the model building must occur in the schools, using the expertise of teachers, parents, consultants and so on.

At the 1994 *Reimagining Curriculum* conference, Nancie Atwell[3] began her keynote address by describing a questionnaire she had to complete as director of the Teaching/Learning Centre. The first question was, "Who develops curriculum for your school? Superintendent, Assistant Superintendent, School District Curriculum Team, Principal, Parents, Other." She passionately pointed out that teachers was not one of the choices. She argued that curriculum development should be the equivalent of "intellectual barnraising" and every teacher should be part of it. Further, a curriculum that is developed by others is static and has the distinct possibility of being boring for teachers. If the teacher is bored by it, there is little chance of it engaging the student. At the same conference, Bobbi Fisher advocated a *generative curriculum* — one that unfolds and evolves in response to the participants. It is not preset but the teacher starts with a framework and then fills in the program once the children start working with it.

The vast amount of material available in the core curriculum and all of the other supplementary documents is both an advantage and a disadvantage. On the plus side, there is a detailed listing of what is to be accomplished in each grade. On the negative side, there is so much information that it easily becomes overwhelming. While teachers often feel that they are floundering or that they are left on their own, there is a whole "industry" that deals with curriculum development.

[1] Roland Barth, *Improving Schools From Within: Teachers, Parents, and Principals Can Make the Difference* (San Francisco: Jossey Bass, 1990), 16.

[2] Sara Delamont, "The Primary School Teacher 1945-1990: Myths and Realities," in *The Primary School Teacher*, ed. Sara Delamont (London: The Falmer Press, 1987), 46.

[3] Nancie Atwell, keynote address at the *Reimagining Curriculum* conference, Portland, Maine, May 13-14, 1994.

Although this industry supports teachers in some ways, it also undermines their confidence and professionalism. As a librarian and as a consultant I observed that the multiple copies of the core curriculum and other official curriculum documents, housed in the library, were rarely used. Many teachers prefer to use commercially prepared materials because they provide teaching strategies, course content and suggestions for student follow-up. Because the core curriculum is just a listing of objectives it is extremely tedious to read and has to be supplemented with more practical suggestions. In order to use the core, teachers would need the skill and time of a superteacher. Many skip the step of reading the core and turn immediately to the content section of a teacher's manual; this hop-scotching through curriculum materials further distances teachers from their school boards, their students and their colleagues. Rather than plan as part of a team and use a generative curriculum, teachers are left to their own devices.

A further problem with the core curriculum document is the sheer quantity of objectives. In 243 pages there are hundreds and hundreds of curriculum objectives; by outlining twelve different curriculum topics the whole becomes fragmented. As teachers wade through the charts, objectives, skills, content and time-lines, all sense of the overall goals of education is lost. It is difficult to visualize and understand the intent of these objectives. The "shape of a human life" disappears in a maze of curriculum objectives. Most teachers are unable to pull the many diverse strands into a coherent program; as Jane Roland Martin says, our aim should be a "unified and unifying"[1] program. The current curriculum documents do not provide a unified program because the range of materials is just too great. It is too easy to have each subject area become an end in itself which leaves the overall vision of the learner pushed aside.

A quick browse through any formal curriculum document leaves a reader bewildered; one is inclined to ask, "Do teachers actually talk like this?". For example, in the language arts section some objectives for the students are: "enjoy recreational, social and imaginative language," "manage various purposes, formats, topics, audiences and situations".[2] Most teachers would read these statements, be generally confused, and not see any connection to the practices in their classes. As stated in Chapter Two, it is essential that we use a common language if we hope to *keep the conversation going*; however, most curriculum documents are

---

[1] Jane Roland Martin, *The Schoolhome: Rethinking Schools for Changing Families* (Cambridge, MA: Harvard University Press, 1992), 57.

[2] Metropolitan Separate School Board, *Core Curriculum: Formative Years Grades 1,2 and 3*, LA3.

written in an obscure and awkward style. The wording must describe the learner in terms teachers can understand; and the discussion must be set in the context of schooling. William Doll says that we should develop curriculum in and through interaction; we should "use our actual minds to create possible worlds."[1] For example, the term "self-directed," which is very common in curriculum documents, can mean anything from using one's initiative in choosing topics for storywriting to the other extreme of completing all assigned worksheets. There must be many examples included so that everyone —teachers, parents and students— clearly understand the intent of the goal.

The connection between the stated objectives and the world of children who are five to nine years old is too tenuous. The directives given by the Ministry of Education bureaucrats often seem to be for a world that does not exist; there is a huge chasm between the reality of day to day schooling and the scenario described in official documents. The underlying question should be, "Is this what children need at this point in their lives?". As I read the objectives I recognize that they all have some value in their own right, but when combined with the thousands of other prescribed objectives they do not specify a program which is what children need and will *keep the conversation going* between teachers and children.

iii. *A Multitude of Methods*

Since Ministry objectives are listed in numerous documents one would assume that there would be a measure of curriculum consistency in schools; however, this is not the case. The core curricula and Ministry documents outline the objectives but must still be cloaked in content. Most school boards suggest broad content areas for each subject; however, there is much diversity in content and actual practice. For example, the grade two social studies program at TCDSB focuses on the school community whereas in another Metro Toronto board it focuses on Japan. Obviously, the two school boards have very different goals for their curriculum. The basic question, "How can there be consistency in programs while encouraging teachers to develop a relevant curriculum?" strikes at the heart of the matter. I will return to this question later in the chapter.

Lesson plans, thematic studies and curriculum units are (a) developed by teachers, (b) produced by local boards and (c) made available

---

[1] William Doll, *A Post-Modern Perspective on Curriculum* (New York: Teachers College Press, 1993), 163.

in commercially prepared texts and kits. In most cases, teachers draw on all three resources; however, they tend to rely heavily on commercially prepared materials since publishers know the market well and recognize the diversity of needs. As a result, despite common goal statements, the range of materials is staggering. On the one hand, this diversity means there is "something for everyone"; on the other hand, the variety means that almost "anything goes." Teachers who are thoughtful practitioners have the knowledge and confidence to choose the most appropriate curriculum materials for their purposes but when teachers are technicians, they simply follow what is given to them or what is most readily available.

The best laid curriculum materials can all be for naught if teachers choose to disregard them or do not understand the theory underlying them. Teachers frequently express dismay at unrealistic pressures and rising demands placed on them, but they have the luxury of a great deal of independence in day to day practice. This autonomy/control cannot be forfeited; rather, it must be balanced with a responsibility to provide the best possible curriculum. Once teachers cross the threshold into their classrooms, they have a great deal of freedom to do as they please. "Their closed classroom doors signal that they are in charge, and they cherish the authority they have over their schedule, curriculum, and classroom management."[1] This freedom has both advantages and disadvantages. One of the problems is that curriculum choices and implementation strategies can be mildly inappropriate or, as I have seen in many instances, highly problematic.

In one junior kindergarten class, for example, in a strongly ethnic area where many children did not speak English, the teacher decided the focus of her winter unit should be the Innuit; she was bored with her standard approach. Although I applaud her decision to try something new, her choice was totally unsuitable for her students. Most of the children diligently completed the maps of Canada and coloured the pictures of Innuit clothing, but this was definitely not what they needed at this point in their lives. A steady diet of inappropriate curriculum leads to very bored children who do not see school as relevant to their lives. If this teacher had not been so isolated, had been part of a team and more knowledgeable, she would have made a wiser choice.[2]

---

[1] Harold Stevenson and James Stigler, *The Learning Gap: Why Our Schools are Failing and What we can Learn from Japanese and Chinese Education,* 163.

[2] In divisional meetings, teachers should be discussing and building their programs based on theory of child development. Primary educators are referred to Sue Bredekamp, ed. *Developmentally Appropriate Practice in Early Childhood*

Many teachers are content to use prepackaged curriculum even if it is not developmentally or culturally appropriate. Since they do not see themselves as scholars, they defer to "experts." (Perhaps, this is part of the reason that schools are vulnerable to fads.) There is a certain attitude towards texts and units; if the material is published then it must be good. For example, primary math programs which are page after page of computation, or spelling programs which have indecipherable tasks, continue to be the mainstay of many math and language arts programs. Teachers continue to use them even though they are a waste of time and turn children off school. Within the last few years the sales of formal spellers have skyrocketed, even though research questions their effectiveness. In the short term these programs keep children occupied but as Donald Graves notes, "in education we've associated busyness with accomplishment."[1] There is a huge difference between completing worksheets and *being involved* in the curriculum, and unfortunately many teachers do not clearly differentiate between the two. Teachers as thoughtful practitioners would approach curriculum in an analytic manner and not be duped by inappropriate programs.

An example will illustrate the problem presented by a wide variance of materials coupled with teachers not acting as thoughtful practitioners. There are many different approaches to language arts instruction. The "Collections"[2] program is a literature-based language arts program with a minimum of ten anthologies per grade, is highly integrated and stresses flexibility, process, choice, multicultural perspectives and student response. Alternatively, the "Open Court"[3] program, a basal reader, uses a controlled, stilted vocabulary, must be followed lock-step, uses a worksheet approach for student response, offers only two or three slim texts per grade, follows a highly eurocentric viewpoint and a prescriptive methodology. The two series are at opposite ends of the curriculum continuum, it is not unheard of for two grade one teachers in the same school to use these different programs. Although research has shown the problems associated with overly structured basal readers, many teachers still continue to endorse and use them. Most well-trained teachers who collaborate, study and keep abreast of research would not choose to use the basal reader approach. As Barth

Programs Serving Children from Birth Through Age 8 (Washington: National Association for the Education of Young Children, 1986).

[1] Donald Graves, *Build A Literate Classroom* (Portsmouth, NH: Heinemann, 1991), 11.

[2] Prentice Hall Ginn Canada, *Collections* (Scarborough: Prentice Hall Ginn Canada, 1998).

[3] *Open Court Publishing, Open Court Reading and Writing.* (Peru, Illinois: Open Court Publishing Company, 1989).

As Barth notes, "mutual visibility is not a hallmark of the teaching profession. Rather, a third-grade teacher on one side of the hall carefully circumvents the teaching space of the third-grade teacher on the other side of the hall."[1] Collegiality, the mainstay of thoughtful practitioners, cannot develop in a competitive, lonely environment where curriculum is an obstacle and dubious practices remain unquestioned.

Apart from the defects of particular curricular methods, there are many problems related simply to having a diversity of approaches. Children who transfer between classes and schools are often confused by the different style of texts and methodologies. Teachers cannot share strategies and materials because programs are often highly dissimilar. Frequently, a rivalry develops between teachers because some feel their methods are superior and consequently become critical of their peers. Parents are baffled because one year their children are memorizing lists of vocabulary words while the next year they are being encouraged to write their own stories using non-standard spelling. In such a case, professional development for teachers becomes a divisive issue because the groups have very different needs.[2] Ironically, both groups of teachers would feel they are meeting the Ministry requirements and fulfilling the core curriculum objectives.

Under such conditions, rather than being a unifying force in the school curriculum hinders the growth of the school as a learning community. Stevenson and Stigler note that one of the strengths of Asian schools is teachers working together on curriculum development. "We need a system that gives teachers opportunities to learn from one another and to benefit from the accumulated wisdom of generations of skilled practitioners."[3] At present, our timetable and our approach to curriculum does not provide opportunities for collaboration. Furthermore, the knowledge base of some of our teachers makes it almost impossible for them to provide a consistent, high quality program. Unfortunately, many teachers do not have the knowledge or skills to develop suitable curriculum; in a system based on thoughtful practitioners, teachers would be given the assistance and guidance through courses, apprenticeship, mentorship programs, divisional meetings and so on to develop the necessary skills. In this way, some of the inappropriate methods currently in use would decline and teachers would have a

---

[1] Roland Barth, *Improving Schools From Within*, 16.

[2] See Susan Church, "Is Whole Language Really Warm and Fuzzy?," *The Reading Teacher* 47 (February, 1994), 362-372.

[3] Harold Stevenson and James Stigler, *The Learning Gap: Why Our Schools are Failing and What we can Learn from Japanese and Chinese Education*, 173.

common basis on which to work together more and learn from each other.

Simply presenting an image of the learner is not adequate; curriculum objectives must be laid out with sample content and strategies, thus making the goals meaningful, realistic and recognizable (and not open to such diverse interpretation). Of course, each school community must work on shaping the curriculum to fit their children and capitalize on their teachers' special skills and interest. Returning repeatedly to the intermediate steps and the vision of an educated person will be the unifying force. Thomas Sergiovanni uses the example of Newton School District in Massachusetts, which has three Core Values central to all curriculum development, classroom practice and so on. "These values affect the way people think and feel and behave ... [they are] so significant that they permeate every aspect of the school organization."[1] Their Core Values, like my intermediate steps, are the framework for all activities and provide the unity for the school experience.

iv. *Grade One is "Real" School*

A final point about curriculum development concerns the crossing of the threshold from kindergarten to grade one. There is a sudden, intense pressure to teach children "academics." By this I mean that primary teachers are "under the gun"[2] to have children reading and writing by Christmas. As a grade one teacher I had numerous parents say to me, "Well real school starts now, no more of that kindergarten playing."[3] Because the primary division is segmented into two very distinct periods, *kindergarten and grades one, two and three,* the expectations for each are clearly different. Kindergarten classes are often located in a separate wing of the building, they are funded differently, their staffing ratio is calculated separately, their hours are unlike those of the rest of the school and attendance is optional. As a result, many parents and some educators believe that school, which they equate with academic excellence, rigour and performance, begins on the first day of grade one. Many children are baffled by the sudden switch from the more low key, activity-oriented kindergarten practices to the struc-

---

[1] Thomas J. Sergiovanni, *Building Community in Schools* (San Francisco: Jossey-Bass, 1994), 72.

[2] John Goodlad, *A Place Called School: Prospects for the Future* (New York: McGraw Hill, 1984), 332.

[3] For further discussion of this strong misplaced emphasis on academics in grade one see David Elkind, *Miseducation: Preschoolers At Risk* (New York: Alfred A. Knopf, 1989), 63.

tured grade one methods. Between June of kindergarten and September of grade one, children do not necessarily leap in maturity and ability; however, grade one is based on the premise that there is this incredible growth spurt. We see here, once again, the consequences of curriculum development which ignores the actual needs of students and the experience and insight of teachers.

Deborah Meier, former principal of the Central Park East Secondary School, an alternative school that uses the notion of community as one of its unifying principles, applies the metaphor of the kindergarten to her high school.

> Kindergarten was the one place —maybe the last place— where you were expected to know children well, even if they didn't hand in their homework, finish their Friday tests, or pay attention. Kindergarten teachers know that learning must be personalized, just because kids are idiosyncratic ... It is, alas, the last time children are given independence, encouraged to make choices, and allowed to move about on their own steam ... In kindergarten we design our rooms for real work — not just passive listening ....[1]

It is not only the culture of the kindergarten class —a supportive, rich environment— but also its approach to learning which must continue into grade one and beyond.

In grade one, the pressure on both children and teachers to meet unrealistic and inappropriate expectations is intense. Teachers often resort to gimmicks or use rote recall methods to show that they are "effective" primary school teachers and many children get turned off the whole school experience by December of grade one.[2] The goals of mutuality and autonomy are discarded because of the great pressure on teachers and students. Many administrators and parents utter the time worn phrase, "grade one is the most important grade"; however, some school practices suggest that they believe otherwise, or that they do not fully understand the needs of young children. And the myths that surround primary teachers as being "soft" cast a long shadow on the primary years. Most primary teachers are hard working, compassionate, caring individuals and many have a good sense of what their children need. Unfortunately, they, like the children, are caught in the tensions of the institution.[3] The needs of primary children (like all students) are complex; simplistic solutions such as more phonics or more

---

[1] Thomas J. Sergiovanni, *Building Community in Schools*, 36.
[2] See Sara Delamont, "The Primary Teacher 1945-1990: Myths and Realities," in *The Primary School Teacher*, ed. Sara Delamont, 15.
[3] See "Primary Educators in Dialogue," *Orbit* 25, 25-27.

spelling indicate a superficial understanding of both primary children and the role of curriculum. The primary school years are an important time in young children's lives and the experiences set them on a certain path. As adults, we have to regard this time as critically important and adjust to the complexity of the situation.

To conclude, the strength of our Ontario approach, its multiplicity of objectives and great variety of materials, is also its weakness. Almost anything can be justified because the guidelines can be interpreted in many different ways. The Taipei philosophy and practice described in the opening quotation is frightening because it reduces all children to a stereotype; and this is the direction in which many government departments of education are heading today. However, from my experiences as a consultant and as a supervisor of practice teaching I find our current situation also unacceptable. There are many hard working, caring teachers who provide excellent child-centered programs throughout the province but many programs fall short of this ideal. We cannot depend solely on the goodwill of the teacher to care for the whole child, nor can we base the system on the superteacher who has the time and ability to pull the scattered curriculum into a coherent program — our children are too important to rely on the luck of the draw. We cannot have a Ministry of Education writing epistles from afar nor can we have teams of school board consultants writing vast documents that no one uses. The answer is not to produce more of the same, the solution is to get in touch with the teachers and the children.[1]

Because something has been done in a certain way for an extended period of time does not guarantee that it is appropriate. Society has changed, needs are changing and curriculum must also change. Sergiovanni has observed that it is difficult to change preconceived notions about content and approaches because "current school practices have been continuously reinforced by the existing theory. As a result, their acceptance has become so automatic that they are considered to be unquestioned truths."[2] If we want fundamental changes in schools then we must begin to question the unquestioned truths.

This extended section on curriculum development has largely focused on the negative aspects of the present situation. What is needed is a positive account of how curriculum should be developed involving both teachers and students to a much larger degree. My recommendations for involvement of teachers will be given at length in Chapter

---

[1] See Alice Yardley, *Structure in Early Learning* (Oakville, Ontario: Rubicon Press, 1989).

[2] Thomas J. Sergiovanni, *Building Community in Schools*, 1.

Seven. We turn now in this chapter to a consideration of the needs and involvement of students.

Curriculum from the Students' Perspective: Giving Children a Reason to Learn

Many parents try to motivate their children to apply themselves diligently to school by pointing out the future market value of success in school. The adults' long lecture to the children includes reference to getting into a good university or finding a well paying job; however, such rationales are remote from the children's lives. Parents should show that they value education and demonstrate their commitment to the children's schooling, but long monologues will not work. Alternative actions such as sitting and reading with the youngsters, setting aside quiet time for them to complete their homework or visiting the school are ways for parents to show that they value education.

The impetus for learning does not usually come from an external source; rather, the motivation must be largely from within the child. The children's interests are the spark:"[t]o be interested is to be absorbed in, wrapped up in, carried away by, some object. To take an interest is to be on the alert, to care about, to be attentive."[1] The learning opportunities in the class should be so powerful that they encourage the children to "apply themselves diligently" to their schooling;, they should absorb them and carry them along. I am using the term "powerful" in the sense that the curriculum helps children make sense of this world. When the curriculum is seen as a powerful personal tool children will develop what Dewey calls the "habit of learning."[2] When learning and schooling are personally rewarding, there will not be a need for external rewards in the distant future. Donald Graves at the *Reimagining Curriculum* conference suggested that we should look back each day to see what we did that was *useful*.[3] His goal is to have schooling be useful: children involved in tasks that matter; learning that lasts; a curriculum that engages us and causes us to struggle; and an approach that brings the outside world into the class. Approaching curriculum from the perspective of usefulness will serve to reconceptualize it as a broad and enduring force.

---

[1] John Dewey, *Democracy and Education: An Introduction to the Philosophy of Education*, 126.

[2] John Dewey, *Democracy and Education*, 45.

[3] Donald Graves, keynote address at the *Reimagining Curriculum* conference, Portland Maine, May 13-4, 1994.

Certainly there are times when children have to practice or drill or copy a note from the board; but for the most part they must see the value of the work and the connections between the various steps. In George Wood's description of schools that work, he observes that "there is a delightful sense of purposeful clutter to these classrooms and schools. They are places to do things in, not places to sit and watch. Real work goes on here, and real products (not endless streams of blue dittos) go home."[1] The children are aware of what they are doing, the steps involved and the reasons for their activities. Wood uses the term "purposeful" whereas Brian Cambourne, who has written extensively on literacy development, uses the term "engagement"[2] to describe the force that draws children into the learning sphere. Whether the terms are useful, purposeful clutter or engagement, there are two central principles basic to learning: *relevance* and *participation*.

When children see schooling as relevant to their lives, there is motivation to continue learning. Although this may be so obvious that it does not need to be mentioned, we have a long history of curriculum that "represents the values of adults rather than those of children and youth, or those of pupils a generation ago."[3] In George Eliot's *The Mill and the Floss*, Tom Tulliver is sent to study with an Oxford scholar. Tom complains that the Latin and Euclidian geometry are far removed from the skills he will need to run the mill. In more recent writing Nel Noddings notes that "in trying to teach everyone what we once taught only a few, we have wound up teaching everyone inadequately. Further, we have not bothered to ask whether the traditional education so highly treasured was ever the best education for anyone."[4]

The problem of developing a curriculum that is relevant is certainly not new! To create an appropriate curriculum, there must be a balance between long and short term needs. Children must find the curriculum interesting and compelling; it must provide them with the skills that they need for their present life; and it must equip them with the skills and attitudes for future endeavours. The clash between the two worlds of now and later makes curriculum development a very complex task; relevance for the present world must often be sacrificed to a degree for longer term goals. Nevertheless, this challenge is not insurmountable;

---

[1] George Wood, *Schools that Work: America's Most Innovative Public Education Programs* (Scholastic Books: New York, 1992), xiv.

[2] Andrea Butler, *The Elements of the Whole Language Program* (Crystal Lake, Ill: Rigby, 1988), 4.

[3] John Dewey, *Democracy and Education*, 241.

[4] Nel Noddings. *The Challenge to Care in Schools: An Alternative Approach to Education* (New York: Teachers College Press, 1992), xiii.

George Wood, Nancie Atwell, Loris Malaguzzi, Vivian Paley, Lucy McCormick Calkins and Donald Graves provide many examples of schools that work from the point of view of children. We need to look to these models for examples, rather than dull, flat curriculum documents written far from the school setting.

The following example will help show how pursuit of academics could easily be made more relevant for children. With the meteoric rise of computer games many children are reading computer manuals and guides, in simplified form, at home. However, in our reading programs at school minimal attention is given to learning how to read nonfiction material of this kind. We largely ignore what the children are reading at home or, in general, what their reading needs are outside the school. Rather we emphasize fiction, often selected by someone other than the children. Even the most reluctant reader will be strongly motivated to learn how to read if the end result is better computer skills. Although this is a simple example it gets to the core of the matter: education cannot be a enterprise that is separate from living. When we splinter living into in-school and out-of-school, both worlds suffer.

A major obstacle to making curriculum relevant for children is that the current impetus for educational reform is being driven by an economic agenda which ignores children's needs. Rather than begin with the economic situation, which is of course crucially important to a country, we must start with the children. If I am correct in my assumption that, if we meet children's needs, they will be motivated to do their best, will value the community and will stay in school, then the school enterprise will be a success. Placing children first will allow the notion of "relevant to their needs" to become the guiding principle of curriculum development. Alice Yardley says that if we want to know the basics and what children need, we have to observe them.[1] Their actions and words will tell us what they need.

Participation is the second critical factor in giving children a reason to learn. The central argument of Piaget's work is that children actively construct their own knowledge base through interactions with their environment. If we understand (and are concerned about) how children learn, what is relevant to them and what motivates them, the curriculum we develop will be based on participation. As Piaget says: "To understand is to discover, or reconstruct by discovery, and such conditions must be complied with if in the future individuals are to be formed who are capable of production and creativity and not simply

---

[1] Alice Yardley described the "basics" in this way at a meeting of the *Canadian Association for Young Children*, Toronto, April 1993.

repetition."[1] School must be a place where children are actively involved in learning; sitting in a desk for long hours or completing prescribed worksheets is not active involvement. Nancie Atwell begins Chapter One of *In the Middle* with the following quote, "the logic by which we teach is not always the logic by which children learn."[2] Participation is part of the "logic" by which children learn.

Another way of making this point is to say that children should not see education as a "spectator" sport, where they are "observers of" instead of "participants in."[3] Rather, children should see that *education is what they do with their lives.* "Holistic teachers try to create learning situations that are connected to life. This implies that the work itself, as well as how it is undertaken, is in agreement with the activities that are part of our daily living."[4] When school provides opportunities for children to live their lives with fullness, they develop the habits of participation. When we as adults become involved in an institution we learn much more about it. For example, when teachers become part of the education council, they learn about the many other aspects of their school. The same principle applies to children; they must be fully involved in their classroom.

Children "need to learn to live in this world, not just know about it."[5] It is not enough simply to be cognizant of certain facts about school and society (indeed, I am not sure that we can learn about the world vicariously); rather, children must be *living their education.* As a result, what is learned in school will help children negotiate life outside the classroom, and conversely what is learned beyond the brick building will assist in formal schooling. This approach bridges the two worlds of home and school and sets the tone for children to lead a full participatory life in society.

In order to have a curriculum that is relevant and participatory, knowledge must not be reduced to facts in books. Learning is going on all of the time children are in school. The formal curriculum may be the "binder," but for children curriculum is everything that happens in their day.

---

[1] Jean Piaget, *To Understand is to Invent: The Future of Education* (New York: Grossman, 1973), 20.

[2] Nancie Atwell, *In the Middle: Writing, Reading, and Learning with Adolescents* (Portsmouth, NH: Heinemann, 1987), 32.

[3] Jane Roland Martin, *The Schoolhome: Rethinking Schools for Changing Families*, 90.

[4] Ralph Peterson, *Life in a Crowded Place: Making a Learning Community* (Richmond Hill, Ontario: Scholastic Canada, 1992), 128.

[5] Jane Roland Martin, *The Schoolhome: Rethinking Schools for Changing Families*, 86.

Implicitly dividing school into the world of the private classroom and the public world beyond its doors, she took it for granted that only the former sphere is a teacher's domain. Learning recognizes no such boundary line, unfortunately. What transpires in the halls and in the lunchroom may fall outside the standard school subjects, but its educational impact is not thereby diminished. Nor is the lesson lost that the way people live together and treat both one another and their surroundings is not nearly so important as how well one knows the facts of history and the formulas of physics.[1]

We should take our clue from children. Creating all sorts of artificial barriers between school subjects or in-school and out-of-class behaviour is not their way. The curriculum should not be viewed simply as twelve distinct subjects; nor should learning be restricted to a specific time of day. Children are always observing, imitating, experimenting and so on. Whether it is the pattern of a spider web in the school yard or the teacher's mannerisms, they acquire a great deal of knowledge without a formal lesson plan. My five intermediate goals suggest that the whole school experience is the curriculum. My emphasis on the culture and structures within the learning environment recognizes the power of the hidden curriculum. My argument for a strong, positive learning community is based on the belief that children learn a great deal from their environment.

Finally, it should be noted that giving children a reason to learn is rooted in the principle that young children must be respected. When a distorted view of academic excellence is placed above personhood, an inappropriate attitude towards children develops. When children voice their frustration about school or do poorly we tell them to work harder; however, if an adult friend echoed the same dissatisfaction with a job or had a poor work performance, we would tell him or her to find a new job or go for retraining. We would not want him or her to be unhappy nor would we want the failing experience repeated frequently. We do not apply this same rationale to children; if they do badly we tell them to study more, pay closer attention, stay after school for extra work but it is unrealistic for them to devote more hours to something that they find either much too difficult or highly unpleasant. When the child is only five or six years old, this counsel makes even less sense. It is almost impossible for children to do well in school if they find it exceedingly difficult or intolerable. Their emotions cannot be detached from their learning. As adults, we must put ourselves in the children's place so that our guidance and support are sensible and realistic. Education for life does not begin with a negative attitude towards

---

[1] *Ibid.*, 167.

school, it starts with a fondness for the whole process. Using common sense and a respectful tone toward children is necessary if we hope to devise an appropriate curriculum.

School as a Way of Life: Linking Curriculum to the Intermediate Steps

In our fragmented education system curriculum has emerged as the core of the entire process. It is not uncommon to hear teachers say "I have to get through the curriculum"[1] which implies that it is separate from other aspects of the school process and that it takes precedence over them. The current testing frenzy reinforces the fragmentation of the schooling process, In a more balanced view, curriculum should be seen *in relation* to the overall goals of education. Educated persons should be able to look back on schooling as a time when they felt a sense of belonging; when they acquired relevant knowledge and skills for work and for adapting to new situations; when they had joyful experiences and a sense of accomplishment. We must return repeatedly to these qualities; both the formal and the informal curriculum must encourage development of educated persons. And as a result of returning to these qualities, we will cease to view curriculum as a formal syllabus and see it rather as a lived and living experience.

Earlier in this chapter I posed the question, "How can we have consistency in process and content while encouraging teachers to engage in curriculum development?". The answer to that question and the question of what type of curriculum is necessary lies in the intermediate steps: they become the unifying and guiding principles. Teachers can vary on actual content while striving to support common intermediate goals. In the Newton School system the Core Values are "powerful value pillars" that provide direction and parameters.[2] When the larger values are the framework and an integral part of the school's philosophy, teachers will aim towards realizing them; although they will individualize curriculum, the intermediate steps will lead to a consistency in approach. Rather than starting with twelve subjects and then devising ways to integrate them, we should begin with a manageable set of goals and ask, "How can the academic program help the child develop a sense of autonomy?" or "In what ways can the curriculum help the child become reflective?" or "How can mutuality enhance learning?" or

---

[1] Sue Bredekamp, *Developmentally Appropriate Practice in Early Childhood Programs Serving Children From Birth Through Age 8*, 63.

[2] Thomas Sergiovanni, *Building Community in Schools*, 75.

"What programs allow the child to exercise some control over content and methods?". This type of discussion expands our understanding of the intermediate goals and helps reconceptualize the curriculum. As a result, the curriculum becomes directly tied to the goals — the relationship is dialectical. The curriculum ceases to be an end in itself, it is connected to the big picture. Roland Martin's central values of care, concern and connection, for example, are unifying principles that enable both diversity and cohesion. She suggests that "it is equally important to note that core is composed mainly of attitudes, skills, and values, not bits or bodies of knowledge."[1]

Academic excellence is definitely a dimension of personhood; children need strong literacy and numeracy skills to lead fulfilled lives. However, the following characteristics of academic excellence show the dialectical relationship between my intermediate goals and, for example, the language arts program: ability to choose books and write on topics selected independently (autonomy); use of books and projects for personal growth (integration); sharing of books and works with others (responsibility and mutuality); self-knowledge about what needs to be learned and how one learns best (reflectiveness); knowing where to go for help and when to offer assistance (responsibility and mutuality); understanding the power of reading and writing (reflectiveness and integration); and being able to apply knowledge to other settings (integration).[2] The curriculum becomes the vehicle for developing personhood instead of being a separate track. Mem Fox endorses this approach to curriculum when she says:

> [o]ur ultimate success as teachers can't really be measured until after our students have left us. If, in their continuing lives, our past students can deal confidently and competently with any real-consequences writing task that confronts them — then, and only then, can we claim to have taught them well.[3]

To develop a comprehensive framework from our vision of the educated person and the five intermediate steps, we must adopt certain guidelines. First, teachers, principals, parents and students must know and understand the overall goal and the intermediate steps. I have tried to make them clear and readily accessible by providing examples set in the context of schooling. Some may disagree with the five goals,

---

[1] Jane Roland Martin, *The Schoolhome*, 84.
[2] This list is an adaptation of Donald Graves characteristics of a lifelong literate person outlined in *Build a Literate Classroom*, 27.
[3] Mem Fox, *Radical Reflections: Passionate Opinions on Teaching, Learning and Living* (San Diego: Harcourt, Brace, 1993), 109.

and over a period of time these goals may change; however, any other goals that are established must be described in the same way: accessible language and lots of examples set in the schooling world.

Secondly, the goals that are identified must not be understood exclusively as "school" goals. They must be seen as having equal validity for life outside the school. A perspective that encompasses both school and society has many benefits: school does not become separate from society; school is seen as a way of life rather than a temporary state; and the curriculum is tailored so it has validity for living.[1] All of this allows children to continue the learning that has taken place in home and in kindergarten. As Dewey said: "[t]he learning in school should be continuous with that out of school. There should be a free interplay between the two."[2] Further, in light of the discussion in Chapter One on our changing society, curriculum must respond to the needs of children living in this society; this can only happen if the school and non-school spheres are closely linked.

Thirdly, and following from the previous point, school must deliberately and systematically build on the learning from home.[3] By the time children enter grade one, they have learned a great deal about negotiating life; however, many of these skills are overlooked because they do not match the objectives in the core curriculum. Instead of capitalizing on what the children bring to school —curiosity, boundless energy, flexibility, enthusiasm, strong oral skills, a vivid imagination and accumulated knowledge— the core curriculum often overlooks these skills and knowledge. The children's natural abilities and acquired skills could easily be used to teach reading, writing, social skills and even neat printing. If school learning was continuous with the knowledge already gained, educators would be building on an established foundation.[4]

Our present situation divides the children's lives into two worlds — in-school activities and life beyond the school walls. This gulf must be closed if we hope to educate towards the five intermediate goals. It is too hard to blend the values and skills from beyond the school yard

---

[1] See John Miller's discussion of Eliot Wigginton's Foxfire projects in John Miller, *The Holistic Curriculum* (Toronto: OISE Press, 1988), 109.

[2] John Dewey, *Democracy and Education*, 358.

[3] For two different perspectives on this topic see Sue Bredekamp, *Developmentally Appropriate Practice in Early Childhood Programs Serving Children From Birth Through Age 8*, 61 and Gordon Wells, *The Meaning Makers: Children Learning Language and Using Language to Learn* (Portsmouth, NH: Heinemann, 1986), Chapter Five.

[4] For further information see, "Reflecting on the Relationship: An Interview with Ada Schermann," *Orbit* 25, May 1994, 30-32.

with the activities within when one is not relevant for the other. As George Wood notes, "give a student a real responsibility and he or she will act responsibly."[1] When children see school as an integral part of living, as opposed to something to be endured or remote from what really counts, their commitment to learning becomes stronger. As Noddings asserts, there must be "a continuity of purpose."[2] In schools that view autonomy, responsibility and friendship as pivotal to learning, there will be greater continuity between home and school. Children who receive the same messages about what is important at home and at school are not forced to shift behaviours between home and school. Schools can become learning centres for the whole community. Loris Malaguzzi says that "learning and teaching should not stand on opposite banks and just watch the river flow by; instead, they should embark together on a journey down the water. Through an active, reciprocal exchange, teaching can strengthen learning how to learn."[3] Our curriculum and the students cannot be on opposite sides of the river, we should be negotiating the river together.

Fourthly, my whole proposal can only be implemented if we take the affective side of life seriously. "Everyone appreciates a person who knows when to hug and when to stand apart. In schools, all kids want to be cared for in this sense. They do not want to be treated 'like numbers,' by recipe — no matter how sweet the recipe may be for some consumers."[4] Rather than have that aspect of the person separate from the curriculum it must become central to the overall goals. This allows for the recognition of the role of self-esteem in learning, and it encourages the growth of the complete person. Schooling should be for the whole individual and not simply for cognitive development.

Conclusion

An essential basis of schooling is a unity of purpose and practice. To accomplish this, curriculum must be viewed as *one of the many dimensions*

---

[1] George Wood, *Schools That Work: America's Most Innovative Public Education Programs*, 46.

[2] Nel Noddings, *The Challenge to Care in Schools: An Alternative Approach to Education*, 66.

[3] Loris Malaguzzi, "History, Ideas, and Basic Philosophy" in *The Hundred Languages of Children: The Reggio Emilia Approach to Early Childhood Education*, eds. Carolyn Edwards, Lella Gandini, and George Forman (Norwood, NJ: Ablex, 1993), 79.

[4] Nel Noddings, *The Challenge to Care in Schools: An Alternative Approach to Education*, 17.

of schooling. It must be conceptualized as "part of" not "separate from." Given the reality of schooling, curriculum is very important; however, we must ask such questions as, "What kind of curriculum will help children and our society develop?" and "How can the curriculum assist us in attaining our goals?". The answer to these questions lies in part with teachers being thoughtful practitioners; the school structure must support this view of teachers and see the curriculum as generative and evolving. There must not be a pre-set curriculum: the fatal flaw of this approach is that it is closed. While having shared goals for schooling, we must adopt an open approach to curriculum which allows for ongoing in-put from teachers and constant adaptation to student interests and needs.

Chapter 7

Drawing on Whole Language Philosophy and Practice for a Reimagined Curriculum

I suggested to her that the metaphor of pendulum swings between two extreme positions is a bad one. Rather there is a continuous struggle in education and in research and theory that relate to education. It's an over-simplification to describe two diametrically opposed systems of belief. But there are basic differences in how people, fact, truth, the purposes of education, teaching, and learning are viewed which strongly define the struggle at any point.[1]

Ken Goodman

The debate over curriculum content and methodologies has been intense; when the focus narrows to language arts the discussion becomes extremely heated. The passion and intensity have reached new heights: for example, in the United States "[t]he pressure ... from the far right demanding that phonics be mandated as the official reading policy of the U.S. government"[2] places language arts squarely in the political arena. Similarly, in Canada parent groups such as the Concerned Coalition for Parents and writers in the popular press continuously lobby school boards and provincial governments for a return to phonics, basal reading programs and standardized tests to measure reading achievement.

The term whole language is becoming less common today; however, the concept behind it namely an emphasis on meaning making a balance of various aspects of the language learning process are still of vital concern. I have chosen not to use the term "balanced literacy" exclusively because the roots of whole language are important for teacher

---

[1] Ken Goodman, "I Didn't Found Whole Language," *The Reading Teacher* 46 (November, 1992), 189.
[2] *Ibid.*, 193.

development. For ease of communication in this chapter I will use the term whole language to refer to this approach to language learning.[1]

It would be simplistic to reduce the arguments between phonics advocates and whole language educators to a debate over methodologies; each position represents a particular worldview, a set of values, a vision of the educated person, a purpose for education and a political agenda. The debate involves a whole host of issues. Susan Church shows this complexity when she says, "I've come to the conclusion that I cannot advance a whole language agenda without also taking on a political agenda — one that entails profound changes in the way we view curriculum, leadership, school organization, our roles and relationships within the institution, and the change process."[2]

In the previous chapter, I discussed the general theory of curriculum development. The next step is to show how to bridge theory and practice; actual curriculum delivery must be addressed. In order to do this, I will focus on language arts education, in particular, the whole language approach. In keeping with the whole language philosophy of integration, I will propose reducing the curriculum from twelve separate subjects to three core areas: language arts, mathematics and the arts. I will then concentrate on language arts for the remainder of the chapter.

A Reimagined Curriculum: Three General Curriculum Areas

From my experiences as a teacher, curriculum consultant and teacher educator I know that curriculum planning and implementation are difficult and can become overwhelming. Nancie Atwell summarizes her own problems with curriculum: "I spent my first six years in the classroom looking for the someone elses who would tell me what to do. I read about the methods of Moffett, Tchudi, and Elbow and applied them liberally to my kids."[3] Atwell and Donald Graves would say, we need a "reimagined curriculum." We need this "reimagined curriculum" for two basic reasons: first, to be consistent with the overall goals of education; and secondly, to simplify planning so that teachers are not so dependent on "the someone elses."

---

[1] Clare Kosnik, *Spelling in a Balanced Literacy Program* (Scarborough: Nelson Canada, 1998)

[2] Susan Church, "Is Whole Language Really Warn and Fuzzy," *The Reading Teacher* 47 (February 1994): 369.

[3] Nancie Atwell, *Side by Side: Essays on Teaching to Learn* (Portsmouth, NH: Heinemann, 1991), 4.

The first step is to reduce the primary curriculum to three main areas: language arts, mathematics and the arts (which includes music, physical education and art). As schools and teachers evolve the curriculum may be further reduced to the single subject of "learning," but at present this would be too large a leap. This dramatic step implies that "more of the same" (just add another course) will not fit into my model. As I showed in Chapters Three and Six, at present there is simply *too much* curriculum, which results in it becoming an end in itself and overshadowing other goals.

There are numerous reasons for advocating a curriculum reimagined along these lines: first, when we deal with just three areas, the curriculum guidelines and materials are *more manageable* and hence teachers may actually use them; secondly, by limiting it to three areas, the curriculum is subtly de-emphasized, thus encouraging teachers to focus on the class as a *learning community*; thirdly, teachers can *focus their professional development* on fewer topics because they do not feel that they have to be "experts" in twelve areas; ease of *communicating with parents* is the fourth reason (writing a report card that addresses multiple subjects results in a document so convoluted that it conveys limited information); fifthly, three broad areas allows for *integration from within*, a more natural approach, rather than trying to create artificial bridges across multiple subject areas; and finally, a simplified core is far more *workable*, it focuses on the *essential* aspects which allows for a less fragmented approach to schooling. When educators deal with fewer subjects, they can concentrate on *how children learn* rather than being caught up in the pressure to get through all of the subjects. Rather than an overloaded curriculum we need to develop as Donald Graves argues a "useful" curriculum, one that makes a difference in the students' and teachers' lives. As my formal curriculum unfolds it should be apparent that it emphasizes *learning* rather than following someone else's list of what should be done in school.

Many theorists and educators would support this more holistic approach to curriculum: John Dewey argues that curriculum should not be a series of subjects isolated from the everyday lives of children; Jean Piaget has shown that "students construct their own knowledge from within rather than have it imposed on them from some external source;"[1] Ken Goodman and Constance Weaver define reading and writing as an active interaction not a series of isolated skills;[2] Brian Cam-

---

[1] Maryann Manning, Gary Manning and Roberta Long, *Theme Immersion* (Portsmouth, NH: Heinemann, 1994), 3.

[2] Constance Weaver, *Understanding Whole Language: From Principles to Practice* (Portsmouth, NH: Heinemann, 1990), 55.

bourne and Donald Graves argue for classrooms where "learning is kept whole";[1] Jane Roland Martin, as noted in Chapter Six, advocates a unified and unifying curriculum; and John Miller et al state that "[t]he problem, then, is that students often are confronted with long lists of facts or skills that are isolated both from each other and, more importantly, from a pattern or context that would connect and give meaning to the information."[2] The cry for a more integrated, natural, holistic curriculum comes from many theorists and practitioners.

At this point some curriculum specialists will be dismayed that I have not mentioned social studies, science, computer literacy and so on in my three main areas. These fields certainly have merit and should be part of the curriculum; many students find them interesting; they help with the development of thinking; and they increase the children's knowledge and skills base. My approach would include these fields but they would be developed *from* and *through* the language, mathematics and arts programs rather than as separate subjects. "[L]ong checklists of skills in all curriculum areas; reading skills continua; standardized testing; division of subject matter ... this chopped-up approach to learning just [doesn't] make sense."[3] We need to free teachers to focus on learning and development of self.

Traditional subject areas would still be addressed in my reimagined curriculum. In the language program, for example, there would be stories on the family such as *The Doorbell Rang, Shoes From Grandpa, Where's Jamie, A Special Trade* or *I'll Love You Forever* through which students would acquire social studies concepts, knowledge and skills. When students assist in writing and publishing the class newspaper, which would be part of the regular language arts program, they would develop computer literacy skills. Much of the substance of the program would be social studies, science, family life, religion and so on; however, the whole language approach would enable us always to keep these specific subjects in perspective. They would not become ends in themselves. The emphasis will always be on learning.

> All educators need to appreciate and understand the role language plays in a system of knowing. Language is a process of symbolization. Language is the vehicle by which we make intuition public and communica-

---

[1] *Ibid.*, 5.

[2] John Miller, J.R. Bruce Cassie and Susan Drake, *Holistic Learning: A Teacher's Guide to Integrated Studies* (Toronto: OISE Press, 1990), 1.

[3] Maryann Manning, Gary Manning and Roberta Long, *Theme Immersion: Inquiry-Based Curriculum in Elementary and Middle Schools*, 4.

ble. This basic process is what education is all about. A theory of language learning is both a theory of learning and a theory of education.[1]

When children read *Albert's Old Shoes*, the story of a young boy
who wants the latest track shoes and is embarrassed by his brown ox-
fords, they would complete activities that cross over into traditional
subject areas. They might graph types of shoes (mathematics), compare
equipment for sports (science), discuss the problems of friendship
(family life), visit the local sporting goods store (social studies) and
participate in playground games (physical education); the various curriculum areas would be addressed but as reactions to or outgrowths from
the book. The children would "revisit" the story many times, and although each rereading would be for a different purpose it would connect
the various activities.

At the *Reimagining Curriculum* conference Atwell gave an example
from her Center for Teaching and Learning where the whole school focuses on just two themes per year. This type of integration is on a much
larger scale and may be the end point to which schools should strive.
Some of the activities Atwell described under the theme of immigration were: a trip to Plymouth where the older students made a slide and
tape show for the younger students; making dioramas and board games;
an excursion to a museum to work with artifacts; creating an archaeo-
logical dig in the sand box; acting out an immigration story; studying
how immigrants brought their holiday traditions to America; making
pizelles and fate cupcakes; learning some Irish music; having a tea and
scones party; writing stories from the immigrants' perspectives; inviting parents into the school to tell their family story; and researching
why immigrants came to America. Such a highly integrated curriculum
crosses subject areas and also is consistent with two principles stated
earlier — curriculum must be relevant and participatory.

In the last ten years there has been pressure to teach language arts
—reading and writing— through social studies and science curriculum,
the reverse of what I am suggesting. The rationale for this approach is
that the content of the lessons and activities would be more interesting
for the children and the skills would be set in a more relevant context.
However, there are three problems with this approach as it has been
put forward. First, it assumes that simply reading books and writing
regularly constitute an adequate language arts program, thus overlooking the complexity and depth of what is needed. Secondly, it assumes

---

[1] Jerome Harste and Virginia Woodward, "Fostering Needed Change in Early Literacy Programs," in *Emerging Literacy: Young Children Learn to Read and
Write*, eds. Dorothy Strickland and Lesley Mandel Morrow, (Newark, DE: International Reading Association, 1989), 153.

that typical classroom teachers recognize and understand the required elements of language arts and will use their own initiative to find materials to support and develop the program. Thirdly, it assumes that all of the traditional content will still be covered whereas in fact we must select content much more carefully than in the past in order to support the goals of education.

Of course, any push for integration —including the one I am proposing here— must provide for the integrity of the various fields, ensure that topics are studied in all their complexity and depth, and afford adequate teacher re-education. However, whereas such reconceptualization and re-training is integral to what I am advocating, it has been missing from the "language through science and social studies" movement. The traditional science and social studies subjects have been left fully intact while language arts has been left to chance and amateurish efforts. For example, I visited one educator who was held in very high esteem by her school board because she used a highly integrated curriculum approach which revolved around science. On closer examination, I discovered that her students were only reading and writing occasionally. They were not becoming acquainted with various literary genres such as poetry, mystery stories or many of the classics and the writing program was reduced to daily journal entries and the obligatory essays about holidays.

If we are to move to a highly integrated curriculum, there must be opportunities to involve the community, a changed timetable and possibilities for vertical groupings. But most importantly teachers must become thoughtful practitioners. An integrated curriculum is a good example of the connectedness between the many points of the three dimensional model; it cannot be adopted unless many other factors change to support it.

The Whole Language Approach to Language Arts

In this section, a language arts program is described in both broad and specific terms. In a single book it would be impossible to discuss mathematics and the arts in the same detail; however, the principles or model I propose for language arts can be applied to them as well. One of Frank Smith's claims is that understanding how children learn to read helps us appreciate the process of learning *in general*.

> When you have covered all the ground, not only have you gained insight into reading, but you also know a good deal about many other aspects of the human intellect, especially with respect to learning. Teachers in other areas find that such an analysis of reading also gives them a deeper un-

derstanding of the problems of comprehending subjects like science, music or mathematics.[1]

In many ways, the language arts program becomes the framework for learning. As Lucy McCormick Calkins says, "literacy is inseparable from living."[2]

To create a rich, diverse, challenging, in-depth language arts program, there must be a pooling of the knowledge of theoreticians, consultants and practitioners. The program that I am going to suggest does not have the prescriptive style of the basal reading programs which "straightjacket" the teacher and students or of the "integration across subjects " approach mentioned earlier. A new type of program is needed which balances structure and flexibility, theory and practice. The approach I am presenting draws heavily on whole language and for ease of communication I will refer to it as a whole language program.

i. *Traditional Approaches to Language Arts*

Traditionally, the term language arts has been used as a general label to cover the subjects of reading, writing, speaking and listening. These four areas were further subdivided into spelling, grammar, phonics, creative writing, reading comprehension, silent reading, oral reading and handwriting. The traditional approach is to teach each of these subjects separately; for each subject there is a list of skills to be taught in a specified sequence.[3] At some point, the "knowledge" from all these subjects comes together and, voila, a literate person. In Chapter Two I referred to this as the building block system. The logic of the process was simple: deal with each area as if it were distinct, have the student achieve a high degree of success with each band of skills and at a certain age the knowledge from one area would easily be transferrable to another. This theory of language learning unfortunately did not work as well when applied to actual children.

> ... both the stage theory of development and a related linear, hierarchical approach to developing literacy severely distort the learning process. While evidence for the idiosyncratic nature of children's literacy devel-

---

[1] Frank Smith, *Reading Without Nonsense* (New York: Teachers College Press, 1985), 4.

[2] Lucy McCormick Calkins, *Living Between the Lines* (Portsmouth, NH: Heinemann, 1991), 3.

[3] For research and programs which adopt this method see Jeanne Chall, *Stages of Reading Development* (New York: McGraw Hill, 1983).

opment doesn't mean there are no trends in how children develop literacy, it does mean that stage theory is far too tidy a concept to account for the messy reality encountered when we observe and document the learning of individual children.[1]

Jo Phenix, who has written extensively on spelling instruction, recounts a story from her experiences as a teacher which illustrates the flaw in the logic of this approach. A comment she frequently used on student report cards was, "Johnny is doing well in the spelling program but his spelling in creative writing is poor."[2] Obviously, the spelling program was not connected to Johnny's writing; she challenges us to rethink why we have formal spelling programs if they do not help children spell when they write. Looking at the issue from another perspective, Goodman notes that we have managed to teach many children to read and write with moderate success but they think of these as unpleasant activities and would choose not to do them if the choice was theirs.[3] Researchers and writers such as Phenix and Goodman question the transferability and the long term value of traditional programs.[4]

The traditional language arts program has many apparent advantages: it is easy to manage, the content areas are clearly delineated, children work quietly at their desks, parents know exactly what to expect from the school and that particular view of literacy is widely accepted. We must draw on some of the strengths of the traditional approach and incorporate them into our reimagined curriculum. There are also major drawbacks to the traditional program: there is rarely any mention of the children's interests or motivation in the language learning enterprise; and literacy is equated with a prescribed set of language skills, "students are rewarded more for correct answers than for critical and creative thinking..."[5]. Mem Fox captured one problem with the ap-

---

[1] Constance Weaver, *Understanding Whole Language: From Principles to Practice*, 55.

[2] Jo Phenix told this story about spelling programs and creative writing at the *Reading for the Love of It Conference*, Toronto, February 14, 1992.

[3] Ken Goodman, *What's Whole in Whole Language*, 36.

[4] Some recent spelling programs have overcome this problem of lack of connection between writing and spelling; for example, *Nelson Spelling* is a program which directly links spelling with reading, writing and speaking. *Nelson Spelling* (Scarborough: Nelson Canada, 1997).

[5] Constance Weaver, *Understanding Whole Language: From Principles to Practice*, 52.

proach when she noted that children did not "ache with caring"[1] about reading and writing.

It is understandable how the traditional approach became so deeply entrenched. Educational research was dominated by behavioral learning theory which in turn governed tests and textbooks;[2] the researchers became the writers of the textbooks which strengthened the links between theory, research and classroom practice. The research was driven by the theory, the theory supported a priori considerations, and the whole system had an empirical research program which only looked at certain aspects of reading and writing. The process became circular and so it was almost impossible to evaluate it carefully. In many ways whole language educators (as described in the following section) have upset this tidy state of affairs by challenging the research, reviewing what is meant by success, confronting notions of literacy and questioning the underlying assumptions and research methods of the system.

ii. *History of Whole Language*

Whole language is an umbrella term which has come to represent a more complex approach to language learning. Although many skilled teachers have used whole language practices for many years the term was first coined in the mid-1980's. The approach was not "invented" by one individual nor was it the domain of one particular group; rather, it evolved from the interplay of theory and practice. Robert Hillerich's definition captures the openness of the movement. It "is not a method of teaching, nor is it a program; it is a philosophy or viewpoint. It can incorporate many different methods and materials, and has, in fact, adapted and moved beyond two of its precursors, Language Experience and Individualized Reading. Hence, as more a slogan than a method, it is subject to as many interpretations as there are proponents."[3] I endorse Hillerich's definition because it emphasizes that whole language is not simply a methodology but involves a complex philosophy. Given my position that we must consider the "shape of a human life," that the factors of schooling are interconnected and that there is need for a general framework, we should be talking about a philosophy of language learning, not simply a methodology for teaching grammar or spelling.

---

[1] Mem Fox, *Radical Reflections: Passionate Opinions on Teaching, Learning, and Living* (San Diego: Harcourt Brace 1993), 22.

[2] Ken Goodman, I Didn't Found Whole Language, 191.

[3] *Ibid.*, 4.

The roots of the whole language movement are highly significant. Its emergence represents one of the few times when theoreticians and practitioners have collaborated on actual school practices. In the 1980's as psycholinguists were studying language development, teachers simultaneously were expressing their dissatisfaction with standard basal reading approaches. Regular classroom teachers organized themselves into district level groups to find a better way to approach reading and writing. They began to analyze their teaching, to develop literature units, to share success stories and to work collaboratively. Ken Goodman, who is often credited with founding whole language, claims that he did not "invent" whole language, rather whole language found him!

> The changes sweeping the schools under the banner of whole language are being accomplished by teachers who have taken the best of the knowledge available to them and built a practical philosophy that informs their decisions and soundly supports their innovative teaching. *They know what they're doing. They know why they're doing what they do.* They're professionals and know what they can accomplish. I learn every time I visit their classrooms.[1]

As the two groups, the academics and the practitioners, converged they found that they had reached similar conclusions: reading and writing are linked; children must read and write daily; students learn how to read and write by reading and writing; and reading and writing are social as well as cognitive processes.

The whole language movement represents: groups from different facets of education talking to one another in the same language; teachers taking control of their own learning and teaching; and the children's needs being given priority. Many books on whole language include chapters by classroom teachers along-side articles by academics and many teachers are beginning to act as researchers in their own classes. This approach to education certainly *keeps the conversation going* and produces a better, more caring, more realistic schooling system. The origin of the whole language movement symbolizes to me the way educational change should be carried out. It shows the possibilities for integrating theory and practice and gives me hope that education will move out of the merely political arena.

The whole language movement is still evolving. There are many groups, such as the *Whole Language Umbrella,* which continue to work out philosophy and articulate practice. The impetus for whole language is not restricted to a single organization or country. New Zealand

---

[1] Ken Goodman, "I Didn't Found Whole Language," 189.

is one of the leaders in the movement — at present whole language is the official language arts policy in that country and writers such Marie Clay and Don Holdaway have been instrumental in expanding language arts programs. Australian writers such as Brian Cambourne and Mem Fox have helped reconstruct policy in a whole language direction. Canada has a mixed approach — British Columbia, New Brunswick, pockets of Ontario and Nova Scotia are leaders in whole language, but of critical importance is the general Canadian resistance to the testing and basal reader obsession of the Americans. The United States has many teachers and writers advocating whole language but the battle in the United States is uphill since 90% of teachers still use basal readers and standardized tests.[1] In Great Britain the *Language for Life* report called for major changes to language arts instruction in light of the "insights into the relationships among language, thinking, and learning";[2] however, the push for a national curriculum has detoured and sidetracked language policy reform.[3] The whole language movement has many obstacles to face because it proposes not just a change in methodology: it offers a new vision of the learner; expands goals for the class; has an emphasis on community; and insists that teachers have more control over their program. More than just a language arts technique, it is a framework for education.

Whole language theorists and practitioners suggest that language arts programs must go beyond a surface set of skills; our success rate, defined as students continuing to love reading and writing, must be our marker. Brian Cambourne suggests that there are three questions central to the issue of literacy: "What is effective literate behaviour?", "How is it best acquired?", and "After you have acquired it what do you use it for?".[4] Whole language practice is being shaped by these questions. The third question is the critical one; if students do not use reading and writing in their daily lives inside and outside of schools we have not helped them lead a fuller, more active and reflective life. The successful language arts program is not gauged by high test scores but by the use, understanding and love of reading and writing.

---

[1] Constance Weaver, *Understanding Whole Language*, 58.

[2] Ken Goodman, *What's Whole in Whole Language* (Richmond Hill: Scholastic, 1986), 60.

[3] The National Literacy Strategy. *Framework for Teaching, 1998*. London: Department of Education and Employment.

[4] Brian Cambourne raised these three questions at an address to the *Consultants/Co-ordinators Association for Primary Education*, Toronto, April 1992.

iii. *Some Elements of Whole Language*

When I began as a primary level student in the 1950s my school used a fragmented, skills development approach to language learning. It was not until I was half-way through high school that I discovered the joy of reading and it was not until I was in graduate school that I realized that I loved to write. Thankfully, I was one of the lucky ones who overcame the effects of my schooling. Some students may thrive on a very structured approach but many do not.

In recent research on emergent literacy, some researchers have concluded that: "literacy is not regarded as simply a cognitive skill to be learned, but as a complex sociopsycholinguistic activity. Thus, the social aspects of literacy have become significant, and literacy learning is investigated not just in the researcher's laboratory, but also in home and community settings.[1] "This broader understanding of literacy is echoed by other writers: Marie Clay believes that "reading [is] a message-getting, problem-solving activity which increases in power and flexibility the more it is practised,"[2] and Constance Weaver argues that literacy is much more than a set of skills.[3] Literacy learning must be placed in a larger context, literacy is not just a specific set of skills to be learned in isolation. For example, the culture and environment of the community affect learning. Many whole language educators are adopting the model of the home, where children learn to speak without formal lessons. Children learn to speak because they are immersed in the family/home, are expected to speak, are drawn into the dialogue and have a genuine reason to speak. These same conditions are being duplicated in school in an attempt to have reading and writing develop more naturally.

Whole language educators have a very broad understanding of literacy; many dimensions are considered and seen as part of the overall curriculum. Jerome Harste succinctly describes literacy as "the process by which we, as humans, mediate the world for the purpose of learning."[4] Schools should help children mediate the world and lead fuller, more responsible lives. The aim of a whole language program is to help

---

[1] Mem Fox, *Radical Reflections*, 8.

[2] Marie Clay, *Becoming Literate: The Construction of Inner Control* (Portsmouth, NH: Heinemann, 1991), 6.

[3] Constance Weaver, *Understanding Whole Language: From Principles to Practice*, 39-41.

[4] Jerome Harste, Kathy G. Short and Carolyn Burke, *Creating Classrooms for Authors: The Reading-Writing Connection* (Portsmouth, NH: Heinemann, 1988), 3.

the child "begin to hear his own voice actively using information";[1] literacy is personal, useful, relevant and cannot be defined in a manual. *Literacy is using language to make meaning.*[2] Whole language then is a way to help children negotiate life, lead fulfilled lives and contribute to the community. It is not simply a set of grammar, phonics and spelling skills to be acquired and applied; rather, language, thinking and learning are one.

As the name whole language implies, "language" as a "whole" is the field of enquiry; the emphasis is on the *understanding* and *use* of language. The language program is for learning language, learning about language and learning through language.[3] Ken Goodman summarizes whole language as follows:

> Whole language learning builds around whole learners learning whole language in whole situations.
> Whole language learning assumes respect for language, for the learner, and for the teacher.
> The focus is on meaning and not on language itself, in authentic speech and literacy events.
> Learners are encouraged to take risks and invited to use language, in all its varieties, for their own purposes.
> In a whole language classroom, all the varied functions of oral and written language are appropriate and encouraged.[4]

One of the aims for the primary curriculum is to teach children how to read. Although this may seem straightforward, actually defining reading is far more complex. There is both surface structure which requires decoding and the deep structure where the meaning of the text is made. It is the latter area where much of the emphasis should be. Certainly, children need many decoding skills such as phonics and sight vocabulary recognition, but this should not be the end point for reading instruction in the primary years. Yes, children need skills! Yes, skills must be taught! No, skills are not equal to reading! Trevor Cairney, who has adopted a middle position in the reading debate, notes that

---

[1] Donald Graves, *Build a Literate Classroom* (Portsmouth, NH: Heinemann, 1991), 16.

[2] There are many writers who would support this view of literacy. See Gordon Wells, *The Meaning Makers: Children Learning Language and Using Language to Learn* (Portsmouth, NH: Heinemann, 1986), 122 and Donald Graves, *Build a Literate Classroom* (Portsmouth, NH: Heinemann, 1991) 13, 27.

[3] Andrea Butler, *The Elements of the Whole Language Program* (Crystal Lake, IL: Rigby Press, 1987), 4.

[4] Ken Goodman, *What's Whole in Whole Language*, 40.

"the act of reading requires the interplay of many text-based and reader-based processes."[1]

Unfortunately, meaning making is often lost in the debates over methodologies; when teachers say that they have to "get through the curriculum," meaning making is not their priority. Or when academics cite reading scores as the measure of success of a program they are not interested in meaning making. As a primary teacher I knew that I had to equip the children with decoding skills but I tried very hard not to kill the love of reading in the process. In order to do this I had a balance of easy books for independent reading, more difficult books for guided reading, big books for shared reading and books read aloud by me. These four kinds of reading experiences made up the program and were a daily occurrence. Reading skills were taught in the context of the stories. On some occasions I assigned worksheets but these were not the mainstay of my program.

When students read trade books independently or they are read to them, there is an opportunity for an emotional response. Traditional basal readers do not allow this response. One year when I had to teach a very structured reading program, the second story in the book was, "Come Curt. Come Jan. Come Curt and Jan." The third story was, " Look Curt. Look Jan. Look Curt and Jan. Come and look Curt. Come and look Jan. Come and look Curt and Jan." This drivel was painful for both the students and myself. Certainly children need easy books to read but these must be balanced with very engaging literature. Books such as *Henry Huggins* by Beverly Cleary, Shel Silverstein's *The Giving Tree*, *The Cat in the Hat* by Dr. Seuss and *Sylvester and the Magic Pebble* by William Steig are rich with images, story, vocabulary and character development; students respond to them emotionally. In my primary class I used fiction and non-fiction books, poems, magazines and newspaper articles, song lyrics, and student-written stories, in addition to readers. I also told the students about books that I was reading — they saw me read and heard me describe the characters and plot of the novel I was reading. Fox says that students must see us weep as we read, this demonstrates the power of the text and our commitment to reading.[2]

As children are immersed in a literary environment, are read to daily, listen to books on tape and watch videos they learn about the many kinds of texts and develop a sense of story, a love of reading, an awareness of the possibility of stories and so on. "In fact, research sug-

---

[1] Trevor Cairney, *Balancing the Basics For the Teachers of Reading* (Sydney: Ashton Scholastic, 1983), 12.

[2] Mem Fox, *Radical Reflections: Passionate Opinions on Teaching, Learning and Living*, 53.

gests that independent reading is the major contributor to reading comprehension and vocabulary growth, as well as to gains on tests of reading achievement. Unfortunately, most children rarely read."[1] Weaver estimates that children spend only 10% of their day reading; to complicate the matter even further, often what they are reading is teacher selected. In whole language classrooms reading becomes an extended, daily occurrence.

A second goal for primary children is to learn how to write; however, this skill is usually seen as distinct from reading. Most teachers consider the goal of writing to be the ability to compose descriptive sentences that are grammatically correct. In a whole language program writing is seen as a process of learning. "Professional writers write to discover; we need to recognize those opportunities when children can begin to listen to themselves, observe, and become conscious of new images."[2] Thus writing moves beyond the surface structure just as reading moves beyond simple decoding. Graves and Atwell both argue convincingly for a connection between reading and writing; children read to write and write to read. Nevertheless, children need to learn to use conventions of writing and employ standard methods of decoding. Having these skills frees children to think about the content and increases their fluency. When children have an audience for their writing, skills taught in context, adults supporting their emerging writing, word banks readily available and personal dictionaries as a classroom mainstay, it is possible for them to write correctly without their interest in the subject being trampled. The conventions and skills are not the ends, they are the means!

For writing to be meaningful children must be writing for real reasons; a daily journal to be submitted to the teacher is not a good reason. When children are involved in projects related to a class theme in which they are vitally interested, they have a reason for the reading and writing. For example, when children conduct interviews with people in the community and then write up the interview as part of a class book on People in Our Community, there is incentive to have a proper finished product. At present, students spend less than 15% of their day in writing activities and 70% of this is spent filling in worksheets.[3] Completing "fill in the blank" sheets has a twofold negative effect: first, it sends the message to children that writing and reading are not

1 Constance Weaver, *Understanding Whole Language: From Principles to Practice*, 37.
2 Donald Graves, *Build a Literate Community*, 52.
3 Constance Weaver, *Understanding Whole Language: From Principles to Practice*, 38.

for real purposes; and secondly, it quickly stratifies the students into contrived groups. When students are writing on a topic of interest to them (and not just teacher assigned stories) we allow them to "keep the life in their writing"[1] and help them see that writing can have a place in their lives.

The great debates between Jeanne Chall and whole language educators that are taking place in the literature may be interesting academic exercises but they overlook the point that there are children in primary classes suffering through torturous lessons that will not help them become fluent readers and writers or develop a love of reading and writing. In Ontario, the Ministry of Education pushed for whole language programs in the 1980s but now they are backtracking. *The Ontario Curriculum, Grades 1-8* has a strong emphasis on skills which quickly leads to drills. The answer is not to discard whole language and return to a "part to whole" approach; rather, the task is to incorporate all that we have learned, with a commitment to providing the best possible language learning program.

iv. Primary Education and Whole Language

The impact of whole language theory and practice is being felt in all divisions but the most significant implications are for the primary division. One concept that has been a mainstay of primary education, reading readiness, has been questioned by whole language proponents. Marie Clay, Dorothy Strickland and Lesley Mandel Morrow claim that when we use an adult's perspective on literacy rather than the children's point of view, our conclusions are distorted. When we see literacy from the children's point of view we realize that they have already built up an effective understanding of language.[2] "Recent research has shown that many children have begun literacy learning before they enter school."[3] The primary division has traditionally planned a series of "reading readiness" lessons which emphasize alphabet recognition and sight vocabulary; however, this approach is now seen to be too limited. The new concept is that of *emergent literacy*; teachers observe children carefully in order to meet their individual needs. There is a recognition that many children have had literacy experiences before

---

[1] Lucy McCormick Caulkins, *Living Between the Lines*, 6.

[2] For a good article on the portrait of young children as literacy learners see, William Teacle, Elizabeth Sulzby, "Emergent Literacy: New Perspectives," in *Emerging Literacy: Young children Learn to Read and Write*, eds. Dorothy Strickland and Lesley Mandel Morrow, 1-15.

[3] Marie Clay, *Becoming Literate: The Construction of Inner Control*, 10.

school which should be built upon; that favourite story books can teach a great deal about plot, schema, vocabulary, drama effects and so on; that reading tests scores do not describe the language skills children use; that when children enter school they have a personal frame of reference; that children must read and write in school and at home;[1] that children can express their literacy in many ways; and most importantly, that there is not a lock-step approach to learning how to read and write. Emergent literacy recognizes that children already have some understanding of language and need some control over their learning. The emphasis is on literacy emerging, not waiting for the prescribed program.

In whole language classes, primary children do not have to wait until they have a high level of competence in certain skills before they become acquainted with "hard" books, nor do they have to delay writing until they have completed the speller. They employ written language from the first day of school, and this changes the way many primary classrooms operate. When children use reading and writing in their lives, their language learning is far more natural and less stilted. Children have a reason to learn because there is an emphasis on full student participation.

> There is a logical interrelatedness of the numerous facets of the design that becomes apparent as the learning events, personal relationships, shared responsibilities, and available resources are synchronized into a working environment. Language, spoken and written arises within an activity. It supports, influences, and enriches learning. The main focus of attention, however, is not on language itself but generally on what is going on — the task, the story, the learning underway.[2]

Whole language does not strongly differentiate between "language" and "learning"; the focus is on using your language.

In the absence of the concept of reading readiness there is no longer a magic moment when children are suddenly ready to read and write. Grade one as the great moment — read by December and write by March — is seen as too artificial. Emergent literacy allows for more flexibility, recognizes that some children are not ready for a formal program,

---

[1] Dorothy Strickland emphasizes this link between reading at home and in school in her family storybook reading program. This aspect of language learning departs from the traditional notion that reading and writing instruction are only in-school tasks.

[2] Martha King, "Behind and Beyond Whole Language," in *The Whole Language Catalog*, eds. Kenneth Goodman, Lois Bridges Bird and Yetta Goodman (Santa Rosa, CA: American School Publishers, 1991), 16.

offers different kinds of support, and accepts that simple trade books can be the "springboard to literacy."[1] Listening to books read aloud and writing dictated stories are seen as meaningful activities, not merely preliminary ones. This attitude helps children see themselves as participating in reading and writing.

Reading and writing are seen as processes that build on one another; as noted earlier, children read to write and write to read. "It is important to foster the child's desire to explore writing at the same time as he is learning to read. Not many discussions of early literacy see these two activities as complementary."[2] Both reading and writing are seen as meaning making processes; through reading, different perspectives are revealed as children gain knowledge about the human condition which in turn enriches their thinking and writing. Through writing, children build on personal experiences and respond to and incorporate stories they have read.

v. *Whole Language Supports the Class as a Learning Community*

Another implication of the emergent literacy research is that the culture of the class is a necessary support to literacy development. Ralph Peterson identifies the connection between the learning community and the curriculum. "Life in a learning community is helped along by the interests, ideas, and support of others. Social life is not snuffed out; it is nurtured and used to advance learning in the best way possible."[3] As children read, respond, write and conference with others about their work, they are linking the processes of reading and writing, sharing their knowledge and growing. Reading and writing open up many doors.

Another benefit of the group is noted by Aidan Chambers:

> Like every other creative activity, thinking requires raw material. I don't know about you, but I find I can never get enough raw material on my own. I take most of what I need from other people. On my own I am just not enough — in experience or knowledge or imaginative capacity or language. To put it another way round: thinking isn't really a self-con-

---

[1] Mem Fox, *Radical Reflections: Passionate Opinions on Teaching, Learning and Living*, 55.

[2] Marie Clay, *Becoming Literate: The Construction of Inner Control*, 96.

[3] Ralph Peterson, *Life in a Crowded Place: Making a Learning Community* (Richmond Hill: Scholastic, 1992), 3.

tained, individual activity at all. It is a shared process. We are all members of the human think-tank.[1]

The students work together on projects, share topics and strategies, experience life together and recount personal experiences. The class becomes a rich cauldron of ideas and experiences upon which to draw. Brian Cambourne outlines eight conditions for literacy learning: immersion, demonstration, expectation, responsibility, employment, approximation, response, engagement.[2] Several of these conditions emphasize the need for children to be in a literate community.

A tremendous advantage of whole language is that it does not lead to ability grouping; all children can participate in the same story and thereby see themselves as readers and writers. The less able children may listen to the story on tape while others may read the book independently. Because the program is not driven by worksheets, children can respond in a variety of ways. All children, regardless of ability, will feel that they are participating in the class community; unlike many systems children are not streamed into ability groups which were determined by a test.

Clay's research has shown that where a child starts out, in a streamed classroom, is where he or she will likely remain.[3] John Goodlad has found that the gap between the high and low group increases each year so that eventually there is almost no way to close it.[4] Traditional language programs make it exceedingly difficult for the class to become a learning community because ability groups splinter the class and undermine the self-esteem of one third of the students. By high school, students who have been in the low group have spent eight years feeling inadequate. I have yet to meet an individual who was proud to have been in the low group or said that the low group was good for him or her. In whole language classes the destructive label of "low" is never applied. In whole language classrooms children work in the large group, in small groups and individually. They work in interest, ability, random selection and vertical groups. The mix is fluid; ability groups as a *permanent* feature of the class have no place in whole language. Ability groups result in unhealthy competition whereas a learning community requires co-operation and commitment. I would hazard a guess that

---

1 Aidan Chambers, *Booktalk: Occasional Writing on Literature and Children* (London: The Bodly Head, 1985), 5.

2 Andrea Butler, *The Elements of the Whole Language Program,* 12.

3 Marie Clay, *Becoming Literate: The Construction of Inner Control,* 18.

4 John Goodlad, *A Place Called School: Prospects for the Future* (New York: McGraw Hill, 1984), 142.

the alienation that many students feel in grades seven and eight can be traced back to ability groups in the primary years.

The storytelling process which is part of whole language classrooms helps the community form in another way. As a teacher I knew that the experience of reading to the children was powerful and magical.

> When books are read aloud to children they experience the excitement of their friends in the story during suspenseful moments. They know the full range of joy, laughter, and sorrow as they hear together the story of Fern, Charlotte, Wilbur, and Templeton in *Charlotte's Web* by E. B. White. As I read the children compose their own images, but the feelings they know together create a literate bond that is unique in human existence.[1]

Sharing the books, dramatizing stories and responding to them helps the spirit in the class grow and strengthens the connecting fibres.

vi. *Myths and Problems of Whole Language*

A whole language classroom does not mean a laissez-faire approach to learning; some teachers in the mid-eighties discarded their readers, filled up the class with lots of books and then became disenchanted when the children were not miraculously transformed into avid readers and skilled writers. There must still be structures, routines and formal lessons because children need direction, routine and specific instruction. Teachers do not abdicate their position in a whole language classroom, they redefine it as thoughtful practitioners. Beside structures and routines, there should be high expectations that the students will become avid readers and skilled writers;   literacy is valued. Without these distinct "attitudes" towards students and learning the whole language approach would become just another methodology.

The chief criticism of whole language has been that it ignores skills. On the whole, however, this charge is unwarranted as Judith Newman and Susan Church state:

> *Myth: You don't teach spelling or grammar in a whole language classroom.*
> *Reality:* Within a whole language framework, these aspects of language are a means to an end rather than an end in themselves. Spelling, punctuation, and handwriting are important because they help the writer

---

[1] Donald Graves, *Build A Literate Classroom*, 79.

to make meaning clearer for readers. Knowledge of grammar is helpful to both readers and writers as they construct meaning.[1]

The problem is that critics of the whole language approach feel that there is only *one* way to teach skills and that is through formal lessons; however, whole language educators feel that this method is too artificial and remote. Nancie Atwell advocates a method called "mini lessons" which is an alternative to standard, predetermined drill.[2] Specific skills are taught to the children (whole class or small group) in the context of what they reading or writing — the lessons are short and specific and are applied immediately in the children's work. Because the mini-lessons arise naturally from the children's work, they cannot be preplanned in a syllabus, nor is there is a worksheet to "prove" that the skill has been addressed. This approach to skills has led many to sharply condemn whole language.

Educators, teachers and academics have been remiss in not helping the public understand whole language. Suddenly such terms as "invented spelling" and "conferencing" were being bandied about and many parents became alarmed. Parents walked into primary classrooms and did not see the staples of language programs —readers, spellers, grammar texts and phonics workbooks— and their children were coming home with uncorrected, often illegible stories. Because many parents did not recognize this as school they presumed language learning was not happening (and in some cases their concerns were justified). Parents wanted the best for their children; when they did not receive satisfactory answers, they judged whole language to be yet another fad which was jeopardizing their children's education. The implementation of whole language from the view of the home-school relationship can only be seen as a catastrophic failure. Parents were not kept informed and were not invited to learn about this approach to language learning.

Part of the reason for the failure to educate parents was that principals and teachers themselves did not fully understand whole language. The transition to whole language takes much time and knowledge; however, some school boards hastened the process without adequately preparing and involving parents and teachers. For example, some schools forbade primary teachers from using readers and forced them to implement a "whole language" program. Because the teachers did not fully understand the theory and practice their language programs were sorely deficient. All those involved —students, teachers

---

1 Judith Newman and Susan Church, "Myths of Whole Language," *The Reading Teacher* 44 (September 1990): 21.

2 See Nancie Atwell, *In the Middle: Writing, Reading, and Learning with Adolescents* (Portsmouth, NH: Heinemann, 1987), 77-83.

and parents— were frustrated by the process. The "top-down" model of these schools revealed their shallow understanding of whole language. Regie Routman says that it takes between twelve and sixteen *years* for a school to become a whole language school.[1] These schools tried to adopt whole language in a few months. Not surprisingly the experiment failed and a series of myths sprang up around whole language.

Since whole language is a philosophy not simply a methodology, the typical process of educating teachers will not work. Whole language requires teachers as thoughtful practitioners and classes as learning communities. Moving in this direction requires a completely different type of in-servicing program.[2] If whole language is to become the philosophical framework, teachers must understand the theory, endorse the assumptions and goals, and be able to discuss the approach knowledgeably and with ease and set up a solid language learning program. Anything short of this will perpetuate the myths of whole language.

Even when properly understood, however, there have been some weaknesses in the whole language approach. Although I heartily endorse the works of Atwell, Calkins and Fox, for example, in some instances I find their positions to be a little extreme. At times their work smacks of literary elitism; it is unrealistic to expect students/adults to carry around a journal for the rest of their lives, or be so moved by a sunset or a rain droplet that they will stop what they are doing and quickly write a poem about it. These expectations are unrealistic given life in our society and the low value it places on literature. Further, these authors need to place greater emphasis on using reading and writing for broader projects which take students into other subject areas. Some children may be interested in the natural sciences and projects should include these areas as well. The Reggio Emilia approach, which revolves around projects, should become part of whole language theory and practice. Another problem with their approach is that it is built on the "superteacher" model; I consider myself a whole language educator and I know as a classroom teacher the amount of knowledge and energy required. This is not a realistic model in its pure form. As a teacher educator I have had numerous teachers and student teachers tell me that they do not like to read and write; although this is sad for them personally it does not bode well for the future of whole language.

---

[1] Regie Routman shared her research findings at the *Reading for the Love of It* conference, Toronto: February, 14, 1991.

[2] For a more detailed discussion of in-servicing for whole language see Clare Kosnik, "A Community of Learners: A Fresh Approach to In-Servicing Whole Language," *Orbit*, 22 (1991): 10-12.

I do not feel that whole language proponents are realistic about the teaching population. Finally, because whole language is based on a controversial theory of language learning, there is considerable opposition to the theory and practices; and most teachers do not have the skills or the confidence necessary to respond to this opposition. (Atwell, Caulkins and Fox are *extremely* charismatic speakers — not typical of most teachers.) Having read a great deal and having had years of practice I still find myself hesitant to defend whole language. When faced with a problem teachers tend to retreat to the safety of their classrooms. Teachers do not have a long history of political activism and at present their morale is very low. Recognizing these problems with whole language is sobering but it is important to be objective about the situation.

Balancing Initiative and Structure within the Whole Language Framework

The challenge is to provide educators with enough guidance so they do not have to be superteachers but not with so much direction that their initiative is stifled. Similarly with children, there cannot be twenty five individual topics being studied simultaneously nor should everyone be required to complete the same program. Whole language curriculum requires a new frame of reference and a different kind of support. Rather than have pages of curriculum objectives in isolation, content in another manual and evaluation strategies in yet another document, school boards must see their role as supporting in-school curriculum development.

Teachers cannot be left on their own to develop their language program (the superteacher model) nor can they be offered a typical core curriculum (teacher as technician). The alternative method outlined below will satisfy the many requirements, is consistent with the notion of teachers as thoughtful practitioners and moves towards schools being a community of learners. Some principles are put forward but it must be remembered that this is an outline, it should not be misconstrued as "the program" imposed from above. It is imperative that teachers be involved with every step of the planning process; this is how they learn about curriculum development, have ownership of the program, improve their teaching skills and develop a relevant program. The outline is only a skeleton which provides some direction and a measure of consistency between schools, classes and grade levels.

I would suggest a five-step process for curriculum development. (The first four steps take place at the school board level but with extensive teacher and local school input.) First, broad "themes" or topics that are to be studied are identified by teachers, curriculum consultants and academics. It is not enough just to identify them; their connection to the notion of an educated person and intermediate goals such as autonomy/control, reflectiveness, integration, responsibility/ care and mutuality is shown. This information plus key concepts for each theme are stated in jargon-free language. Secondly, an extensive bibliography is compiled listing titles of books and teacher resources including records, magazines, videos, cassette tapes, books (fiction and non-fiction), computer programs and suggested field trips. Thirdly, an outline is developed of activities (NOT just worksheets), some strongly recommended and others optional. Fourthly, a short list is drawn up of skills that flow naturally from the activities. This approach to curriculum has the benefit of placing skills and evaluation in a specific context. Finally, moving from the school board level to the local schools, teachers in small groups, most likely with the assistance of consultants and academics, take this information and decide which topics are to be studied, approximate timelines, other activities, possibilities within the topics, strengths of each teacher, specific needs of the community and resources within the community. The material provided by the school board is only a jumping off point for the local teachers. These planning meetings become an integral and regular part of the school structure.

In Atwell's Centre for Teaching and Learning, the teachers meet every week to reflect, share, modify and plan. In this way the theme evolves as the students are working on it. The theme is not a prescribed unit of study, it is an overarching topic that includes individual projects, group work, formal lessons, responses to books, field trips, dramatizing stories, sharing information, making videos, interviewing key individuals, making class books and doing art work. In one way the approach is prescriptive because teachers choose some of the general topics; but hopefully enough flexibility is built in to accommodate all needs.

Possible themes are: interesting people (favourite author, historical figures, role models, leaders in politics, music and education); interesting places (my community, my city, my homeland); alive (plants, animals, people, the environment, in the woods, the sea, adaptation); inventions; story (my story, our story); mysteries (of science, behaviour, weather watch); and technology in my life (toys, computers, machines, television). In some schools teachers may decide to do only three themes whereas in others they may elect to do six themes. Teachers may decide to repeat a theme each year; for example, the topic of favourite author might become a yearly event in some schools. Because of my commitment to vertical groupings, I would want some themes that could accommodate the whole school. At first teachers will need a great deal of assistance with planning of this sort; it requires a new way of thinking about curriculum, a willingness to collaborate and a re-shaping of practices. They may definitely draw on many of the re-sources currently in use, but they will be putting them together in a dif-ferent way. Traditionally, schools have not used this "teacher as cur-riculum developer" approach so new ways will have to be learned.

At Atwell's Center for Teaching and Learning the entire school (kindergarten to grade six) is involved in the same themes. Since the school's inception in 1990 there have been two school-wide themes each year: community and change; systems and structures; energy and explo-ration; inventions and immigration; marine study and migration. The teachers meet in the spring and through consultation decide on the themes for the following year and then the process of gathering re-sources and communicating with parents begins.

With this approach, as noted earlier, the skills to be developed are written in a specific context. This helps teachers better grasp the direction of the program and the vision of the learner. Having key con-cepts, titles of resources, tasks and evaluation procedures all in one place makes the program less fragmented. On a deeper level, this ap-proach has a high level of consistency between theory and practice be-cause the overall and intermediate goals for the individual are embod-ied in actual school practice; skills and attitudes are linked to the ac-tual content; and real opportunities for students to apply their knowl-edge are suggested. No part of the curriculum process or the curriculum itself is isolated from other aspects of schooling. This approach is both comprehensive and open-ended. It integrates the philosophy of whole language while providing a framework in which teachers can work.

Whole Language
Supports the Intermediate Goals

For a philosophy of education to be viable, there must be a consistency between theory and practice. My vision of the educated person and my description of a proposed program (necessarily selective) have been provided. At this point, I will attempt to demonstrate the congruence between theory and practice by showing how whole language supports my five intermediate goals for schooling.

a. Autonomy/Control

Because a whole language classroom is open-ended and requires active participation from the students, the goals of autonomy/control are fine fibres running throughout the program. Children have many choices in both their reading materials and their writing; although some of the central texts may be preselected, children have the opportunity to read books of their choice every day and write on personally selected topics regularly. The children also have the opportunity to choose the style and form of their writing; for example, they can use poems (traditional, alphabet, acrostic or shape), invitations, short books, songs, rhymes, mystery stories, narrative, diary entries and so on. The choice is extended to include the option of reading and writing on their own or with other children. (Less able students have the opportunity to dictate their stories to the teacher or to other students, to work with an older "buddy" student, to record their story on a tape or to illustrate their story in various mediums and so on.) Since the literature component is influenced by the children's interests and the follow-up activities are not predetermined, students have both autonomy within and control over their work.

When students select and complete projects of their choice they grow as autonomous individuals. Self-selected projects provide a personal reason to read and write; for example, when a child explores the topic "magic" (within the theme of mysteries) he may learn about a famous magician, locate a store that sells props for magic shows and choose to put on a magic show for the class. The teacher guides, assists, supports and encourages the child's learning — the student is not entirely on his own.

Encouraging a child to select and complete a project on magic represents and requires active, participatory learning. The child has to *initiate* the project, which is one of the first steps in controlling one's own learning; if the impetus does not come from within, the work will in fact be the teacher's curriculum. Selecting and starting the project are personal and meaningful acts for the child; at that moment, magic is especially important to this youngster. As he reads books, writes up the program, makes notes and designs the invitations, a great many *skills are being acquired*. To be autonomous and have control over one's own learning, it is necessary to have skills; without an adequate reading and writing system the child would be overly dependent on the teacher. As the child works on his magic show, he is keeping *life in the learning process*; the activities do not become "flat" as so often happens when they are preselected. Autonomy requires enthusiasm which is often in short supply in more structured classes. When the child presents the magic show many things happen; he *shares his knowledge* with his peers, and through their applause and responses he feels that his work is valued. The validation by his fellow students confirms his growing sense of self. Although a central goal of schooling is to have children recognize that their projects are valuable to themselves, it is also important to have recognition by one's peers. Ironically, as children have the chance to explore a personal interest within the framework of the school, they feel more *connected to the school* because their work is not remote from their life. Autonomy and control do not distance children from the schooling process; rather, they add depth and meaning to the experience.

b. Reflectiveness

When children read and write in a natural manner on a daily basis they draw on their own interests and experiences. In some circumstances the teacher assigns a specific task but most of the time children have considerable choice. Although themes have been identified, they were chosen because generally children find these topics interesting and within each there is a range that allows all students to be accommodated.

Writing does not come easily for most children; to help the process, children begin telling their stories. The oral recounting has the advantage of helping children develop a "sense of story"; but on a deeper level it is an opportunity for children to reflect on their lives, their experiences, their dreams, and their disappointments. It is difficult for youngsters to be pensive; sharing their stories is one way to help them turn inward. After they have recounted their stories, they often want to write them. The writing takes many forms (a picture, a plasticine model, a model made from Lego, or more traditional styles of poems, diary entries, group chart stories, rough drafts, lists of words); unlike in traditional writing programs, not all of these are reworked into "finished" products. Some of the writing is only exploratory and fills a need at a specific time. As the year progresses, the students' writing folders become filled with many different entries. It is important for children to return to these and reread them. As children reread their stories, it is not unusual to hear them comment (or shout out) "Oh, remember when that happened" or "That was so scary". Revisiting their stories gives them a sense of accomplishment, strengthens their sense of self as writers and individuals and gives them a chance to revisit and reflect on their stories.

> When our students turn back in their traces to reread and reflect, we teachers must be very careful not to assume that this rereading and rethinking should necessarily function as an impetus for revision as we have known it. After youngsters read and share their entries, we must not hurry them into a constricting process of adding to or repairing their

entries. But the rereading can lead toward re-visioning in the broadest sense of the word.[1]

Since the whole language reading and writing approach does not emphasize the finished product, students and teachers have the opportunity to explore and develop, within the process. For example, when children have to decide what they like to read or what is "good" for them, they have to reflect in general on what they value. Eventually they may come to understand why a particular series of books —those of Dr. Seuss, for example— hold a special interest and pleasure for them.

Another aspect of whole language that helps to develop the quality of reflectiveness is the opportunity to collaborate with others. As the children progress they are able to participate increasingly in literature response circles or small conference writing groups. "Talking about a piece of literature with others gives readers time to explore half-formed ideas, to expand their understandings of literature through hearing others' interpretations, and to become readers who think critically and deeply about what they read."[2] As they work in these groups they have to offer opinions, support their peers and provide a response to a text; they learn to be thoughtful about the stories and sensitive to the feelings of others. For example, when a student has written a story about the death of a grandparent, she may share it with a friend. After she has read the story, her friend must think about the story and respond. The story may trigger memories of the loss of her own grandparent and the two students may engage in a discussion about death, funerals, feelings and so on. Participating in the discussion helps both students become more reflective.

Conferences about books and stories with peers require many skills and for all children the process is challenging. Some youngsters are not able to handle small group sessions until at least the end of grade three. Rather than discard this activity the teacher can modify it; for example, she can play a fuller role in the group until children are able to work with just another student. Or she may partner the children with older students or have them discuss the story in the whole group setting. Through these modifications, the teacher guides the children along the path of becoming more reflective.

Literature deals with feelings and values. When children read or are read to they become engaged with the plot and, in a good book, they

---

[1] Lucy McCormick Caulkins, *Living Between the Lines*, 63.

[2] Jerome Harste, Kathy Short and Carolyn Burke, *Creating Classrooms for Authors: The Reading Writing Connection*, 293.

"know" the characters; through the reading they possibly identify with the character, react to the events and probably evaluate the action. "It is psychologically impossible to read something without experiencing a response. We may fall asleep with boredom; but that is a response."[1] Reading provides them with images for thought and reflection. At the end of the story the children have a chance to discuss it; participation in the dialogue helps them reflect on the plot and characters of the story. Usually in discussions children will say what they would have done in a similar situation and this mental role playing helps the individual explore possibilities. In a whole language program, the abundance of stories provides children with a great deal of "raw material" for what Northrop Frye has called an "imaginative store."

c. Integration

As we saw earlier whole language theory and programming requires a fundamental change in the way schools approach learning. It involves a move beyond subject specialties and specific learning outcomes, and a recognition that the social and structural environment of the class influences the curriculum activities and hence the learning that takes place. A connection is established between the goals of the individual and the learning community on the one hand and the curriculum on the other; the two are not distinct spheres. When in recent years some teachers have added "literature circles" to their classes, they have been very disappointed that the students have not engaged in discussions similar to the examples outlined in the manual; and they have tended to blame the students, the manual or the academics who created this new fad. What these teachers have not realized is that the new demands placed on the students have not been continuous with regular class practices. Children who have been used to the steady rhythm of worksheet completions are uncomfortable with the demand to be spontaneous and imaginative. Integration requires a consistency in practices and ideology.

Integration also means that the educator's understanding of knowledge and learning does not change from subject to subject. For example, there is a huge difference between environmental studies which focuses on individual awareness and responsibility and a basal reading program which expects conformity and convergent thinking. The children may become highly confused when they switch between these two systems. Kathy Gnagey Short's response to teachers who have had problems with whole language methods emphasizes the need for teachers

---

[1] Aidan Chambers, *Booktalk*, 11.

to examine their understanding of learning and knowledge. If learning is equated with outcomes based education, many whole language activities will be considered trivial or unnecessary.

> I wonder if they have added a new method to their classrooms instead of taking a new perspective on learning. It is not until we, as educators, focus on the broader learning contexts established in our classrooms and consciously think through our own beliefs about learning that we are able to effect change.[1]

Gnagey Short's response has two critical elements: a realization that the teacher's definition of learning will likely influence the choice of curriculum activities, and a recognition of the importance of the link between the class environment and the curriculum. Her second point emphasizes the interconnections between the elements of the school experience. Whole language is not just an "add-on"; it is a philosophy and methodology that requires us to consider the way the many pieces of the daily routine of schooling fit together. In order to have children participate in the many activities described throughout this chapter (and for them to be meaningful), the climate and culture of the class must be supportive of whole language methods. For example, in the proposed technology theme in grade three the children will focus on television. One aspect that might be examined are the techniques used in TV commercials. After children have watched sample commercials, they will discuss the methods used by advertisers. This dialogical method will only be possible if children have had experiences participating in dialogues, feel that the class environment is safe, have had experience examining other materials critically and know that the teacher sees this as a legitimate learning activity. When these aspects blend together, the discussion or activity has the potential to be rich and meaningful.

Harste's definition of literacy implies that reading and writing are skills for living, not just tasks to be completed for a specific subject. This perspective enables educators to see language or literacy from a multidisciplinary perspective, thus allowing for a more natural integration of the curriculum and also a recognition of the moral and social dimensions of schooling. School (the curriculum) is integrated into the lives of the children, is influenced by the surrounding community and supports the children's lives. As Jane Roland Martin notes, drawing on Maria

---

[1] Kathy Gnagey Short, "Creating a Community of Learners," in *Talking About Books: Creating Literate Communities* eds. Kathy Gnagey Short and Kathryn Mitchell Pierce (Portsmouth, NH: Heinemann, 1990), 35.

Montessori's work, "school is not an asylum."[1] As children bring themselves into the reading and writing programs and are involved in meaningful projects, the harsh physical and psychological barriers that
have long separated schools from the real lives of children will soften.

d. Responsibility/Care

Whole language programs strive to balance individual growth and the
development of the group. A key aspect of the whole language approach is that children frequently share their work, in its many stages,
with their peers. They will do this, however, only if they value the
group, both as a means of their own learning and as a way of helping
others.

Children must feel responsible not only for their own learning but
also for that of the group. In this book I have stressed repeatedly the
need for children to develop a consciousness of the class as a learning
community. This awareness and its accompanying actions cannot be
taught directly; however, a well balanced, thoughtful curriculum can
foster a sense of responsibility and caring for the community.

In my own teaching at the primary level, I would start off each
writing class with students reporting on their progress. Some children
would state their topics, others would describe their bookmaking projects and so on. This brief reporting was more than a classroom management technique. When children share their topics and approaches
there is the implicit understanding that others can "borrow" or "use"
this information in their own writing. A good idea does not remain one's
personal property or symbol of success; rather, it becomes part of the
group's repertoire of skills. For example, a young student wanted to re-
copy her completed story into a "big book" format with painted illustrations. I agreed to this proposal, she completed the book with help
from other students, and this type of book was then a model that could
be copied by other students.

Given the nature of the proposed language arts program, teachers
cannot single-handedly orchestrate and implement all aspects; the demands and tasks are shared with the students. In whole language programs students learn to share their work, discuss, collaborate and assist
less able students. In order for collaboration to be part of the community's structure, children must have the skills and opportunities to be active participants in the class and must value these methods; joint efforts help children see themselves as responsible for self and others. As
students work collaboratively, they have the opportunity to "encounter

---

[1] Jane Roland Martin, *The Schoolhome: Rethinking Schools for Changing Families*
(Cambridge, Harvard University Press, 1992), 12.

the world in interesting, complex and critical ways"[1] but also to be actively involved in the class; to share in each other's success; and to gain language skills within the context of day to day life. All of which allows children to develop a sense of responsibility for others both as individuals and as a group.

The story of Oliver and Brian provides an example of a learning partnership. Oliver, a young grade three student, had extreme difficulty reading and writing. I noticed that he liked Brian, an extremely able lad, who preferred to work on his own. I approached Brian about helping Oliver, and though he was at first reluctant, he finally agreed. The two boys worked together and Brian helped Oliver sort out the beginning, middle and end of his story and printed it on chart paper. When Oliver read his story, with a great deal of assistance from Brian, both boys were beaming with pride. This activity led to a fast friendship; it helped Brian become more actively involved in the class; Oliver looked forward to storywriting and he felt that he was a reader and a writer. Both youngsters cared about the friendship and stories; the skills and attitudes of responsibility for others developed through the curriculum and spilled over into everyday life. Certainly there were times when the boys worked on their own, but they also continued to work together.

e. Mutuality

As we have just seen, for whole language programs to be viable the group of children must become a collaborative community. True collaboration cannot be forced, it is developed through shared projects, mutual affection, a willingness of spirit and common needs and values. In my definition of mutuality, I stressed the aspect of affecting and being affected through the connectedness, the give and take and the reciprocity of relational living. From the many examples cited, it is apparent that the children's involvement in the program leads to a connectedness, a give and take. Obviously, Brian and Oliver's relationship was complex and reciprocal. I observed that Oliver was affected by Brian's willingness to persevere when there were problems and Brian was affected by Oliver's keen sense of humour and ability to converse freely and easily.

When curriculum is not an end in itself, when it is placed within the larger framework of education, we can draw on the social aspects of learning. Working in small groups helps children get to know one another and also learn how to learn. Literacy is not a specific skill, such as learning to load a disc in the computer; there is a whole social dimension to it. Collaboration in learning has many benefits. First, when

---

[1] Ralph Peterson, *Life in a Crowded Place: Making a Learning Community*, 80.

children see each other as resources, they look beyond the surface and appreciate a dimension to the student's personality not previously evident. Secondly, they become accustomed to joint problem-solving; in life most challenges are shared with others — husbands, wives, colleagues, siblings and so on. "Learners can end up knowing more as they work through a process of inquiry, even though they do not immediately solve the current problem."[1] And thirdly, being able to draw on each other's expertise helps children feel that they are contributing group members thus enhancing their sense of self.

Frank Smith asserts that the class should be seen as a literacy club. Members are expected to participate actively in the club, and the notion of being part of the community is another invisible fibre holding the group together.

> Children join the literacy club with a single unqualified reciprocal act of affiliation. There are no dues to be paid, no entry standards to be met. A mutual acknowledgment of acceptance is all that is required. Children who join the literacy club take it for granted that they will become like the more experienced members of the club; they are the same kind of people ... Expectation does not guarantee learning, of course, but it makes it possible.[2]

The children's language skills have a greater possibility of improving when they feel they are part of a literate community. The literacy club and the curriculum are mutually supportive. Enzo was a student who found reading and writing very difficult. Nevertheless, he was able to enter the literacy club in a most unusual manner. He became the class expert on sewing student-made books. After he showed a student how to stitch the pages together, he usually listened to the student's story. Enzo found the regular curriculum extremely challenging but he was pleased that he could still be part of the class. As the class specialist in this one area, he felt good about himself; through these repeated positive interactions with others his sense of self was stronger and eventually we were able to work on more traditional skills. The friendships and feeling of acceptance by the group eased his way to the more difficult tasks. In a whole language class, the group of students are a team, each with specialized skills. This allows the whole to be much greater than the parts. "Students leave the school with the experience of having been a part of something greater than themselves, realizing the strength that lies in working together for a common goal."[3]

---

[1] Kathy Gnagey Short, "Creating a Community of Learners," 42.
[2] Frank Smith, *Reading Without Nonsense*, 124
[3] George Wood, *Schools That Work* (New York: Penguin, 1992), 118.

Conclusion

The whole language approach is clearly consistent with my general goals for schooling; it supports children becoming educated persons, gives them responsibility for their learning and for the community, fosters mutuality, allows children an element of control, integrates school with the rest of life and in general promotes children's well-being. Much of the whole language approach must be included and allowed to shape the direction of schooling. There is a great deal of work to be done, however, if schools are to become whole language learning communities. The strength educators will need to sustain the movement will be great.

As inspiration we can turn to Bruno Bettelheim, a true advocate for children.

> Depending on how we handle such daily interactions our children's personality and their relationship to life will take one of several courses. No single event need have specially great impact but it is amazing how ... little experiences make up, in the long run, a good life or a pretty miserable one. And all this occurs without anything terribly important having happened, good or bad.[1]

It is the little things of daily schooling that add up to a successful or failed school experience. As thoughtful practitioners creating a community of learners within a whole language framework, we have a chance to make schooling successful for many more children. The disillusionment that is plaguing public institutions should not be allowed to seep into schools any further; otherwise, it will lead to a backlash whereby we may lose all we have gained in recent decades. We must fight to save what we know is important and good for teachers and children.

---

[1] Marie Clay, *Becoming Literate: The Construction of Inner Control,* 47.

Chapter Eight

The Home-School Partnership

Because home is the hidden partner in the education of our young, we tend to forget how much of who we are, how we act, and what we know was learned there when we were very young.[1]

Jane Roland Martin

Throughout this book I have argued that education is a complex, interconnected process: for example, curriculum is value laden, the teacher's style influences the children's attitude toward the subject, and the general perspective of the class towards school affects the rate and quality of learning. Although the children's homes may be physically separate from the actual school, the "home" is another factor that affects education. Homes have many different configurations but one thing that is constant is that no matter what the dynamics or values, the "home" is another point on the three dimensional model of education. Children are not blank slates waiting to be filled by the official curriculum; rather, they are part of a family which has shaped who they are, and when they arrive at school they bear the marks of this upbringing. Traditionally, educational theorists under-estimated the role the family plays in the children's "success" in school. There are token gestures, such as a slightly lower pupil-teacher ratio for schools that are deemed needy, but on a deeper level, education has failed to realize that the home is a partner in education, an associate which cannot be ignored.

The doors of the school are not as tightly shut to parents as in previous generations but the relationship between the two worlds is often very tenuous because neither side has embraced the notion of a collaborative relationship. For example, schools often restrict parent involvement in schools to fund raising activities. But on the other hand, parents often send their children to school unwashed, unfed and exhausted, presuming that the school will provide the basics of food, clothing, shelter and love. There are many reasons why the relationship is troubled, defensive and awkward; however, this should not de-

---

[1] Jane Roland Martin, *The Schoolhome: Rethinking Schools for Changing Families* (Cambridge, MA: Harvard University Press, 1992), 18.

tract from the central issue that the home and school are partners. They may not choose to be bedfellows but they are.

In this chapter, I will examine the home-school connection. I will first discuss the current situation; although I will make some general statements which may not characterize all parent-school relationships I feel that they are quite typical. Secondly, I will discuss the reasons why it is important to have a strong link by considering two aspects: continuity of people, place and purpose and schools as multipurpose institutions. And finally, I will show how a healthy, positive school-community relationship supports my goals for education.

Moving From an Uneasy Alliance to a Partnership

Much of this book has drawn on my personal experiences as an educator. In every example, principle and assertion, I feel that I have been "true to myself" because I have stated what I believed and how I carried out my professional responsibilities as a teacher. However this section on the value of the home-school connection is exceedingly challenging to write because as a classroom teacher I often wished that parents would leave us alone. If they did their job as parents, we could do our job as teachers. The ideal parents would be those who sent their children to school prepared to learn and only visited the school when invited. At the time, I knew this was an inappropriate attitude but given the circumstances these feelings were not unreasonable. While I had many positive encounters with parents and in some cases built a strong bridge between home and school, this constructing and nourishing took a great deal of time and energy — both of which were in short supply. Of greater significance, it seemed to me, were the problematic relationships. I vividly recall parents screaming and raging at me (some in a drunken state) or dashing off to the principal to voice their displeasure about my classroom practice without talking with me first; and parents who were so neglectful or abusive toward their children that the school, on my request, had to contact the Catholic Children's Aid Society. After a few such incidents, teachers start to build a wall around themselves, partly out of self-protection and partly out of disrespect. In the recent work action in Ontario, many teachers did not feel that parents supported them. Most novice teachers do not start out being "separatist"; but a few meetings with headstrong, difficult parents, a lack of support from administrators, and staffroom banter that reinforces a negative attitude towards the community result in most new teachers sliding into the position that parents are a problem.

> All of us begin our work in education with a 20/20 personal vision
> about the way we would like a school to be. This is what we value and
> are prepared to work and even fight for. That is why we became educa-
> tors. Then, by about December of our first year, something devastating
> and apparently inevitable begins to happen. Our personal vision be-
> comes blurred by the well-meaning expectation and lists of others.[1]

Certainly not all parent-teacher relationships are characterized by
distrust and disrespect, but the relationship at best could be called an
uneasy alliance. As I noted in the chapter on *The Thoughtful Practitioner*, the barrage of articles in the press that question and attack
teachers and accuse them of limited capabilities and careless attitudes
undermines a chance for a peaceful coalition. The solution is not to try to
glue the pieces of home and school together; rather, a new conception of
the relationship must be developed. It must be a *thoughtful partnership*: each party has strengths which should be recognized by the
other; each party has a stake and responsibility in the association; and
the partnership has a well articulated, shared purpose, the well-being
of the child. My proposed partnership will be different from previous
ones because the division of labour will not be clear cut and the partnership will be characterized by flexibility. The motto for this partnership is "caring for our children is everyone's responsibility"; schools
cannot be totally responsible for education nor can parents be fully responsible for custodial functions. In some instances, schools will assume
a greater degree of care by providing breakfast, on-site daycare, after-
four programs and so on. Similarly, parents will be expected to assist
with their children's education by supervising homework, taking the
children to the Public Library weekly or listening to their youngsters
read aloud. The areas of responsibility for the two groups will blur and
the relationship will be built on a foundation of greater understanding
of each other.

In Chapter One I identified some of the changes occurring in society.
These have a major impact on children. As a result of the radical
changes in the family set-up, and in response to our knowledge that
children learn best in a safe environment, I feel that schools have to become more homelike. By this I mean that the physical setting must be
comfortable and conducive to relationship building (between children,
children and teachers, teachers and parents, teachers and administrators), sharing meals together must be a regular occurrence, places for
quiet time must be available, a mixing of age-groups must be a common
occurrence, extra curricular activities such as dance and music should be

---

1 Roland Barth, *Improving Schools from Within: Teachers, Parents, and Principals
Can Make the Difference* (San Francisco: Jossey-Bass, 1990), 148.

part of the regular school day and the timetable must not dictate all modes of action. Schools will not replace the home nor will they attempt to duplicate it; rather, they will integrate some of the best features into their way of being.

> First, we must understand that the school, like the family, is a multipurpose institution. It cannot concentrate only on academic goals any more than a family can restrict its responsibilities to, say, feeding and housing its children. The single-purpose view is not only morally mistaken, it is practically and technically wrong as well, because schools cannot accomplish their academic goals without attending to the fundamental needs of students for continuity and care.[1]

As the school becomes more of a multipurpose institution, the division of labour between home and school will soften. Until we start to view home and school as a partnership, too much energy will be expended in protecting turf and criticizing each other's shortcomings.

In July, 1993, I organized a focus group of professors of education, principals, consultants and classroom teachers to discuss issues in education. The one area upon which this diverse group could agree was the failure of schools to communicate to parents and the general public what they were doing. Classroom teachers often cannot adequately explain their curriculum choices to parents nor do schools alert the community to the crushing social problems with which they must deal. This failure to articulate clearly what is actually going on in schools was seen as one of the most critical factors in education. The focus group members felt that school reform must deal with this breakdown in communication immediately. In my proposed home-school partnership, the conversation between home and school must be continuous because, as Dewey said, a community needs communication.

Three Levels of Relationships

The partnership between home and school operates on three levels, all of which are interconnected. First, at a general level there is a relationship between school and society. Schools cannot have a mandate distinct from the rest of society nor are they immune from social and cultural influences. Schools cannot forge a path of their own, they are deeply rooted within the culture of the society. Thus, our expectations for schools must be matched by our hopes for the larger society.

---

[1] Nel Noddings, *The Challenge to Care in Schools: An Alternative Approach to Education* (New York: Teachers College Press, 1992), 64.

On a second more local level there is a relationship between the school and the surrounding community. Each community is unique: in its needs, its degree of cohesion, its diversity and the way that it views the local elementary school. For example, Blythwood Public School, which is in a wealthy suburb of Toronto, reflects the aspirations of its community. Parents consider it to be a "good" school because it has high academic standards, social expectations for the students, a principal who is responsive to the parents and a thriving program for gifted children conducted by parents. As a result the community views its school positively. At the other end of the economic spectrum is St. Paul's school which is also seen as a "good" school but for completely different reasons. It has a strong outreach program to the needy community, a breakfast program, strong links with the church, parent education programs and so on. In both of those local communities, the school responds to the community's needs in a certain way. Obviously the needs of St. Gregory's prosperous community are very different from those of the poorer St. Paul residents. George Wood wonders, "Why do we rush to impose uniform solutions to non-uniform school houses?"[1] Each community must work out what is right for its members; not only, does this help make the school more responsive to the community's needs, but the process itself helps bring various groups together and re-inforces the notion that education is a partnership.

The climate of the community flows through everything the school tries to do. The children come to the primary class with a whole set of experiences that are rooted in the given community. As a result, the economic viability of the community members and the social attitudes impact on the school. Two examples will help illustrate this point. In a northern mining community which has experienced extremely high levels of unemployment there is a defeatist attitude among the community. Teachers note that the children come into primary school talking about unemployment, families losing their homes and older siblings dropping out of school. At a young age they feel their situation is hopeless. The school by continuing with its traditional curriculum is failing to respond to the needs and pain of its community. I am not suggesting that schools must be involved directly in economic reform; however, they must be aware of the larger community and adapt their curriculum and programs accordingly.

The second example is very different in nature but once again shows how the climate of the community runs through the school. In a school where I taught there was a very poorly run daycare centre adjacent to

---

1 George Wood, *Schools that Work: America's Most Innovative Public Education Programs* (New York: Penguin Books, 1992), xxii.

the school. Although the quality of care was questionable the centre was very busy because it was convenient, had extended hours and reasonable rates. When the students from the daycare came to class, they were far more rambunctious, cranky and aggressive than the other children. As a group of teachers we complained about the centre among ourselves but we never moved beyond staffroom griping. In hindsight, I realize that we should have tried to work with the daycare personnel to help them with their programs. Perhaps one of us could have been a liaison person with the centre, or we could have invited some of the daycare workers to our divisional meetings or professional development sessions. These small actions could have helped both the school and the centre run more smoothly, but more importantly the children would have benefitted from an improved daycare centre. It is not enough for schools simply to recognize a problem, the next step must be to respond to it; schools simply cannot continue to disregard the community.

The third and most specific level of partnership is the relationship between the individual teacher and the parents. This partnership is influenced by the other two levels but, being at the grassroots, it has the potential to move beyond the other two. Once again, the primary division becomes critical to the success of other aspects of schooling. Since primary teachers are the persons who make the first contact with parents, they set the tone for the relationship between home and school. Through their actions teachers can either establish a welcoming posture or subtly send the message that parents are not welcome. Most parents of young children are very keen and readily attend meetings and open houses; but as the children progress through school the parents' enthusiasm and participation tend to dwindle. Certainly, as parents become less anxious about their children their excitement often dissipates but in this case I feel that the school has lost the opportunity to communicate and connect with the parents. Further, children benefit from the closer relationship between home and school.

> The child can benefit particularly in the mental area, because a child has to feel secure. If children are not secure, they're not going to reach out for experience. If a child is shy, is insecure, then the parent might have ways of helping the child that would be good for the teacher to know about, the teacher might have ways of helping the child that would be good for the parent. They have to be on the same wavelength.[1]

---

[1] Ada Schermann, "Reflecting on the Relationship," Orbit 25 (May 1994): 31.

Helping Teachers in the Home-School Relationship

Since individual teachers are the persons in contact most frequently with parents, they should be given guidance in dealing with parents and made aware that building a strong relationship with the community is a vital part of education. Somehow the attitude that we must have parents as partners gets lost in vision statements and curriculum documents. Building a partnership should not be an additional duty for teachers, otherwise it will be resented and done in a haphazard manner; rather, it must replace other duties. For example, if primary teachers were relieved of classroom duties for two half-hour periods a week, which were designated as "home-school" time, they would have many opportunities to meet with parents, send home messages, newsletters, curriculum outlines and so on. Parents would know the teacher was available at this time and could make an appointment to see him or her. During this time teachers could meet with other teachers and administrators to discuss the community's needs or ways to communicate most effectively with parents. Certainly this would be costly. But I would suggest, for example, that we could discontinue the Heritage Language program in schools, which is costing millions of dollars and seems to me to be a dismal failure, and use those funds for such a home-school program. With this funding, music and art teachers could be hired to relieve teachers of their duties for these periods.

If we value a home-school partnership, teachers must be given assistance and the opportunity to develop the necessary skills. As professor at a faculty of education, I know that ways to communicate effectively with parents are only mentioned incidentally in the preservice programs. As a result, novice teachers are often at a loss in dealing with parents and in a way are "set up" for confrontations. Systematically addressing the home-school partnership, including ways to communicate with parents, how to understand one's community and the place of schools in society, should be part of all preservice programs.

In schools, all teachers should be part of discussion groups that address the topic of home-school partnership. Every primary division meeting should include some discussion of the home-school partnership; as teachers share information about public library programs, bus schedules and families in distress, they would be placing the school in a larger social context. These discussions would also reinforce the notion that teachers are a community of learners because experienced teachers can act as mentors for novices who are preparing for their first set of interviews while also reflecting on their own practices.

A strong link between home and school is contingent on teachers being thoughtful practitioners. When teachers are confident of their programs, understand the rationale for and the theory underlying the approach and have made choices about the curriculum, they are able to explain their programs clearly to parents. When teachers are involved in setting classroom goals, school objectives and so on, they have a much deeper understanding of and connection to the school. Further, when teachers have been trained to observe children, interpret their observations and then translate their findings into appropriate curriculum choices, they have a much firmer grasp of the situation. At present, many teachers do not have this high level of expertise and resort to using jargon when faced with difficult questions; this gives the impression either that they do not know their job or that they are evading the issue. School boards, faculties of education and local schools must help teachers become more fluent and confident in meeting with parents.

Ongoing communication between home and school is essential; since this takes a great deal of work it should be integrated into other projects: it should not be an "add-on." For example, as part of the monthly class newsletter, there could be an outline of ongoing and upcoming curriculum themes, projects, a message from the teacher and so on. This newsletter, which is already part of the language arts program, could become a vehicle for disseminating information to parents and would also illustrate to the children the importance of the home-school relationship. Initially, building these bridges will be challenging, but schools must be committed to the partnership and devote their energy to the project until it becomes part of the way schooling is conducted. Some activities which are very time consuming, such as preparing for the annual Science Fair or Spring concert, may have to be postponed while educators spend their limited time building the partnership. Formal curriculum nights, parent teacher interviews, regular contact by phone, newsletters, less formal meetings, active Parent-Teacher Associations, parent volunteer training programs, outreach programs and the Education Council are all ways to help *keep the conversation going* between home and school.

It should be noted that most parents are also very busy and have limited time; as a result, educators must be sure that they use their time with parents wisely. Parents cannot be expected to attend meetings frequently, sit through long sessions outlining curriculum in detail or help in planning daily activities. They do not have the time or the interest; therefore, educators must ensure that their message is succinct and clear. For those parents who want more information, however, teachers should be available.

There is a danger in opening up the school to the public that teachers may be subject to unjust scrutiny and abuse by some parents. There is also the problem of parents just "dropping in" on the teacher — primary classrooms are busy places and parents cannot simply walk in and expect the teacher to meet with them immediately. Guidelines must be established and teachers must feel that they have the support of the administration when dealing with parents. Many parents feel that teachers are their employees because they pay realty taxes; to counteract this attitude, I feel that teachers should show they have spent years preparing for their job, that they are professionals and that society needs their services. Two small steps could be: first, teachers should display their university and college diplomas and certificates in the class; when a teacher completes a primary methods program or a Master of Education degree this information should be included in the newsletter. And secondly, schools should have a designated "public relations" person on staff who will contact the local newspaper, radio or TV station to cover a special event that is occurring in the school. All of these individual projects that I have mentioned help to build a partnership between the home and school on the three levels of contact.

Continuity in the Home-School Partnership

A fruitful partnership demands a level of consistency in both philosophy and practice. In order for this partnership to be viable there must be a continuity of many different facets. Nel Noddings in *The Challenge to Care in the Schools* suggests that there should be a continuity of *people, place* and *purpose* within the school[1] and I would extend her notion to suggest that there should be a continuity of these same three aspects between the school and the larger community. I have already discussed the need for shared purposes between home and school. Here I will focus on continuity of place and people.

i. *Continuity of Place*

Continuity of place is important for young children in part because it provides them with a measure of security. When youngsters can easily walk to their local school with other neighbourhood children, they are taking the initial steps of connecting to and being responsible for their community. As schools become centres for the community, it makes sense

---

1 See Nel Noddings, *The Challenge to Care in Schools: An Alternative Approach to Education*, 64-73.

that children attend their local school for both regular schooling and after-school programs. A further way to help children feel connected to the school is to have daycare centres in the school; it is one less adjustment that they have to make. In France, every local elementary school has daycare facilities adjacent to (or within) the school building; the centres do not simply share the same physical space with the school; the childcare workers collaborate with teachers in the local school.[1] This co-operation creates a bridge for children when making the transition from one location to another. When parents "shop around" for a school or are forced to have daycare in a location other than their neighbourhood, they place undue stress on their children. I have taught children who have been in six schools by the time that they are in grade two and it is extremely difficult for them to feel connected to any one place. Children who live with grandparents in one part of the city from Monday to Friday and with their parents on the weekends have problems adjusting to the various settings. These continual moves are very difficult for children.

A continuity of place does not imply that children attend the same school from kindergarten to the completion of high school. I visited a school in New Brunswick which was a combination elementary and high school; from discussions with some teachers, I realized that this arrangement is very difficult for the older children. The intermediate students need a break, both symbolic and physical, with the elementary school; however, that does not mean that the move to high school should be absolute. High school students should have the opportunity to return to their local elementary schools for reunions and festivals and to work with the younger children. As "co-op" courses become more commonplace in high schools, it would be beneficial if all senior students had the opportunity to work in their former elementary school for at least one term. For some students, this might help ease the anxiety of the transition years. When primary children work with older students they appreciate and benefit from the individual attention; the mixing of age levels, more typical of the home, will reduce the stratification in schools.

ii. *Continuity of People*

In order to build a strong relationship between home and school there must, as far as possible, be continuity of people. Since teaching is rela-

---

[1] For a more detailed discussion see Ian D. McMahan, "Public Preschool From the Age of Two: The *École Maternelle* in France," *Young Children* 47 (July 1992): 22-28.

tional it becomes very jarring, especially for young children, to become acquainted with, connected to and then separated from their teacher every year. The same is true for parents; it is difficult for them to become familiar with their children's teacher and form a relationship in a short period, all the while knowing that this procedure will have to be repeated next September. How often have we heard parents struggle to recall their child's teacher's name? They may say "Oh, last year the teacher was Ms. Smith but this year it is ...". When teachers have the same group of children for at least two years, they have the time to develop a relationship with parents; repeating the procedure every year is tiresome for everyone involved. As a teacher in one school for many years, I found that the parents of children whom I had taught previously would stop in and visit me when they were in the school. Often, I had taught two or three children in the same family and they felt a strong bond to me. Seeing familiar faces helps to make the school less imposing and a more inviting, homelike place.

It is not just the teachers who can provide continuity of people: longstanding members of the community can provide stability, a history of and insight into the area. For example, one of my student teachers, for a unit on the community with our grade two students, invited some long-time members of the community to come to class and share their pictures and talk about the changes in the area. The experience was delightful for the senior citizens and the children learned far more about their community than if they had simply studied a textbook. This added dimension helped them to feel "connected to" the visitors and their community.

The policy of many school boards of transferring principals every five years and vice-principals every two years impedes the growth of a strong partnership. The rationale that administrators should have varied experiences has some validity; however, the disadvantage of this regular rotation is that administrators do not have time to build solid relationships with many community members in the given time (usually they only get to know the difficult parents). It is very easy to slide into the attitude of "why bother to put down roots since I will be moved in a few years." In smaller communities the principal is often assigned to a school indefinitely and as a result feels a strong sense of ownership of that school and responsibility to that community. Perhaps, our urban schools should follow the example of smaller communities on ways to connect with the community. The principal sets the tone for the school and when he or she reaches out to the community, that attitude will trickle down to other staff members and many links will be forged in the principal's shadow.

Schools As Multipurpose Institutions

Through partnerships with other agencies, groups and institutions there will be more opportunities for schools to become central to the community. There are two basic reasons for advocating this extended role; first, it would be economically sound for school buildings to be put to much greater use. It seems highly inefficient to be operating for only part of the day, five days a week and for only ten months of the year. (I am *not* advocating a twelve month school year but schools could be used for other programs.) School buildings (capital start-up and maintenance) require such a tremendous amount of money that it seems a low return on the investment to have such limited use. Schools are beginning to be used more frequently for adult education; however, this use is partial and haphazard. I recognize that there is a problem when other groups use day-time classrooms and school facilities: there is often theft, vandalism and disruption and many teachers are very hesitant to allow others to use their classrooms. However, in a true partnership, the schools will not simply be landlords and the visitors tenants. There will be a notion of partnership and hence responsibility from both groups so that these wayward behaviours will not be commonplace.

Schools are busy places with an extensive internal mandate; they cannot assume the role of community leader, *on their own*. Nevertheless, they can make links with other organizations that are already in existence. Buckminster Fuller advocates the principle of synergy or "pursuing several goals at the one time,"[1] and this should be the way schools see themselves — collaborating with other groups and pursuing many goals at once. For example, schools could establish links with the local YMCA. Since both schools and Y's tend to be centrally located, it would make sense that they share a common building site and programs. The costs would be reduced because there could be shared facilities such as the auditorium; personnel could work collaboratively on some programs; extended care of the children for either daycare or after school programs could be arranged on-site; teachers would be encouraged to use the Y facilities which would promote a healthy living style; and using the facilities would help them connect to their school community area. The community perception of the school would be enhanced because it would not be seen as serving only a limited purpose. Certainly, there would be issues of insurance, funding, security and so on that would have to be resolved; however, the benefit of combining with

---

[1] Clive Beck, *Better Schools: A Values Perspective* (New York: The Falmer Press, 1990), 9.

other organizations should provide sufficient incentive to overcome such barriers.

Schools, by establishing partnerships with other community agencies or government ministries, could be centering forces. As school populations fluctuate there is surplus space in school buildings; it should be possible for other organizations to use this space. Groups such as support services for immigrants or re-entry training programs for adults could share the school facilities. These collaborative ventures form a bridge between the school and the community.

To become more multipurpose, schools have only to look in their own backyard; schools should become more involved in teacher training. I was involved in setting up a "school based" teacher education model between the Toronto District Catholic School Board and the University of Toronto, OISE/UT. A group of thirty preservice teachers were "housed" in an TDCSB school: two days a week they had lectures at the home school, they studied on campus for one day and for the final two days they worked in either the home or neighbouring schools. The program was a huge success because the student teachers were quickly immersed in the life of a school, the teachers in the home school participated by either attending lectures, giving workshops or acting as associate teachers and the children benefitted from the additional attention they received. The school based model added another dimension to the home school because it went beyond simply dealing with children. The staff felt very special that their school had been chosen as the home school and they responded warmly to the teacher trainees. Many of the problems that could have hindered the program such as staffroom congestion or funding did not materialize; the commitment to the program and the sense of a partnership motivated everyone to find a solution. And we did!

Partnerships will often enable schools to become more multipurpose without actually having to develop many programs themselves. As more services are available in and through the school, the school can become more central to the community; in its current state, it has limited access and services. When both adults and children use the school, its purpose, power and connection become stronger.

The Partnership Supports
The Five Intermediate Goals

In this final section, I will examine the ways that the proposed partnership supports my five intermediate goals. Since the notion of the schools and the community in partnership is a radical departure from our present system, it is important to show that this direction is consistent with my overall vision of the school. This discussion provides yet another perspective from which to view the goals.

a. Autonomy/Control

A partnership does not necessarily preclude a sense of autonomy or a measure of control; an association implies two distinct groups coming together for a shared purpose. As each group exercises choices there will be less resentment towards the other; more opportunity for each party to grow; and the partnership itself will develop. In the curriculum chapter, I provided the example of the young student who had the opportunity to complete a project on magic; by exploring a personal interest within the framework of the school he feels more connected to the school. The same attitude should be applied to the home-school partnership; when schools feel that they have a measure of autonomy (not full autonomy) they can bring an open mind and a willingness to participate in the partnership.

At present, many educators feel that educational reform is being driven by political and economic agendas; many of the proposals for reform are not rooted in the education community. For example, the implementation of standardized tests for grades three and six students in Ontario was certainly not a recommendation from teachers and principals. When educators feel that they are deprofessionalized and treated like technicians, they lose their sense of autonomy which then leads to a loss of professional self-respect. The sense of helplessness —the feeling on the societal level that the problems are staggering and on a personal level that "I just cannot do anymore"— causes many teachers to feel that they have limited control over their professional duties. Roland Barth notes as we have seen, that there is intense pressure on teachers to perform and meet someone else's "list" of objectives. It is not just that these lists are produced outside of the school community; by their nature they subtly imply that educators should not have the freedom to plan for themselves.

> Add to the highly routinized work of schoolpeople the expectation to do more with less. More pupils per class, more evidence of pupil achievement, and more energy in a climate of decline in the numbers of students, in test scores, in the number of jobs, in resources, in morale, and in public confidence... The message is pretty clear: Teachers are encountering times probably more difficult than at any period in American history. The social value of their work, which has fuelled them through past difficulties,

is no longer able to provide sufficient compensation and professional invigoration.[1]

Educators must feel that they have a measure of autonomy on all three levels, those of school and society, school and community, and individual teacher and parents; and with this confidence they will come to the partnership with a healthy, strong, positive attitude. (And in turn, they will pass this confidence and positive outlook on to their students.) A degree of autonomy and control implies that educators have an expertise —they know what needs to be done and how to do it— whereas externally determined objectives and lists suggest that school people are not capable. A partnership cannot be based on the premise that one group is not competent; such an imbalance of power undermines the formation of a healthy relationship.

b. Reflectiveness

A genuine partnership requires both groups to consider their needs and strengths and develop a method to communicate this information to others; this wisdom then becomes part of the shared knowledge base. As schools and homes pause to consider their own situation —what they can bring to the partnership and what they need— the tone of the conversation changes. At present, the discussion is often defensive and confrontational; this posturing makes communication and community very difficult. On all three levels, schools must think about what they can realistically bring to the partnership and they also must consider their needs (and the answers must be in the realm of the possible). As they bring this information to the discussion table the ensuing plans have a greater chance of being successful. The knowledge of what schools can do and what they need allows everyone to be setting goals and strategies in a far more realistic atmosphere unlike the rarefied climate of ministries of education.

As a teacher I was never really asked what I needed to do my job (other than consumable supplies), nor did anyone inquire as to my strengths. These are lost opportunities. Similarly, I would assume that parents, communities, school boards and so on do not engage in the soul searching that is necessary for the development of the individual, the group and the partnership. At present, the expectations for schools are often so unrealistic that the schools are set-up for failure before they even begin the task. For example, some parents often want teachers to discipline their children because they are not able to control them at home. But equally, teachers often have unrealistic expectation for par-

---

[1] Roland Barth, *Improving Schools from Within*, 12 &13.

ents; for example, some teachers want parents to have a Judeo-Christian, Western European worldview. If both groups, parents and teachers, stopped to reflect, they would realize that many of their expectations, for themselves and for others, are inappropriate.

Many of the examples that I have provided such as mentorship programs, teacher's twice weekly home-school periods, and joint community-school projects require individuals and institutions to be reflective. The motto that I proposed, "caring for our children is everyone's responsibility," should help individuals turn inward to discern what they can bring to the partnership and outward to discover what the needs are. Just as individual classes should have their motto posted in the class, so too should schools display this motto and act as thoughtful partners.

c. Integration

The concept that schools are part of society has been a recurring theme in my book; given this premise, there must be a high level of integration between school and society, on the three levels. I have shown that constancy of purpose, place and people is a necessity. Another perspective on integration is the recognition that the political and economic spheres of the larger society depend on schools to prepare children; these agendas are integrated into the school process. However, the domestic sphere, a critical aspect of a healthy society, is often overlooked in the integration of the larger social context into the school.

The domestic sphere is very complex because it addresses the physical, emotional and cognitive needs; the home nurtures, educates and socializes children. The domestic agenda is often equated with the traditional skills of homemaking, cooking, caring for the young, providing a refuge from the demands of the workplace, tending to gardens, the pursuit of hobbies and so on but care and affirmation are also necessary to developing a sense of self. Through the home the children feel grounded while acquiring skills for life; both the individual and society grow and prosper. I propose integrating some of the domestic agenda into the curriculum because it helps children become well rounded individuals; educated persons must be fluent in the traditional domestic skills too. By integrating these skills and tasks into the curriculum the whole child is addressed and the links between home and school are strengthened. Because my proposed curriculum is one that is highly participatory, relevant to life and flexible, there is certainly place in it for the domestic sphere. Jane Roland Martin notes that in her ideal Schoolhome the domestic sphere is simply part of schooling. "Vocational or professional training is not the issue here. Citizenship is. Each day, every child does some domestic work, not in order to be qualified for careers in food-related industries but because the daily life of the Schoolhome requires this commitment."[1]

The domestic is a necessary part of life, for both males and females, and schooling should not shy away from activities that are often not seen as part of their mandate. Jane Roland Martin recognizes that homes provide the basics, the mores of society, and this "curriculum ... inducts our young into human culture."[2] However, she takes the argument a step further by asserting that the silent partner, the home, provides the basics which then allows schools to pursue the more complex and socially acceptable goals of "achieving economic viability, becoming a good citizen, and acquiring high culture — [these] make sense only for people who have already learned the basic mores of society."[3]

The domestic sphere, which makes so many other goals possible, must be recognized and integrated into our primary schools. If homes are not able to provide as full a complement of the domestic as is "necessary," primary education must make this agenda a priority. The first step is to find ways to incorporate the domestic sphere into the school mandate and the second stage must be the communication of these goals to the larger public. In our justification for its inclusion, educators must stress that the domestic is as important to our children as the political and economic. Given the turmoil of many children's lives, if schools do not provide the traditional skills of the domestic sphere this basic grounding will be neglected; taking the argument one step further, I wonder how these youngsters will be able to provide daycare for their own children.

d. Responsibility/Care

It seems redundant to ask "How does a partnership between school and home support the intermediate goals of responsibility and care?" because a partnership implies that there is responsibility and care. These twin values are the basis of the partnership while also being goals of the partnership. However, when we move beyond the surface question it becomes apparent that our interpretation of the term "partnership" influences our answer. First, a partnership that is based on the two values of responsibility and care has a certain dynamic. When an alliance is based on an imbalance of power or a dominant/submissive model only one partner may care about the well-being of the relationship; however, my partnership is based on two parties both feeling a strong sense

---

[1] Jane Roland Martin, *The Schoolhome: Rethinking Schools for Changing Families* (Cambridge, MA: Harvard University Press, 1992), 157.

[2] Jane Roland Martin, *The Schoolhome*, 29.

[3] *Ibid.*, 30.

of responsibility for the healthy survival of the whole. Secondly, an interpretation that assumes that caring is reciprocal suggests that the partnership is self-generating.

In an earlier discussion, I noted that caring is not simply a one-way interaction; rather it is two-way because, as Noddings says, the recipient must respond to the caregiver and also the caring must be two way. This reciprocity of interaction seems to be one of the elements that is missing from our current uneasy alliance. All too frequently, schools or the community do not respond to the care that is given to them or their response completely overlooks the other's initiative or needs. The dialectic breaks down repeatedly. In order to continue the cycle of caring, the cared for must receive the actions or words, then responds in an appropriate manner, which the caregiver then receives and respond to and on and on. Often schools send out messages that they care but the signals and actions seem to be swallowed into a black hole. Similarly, parents feel that their caring actions are not recognized by their partner. Both groups send out signals but the responses they receive either do not match the intentions or suggest that the actions are not good enough. For example, it is important in primary school to identify children with learning disabilities. If I suspect that a student is experiencing unusual problems, I work with her individually, make detailed observations and notes, modify the program, contact the consultant and, if all of this is insufficient, complete a detailed Board form for Special Education testing; this process takes a great deal of time and commitment. However, often when I contact parents to discuss my concerns, they immediately question my motives and abilities; my message to the parents, although often understandably unwelcome, is not received as a message of care and is not responded to in an appropriate manner. My caring about the child and my sense of responsibility are often rebuffed. When this rejection occurs repeatedly the caring and responsibility which are at the core of the partnership erode. Most parents and educators have the best of intentions. Schools and parents must find a way to receive each other's messages such that we can *keep the conversation going*.

In a partnership children are enculturated into a particular way of being and doing. Caring becomes a way of life. Children can only learn about responsibility and care if they live it and they only learn about partnerships if they are part of one. Through extended partnerships between parents and teachers/ administrators, children will see a co-operative, collaborative model of living. It is not just the content of their schooling but the context of their schooling experience that is a powerful educator for children. "Thus, when children are reminded day after day, year after year, that the most important thing they can do in school is to sit quietly, obey the teacher, and repeat back verbatim what they have been told, they are learning patterns of thinking and behaviour that will stay with them for life."[1] However, when children are actively involved in their community, day after day, with the same people and with the same purpose, those patterns of behaviour will stay with them long after the final school bell rings.

e. Mutuality

Just as responsibility and care are an aspect of the partnership so too should mutuality be an integral part of the way schools and the community interact. A partnership allows each group to affect and be affected by the other in a spirit of mutual support and empathy. Through this type of relationship one gains a better understanding of the other; a partnership cannot thrive without this knowledge. Mutuality, like care, implies that the relationship is dialectical; through interchanges, shared activities and common goals there will be many opportunities to impact on the other's perceptions and activities. The partnership provides the forum for interaction (and growth); without an acceptance of the dialectical nature of education and mechanisms for its development the chance for exchange decreases. For example, a grade one student, Amy, was experiencing problems in turning her attention to the given task; when I talked to her parents, with whom I had a good relationship, they gave me some suggestions on ways to motivate their daughter. Their advice was sound and I integrated it into my teaching practice, and as a result Amy's behaviour improved. This example is from the level of the individual teacher and parent relationship and although it is simple it represents the free flow of dialogue and the two-way empathy that mutuality emphasizes.

Since teaching is much more than "just a job" I have asserted that friendships and collegiality are necessary goals for which to strive. As the school becomes more of a multipurpose institution and opens its doors to partnerships, there is a greater chance for the individuals involved to feel a deeper sense of connection to each other and the community. Often teachers feel very isolated both within the school and in the community. At present, many parent-teacher relations are characterized by formality and awkwardness; this distance inhibits the possibility of a sharing of information about the child and the chance for a more collaborative effort. There must be a comfort level that allows for discussion. A comment often heard from parents and teachers when describing a positive relationship between themselves and the principal

---

[1] George Wood, *Schools that Work: America's Most Innovative Public Education Programs* (New York: Penguin, 1992), 128.

is "he listens to me." And one can only listen if there is a measure of trust, empathy and genuine friendliness. This willingness to listen and the belief that the other will respond makes for a solid and rich relationship.

Since the school is a community of learners, the opportunities for learning will depend on the people involved. Usually, the greater the number of people included, the greater the chance for learning. As noted earlier, Nancie Atwell's school has an "open door" policy to the community. The parents and community members often worked with the children — they brought their expertise into the class. She had fishermen, bankers and carpenters work alongside teachers either to assist children in their daily activities or to give special presentations. Not only does this diversity make for a rich curriculum, it also helps both teachers and students learn about other trades, attitudes and possibilities. And most importantly, these interactions with others help everyone learn a great deal more about the human condition which is essential to schooling. Learning about others while developing a sense of self are integral aspects of mutuality. "In actuality, part of what it is to be one's own person is to take the needs and points of view of others into account without losing sight of oneself."[1]

Once again, children will see the goal of mutuality modelled by their parents and teachers. They will see the reciprocity, the exchange of information, the warmth, the camaraderie and even the humour that are all part of healthy relationships. As the children move through the school divisions, they will witness a relationship that sustains and is sustaining. For the children, the teachers and the parents, the school will become a less alienating place when collegiality becomes a way of being and doing. They will be involved in "life activities" which are "learning situations that are connected to life. This implies that the work itself, as well as how it is undertaken, is in agreement with the activities that are part of our daily living."[2] The inclusion of mutuality in home-school partnerships allows children to be involved in life.

---

[1] Jane Roland Martin, *The Schoolhome*, 178.

[2] Ralph Peterson, *Life in a Crowded Place: Making A Learning Community* (Richmond Hill, Ontario: Scholastic Canada, 1992), 128.

Conclusion

The home is a powerful force in children's development. We no longer can afford to ignore its influence; schools cannot do it all, society is too complex for schools to be "going it alone." Further, the few token gestures that are frequently offered to parents no longer seem appropriate. The intense (and often fanatical) grassroots involvement and the public scepticism towards schools mean that building partnerships will not be an easy task; teachers are wary of parents and have been much maligned by the public. Healing the wounds and building bridges will take a great deal of gumption, courage, hope and skill.

What makes the task even more difficult is the lack of a "good" model for the home-school relationship. The present arrangement is fraught with problems — we often seem to lurch from crisis to crisis. As a society we have to figure out what we want from this relationship; granted each community will work out its unique version, but we need to develop an arrangement that is suitable for most parents and teachers. We need to design a thoughtful partnership, based on respect, trust, collaboration and filled with humour and good intentions. Of all the areas that have been addressed, the home-school relationship is probably the most challenging. For the children, though, we must take the first tentative steps to a healthier, stronger relationship embracing the motto that caring for our children is everyone's responsibility.

Conclusion

Some Future Directions

> *However, the question is: How do we get there (to the ideal, whatever it is) from here? I am proposing that, first, we must identify the basic human values, the things that ultimately make life good and worthwhile, the things we really need ... Secondly, we must attempt to move the present school system —and, necessarily, the surrounding society— toward these values and away from inequitable, destructive and unduly expensive forms of living and learning. And thirdly, as we proceed, we must dismantle those elements of the school system which are inherently incompatible with human well being or 'the good life'.[1]*
>
> Clive Beck

Clive Beck's basic question "How do we get there from here" is the crux of many educational discussions. The previous chapters have provided a general direction and some specific answers. By showing the complexity of the situation, I have demonstrated that there is no easy answer or particular formula for achieving school "success."

In this brief closing section, I will not try to summarize the argument and conclusions of the foregoing chapters. As we have seen our topic is vast, and to attempt a short summary would fly in the face of my fundamental notion of the complexity of schooling. What I will offer, rather, are a few strategies for beginning the process of change. My discussion of education is both descriptive and prescriptive: as description, it analyzes the present situation (on both a school and a societal level) and shows that all the variables of schooling are interconnected; and as prescription, it proposes ways to realize the ultimate goal of well-being. Because it talks about the present, the future and the interconnections within, my approach is comprehensive. However, academic coverage is not enough; we need hope, realism, experience, open minds, patient hearts and clear vision if we are to alter significantly the school experience for most children and change the way we talk and

---

[1] Clive Beck, *Better Schools: A Values Perspective* (New York: The Falmer Press, 1990), 193.

think about education. As school communities enter the process, they are taking the first steps for growth and change.

Schools must respond to the changes in society; however, we must resist the fads, gimmicks and "snake oil sellers" that continue to plague our system. In order *not* to be duped by the slick or the fanatical we must have thoughtful discussions in government ministries, school boards, staff rooms and parent teacher conferences. To have such discussions the participants must be well informed and well read; we must have the courage to direct others to sources of information and to be their guide so that they have the knowledge to make informed and responsible comments.

The ultimate aim of well-being and the five steps of autonomy/control, reflectiveness, integration, responsibility/care and mutuality must permeate every educational conversation. These terms must be part of our conceptualization of and language about schools. To give an analogy, just as everyone knows that we invest money in a bank in order to gain interest, we must have the same level of familiarity with the ultimate and intermediate goals of schooling; everyone must know that schooling is to encourage well-being, reflection, mutuality and so on. We would become suspicious of a banking institution that was not generating interest or was using terminology we could not understand; so too should we distrust any school that is hindering well-being or talking in a unfamiliar dialect. Every discussion of schooling must come back to well-being; the ultimate and intermediate goals must be posted in every school, be part of every school document and be part of our "values pillars." The logo for schools might even be a picture of a cube with the outline of a person superimposed on it thus reminding us that all aspects of the process are interconnected and schools must be concerned with each person's well-being. We cannot deal with fragments in isolation nor can we forget the child.

Educators are key to the change process. They must begin to see themselves as professionals and as thoughtful practitioners. The de-professionalization that leads to teachers being technicians begins in teacher education programs. Rather than being welcomed into the profession, each new group is spoon fed, talked down to and controlled so that their creativity is stamped out of them. Preservice students quickly learn to follow the rules and not think. As a result, novices are not encouraged to be critical and sensitive, gather a sense of the big picture, control their learning, see the connection between theory and practice and so on. A first step in rectifying the situation, which would have a domino effect, would be to move teacher training into schools —mentor teachers, principals and professors would all participate in the induction and training. The general climate must be caring, academic, professional, critical and welcoming. A complete overhaul of teacher education would benefit the preservice candidates and also result in local schools becoming learning laboratories for children and adults. John Goodlad advocates "centers of pedagogy" which are "an inquiring setting for the education of educators that embraces schools and universities ... where the art and science of teaching are brought to bear on the education of educators and where the *whole* is the subject of continuous inquiry."[1]

For our teachers currently in the system there must be many ways to help them make sense of teaching: the system must support their growth as thoughtful practitioners who take responsibility for their own professional development. Teachers must be encouraged to tell their stories both orally and in print. As the general public reads these stories they will gain a better understanding of the challenges facing teachers and as colleagues read them they will feel the kindred spirits of their peers. Encouraging teachers to read others' stories is one way to invite them into professional literature. Sabbaticals, study leaves, long and short term professional development, visiting other schools, academic book clubs and attending and presenting at conferences must become commonplace in the profession. It is imperative that teachers see alternate models, interact with others and gain confidence and a deeper understanding of teaching and schooling.

One way to help address the complex problems of schools would be to hold multidisciplinary conferences. Rather than having small academic societies, which are remote from the reality of schooling, with people presenting papers that are often inaccessible to practitioners (and even to many of the academics themselves), I would propose a model where everyone would speak the same language and address the same issues. In multidisciplinary conferences individuals from a variety of specialities such as philosophy, curriculum, educational administration and child psychology, along with practitioners, parents, preservice teachers, politicians and so on would come together in a workshop format. There would be some keynote addresses but the bulk of the conference would be devoted to meetings of small teams or groups composed of different specialists working together. Rather than follow the traditional format of individuals presenting papers, each person would bring his or her research and expertise to the group and from the discussions they would write a joint paper. Since each group would have the responsibility for producing a collaborative paper, the onus would be on them to work together; through this process they would gain a better

---

[1] John Goodlad, *Educational Renewal: Better Teachers, Better Schools* (San Francisco: Jossey Bass, 1994), 10,11.

understanding of the multiple issues involved in schooling. The papers that emerged would be rich, complex, less specialized, written in a language understandable by all, and integrative of theory and practice. This collaboration would lead to more informed practice, academics becoming involved in real school issues and practitioners sharing their expertise while becoming researchers themselves. Individuals might continue to meet with their specialized societies, but they would be encouraged to branch out and meet other groups. This concept of a multidisciplinary approach could be extended to government ministries, partnerships between schools and business, links between elementary and high schools and so on.

These, then, are some suggestions for implementation of what I have been proposing. However, as the opening quote of the book from Alfred North Whitehead reminds us there is no simple formula for education. The only way to bring about appropriate change is to *keep the conversation going*. When parents, teachers, students, administrators, politicians, academics and business leaders work together, our system will continue to evolve in a healthy direction. By involving children in the discussion and having our focus on their well-being we will *keep the conversation going* between schools and students. When children, teachers and parents feel that schools are joyful and nourishing communities we will know that our conversations have been fruitful and worth the struggle.

Bibliography

Aries, Philippe. *Centuries of Childhood: A Social History of Family Life*. New York: Vintage Books, 1962.

Aronowitz, Stanley and Henry Giroux. *Education Under Siege: The Conservative, Liberal and Radical Debate Over Schooling*. Amherst, MA: Bergin & Garvery, 1985.

___. *Postmodern Education: Politics, Culture and Social Criticism*. Minneapolis: University of Minnesota Press, 1991.

Atwell, Nancie. *In the Middle: Reading, Writing and Learning with Adolescents*. Portsmouth, NH: Heinemann, 1987.

___. *Side by Side: Essays on Teaching to Learn*. Portsmouth, NH: Heinemann, 1991.

Barth, Roland. *Improving Schools from Within: Teachers, Parents, and Principals Can Make the Difference*. San Francisco: Jossey-Bass, 1990.

Beck, Clive. "Is There Really Moral Development." *Journal of Moral Education* 18, October 1989.

___. *Better Schools: A Values Perspective*. New York: The Falmer Press, 1990.

___. *Dialogue and Democracy*. unpublished manuscript, 1993.

___. *Learning to Live the Good Life: Values in Adulthood*. Toronto: OISE Press, 1993.

Bellah, Robert, Richard Madsen, William M. Sullivan, Ann Swidler and Steven M.Tipton. *Habits of the Heart: Individualism and Commitment in American Life*. New York: Harper and Row, 1985.

Bernstein, Richard. *Beyond Objectivism and Relativism: Science, Hermeneutics and Praxis*. Philadelphia: University of Pennsylvania Press, 1983.

Bettelheim, Bruno. *The Uses of Enchantment: The Meaning and Importance of Fairy Tales*. New York: Alfred A. Knopf, 1975.

Booth, David and Carol Thornly-Hall eds. *Classroom Talk*. Markham, Ontario: Pembroke, 1991.

___. *The Talk Curriculum*. Markham, Ontario: Pembroke, 1991.

Bradley, Leo. *Total Quality Management for Schools*. Lancaster, PA: Technomic, 1992.

Bredekamp, Sue ed. *Developmentally Appropriate Practice in Early Childhood Programs Serving Children From Birth Through Age 8*. Washington: National Association for the Education of Young Children, 1987.

Burns, Robert. *The Self-Concept in Theory, Measurement, Development and Behaviour*. New York: Longman, 1979.

___. *Self-Concept Development and Education*. Toronto: Holt, Rinehart and Winston, 1982.

Butler, Andrea ed. *The Elements of the Whole Language Program*. Crystal Lake, IL: Rigby, 1987.

Bye, Marshall. *Holt Mathematics System, Book 1*. Toronto: Holt Rinehart and Wilson, 1980.

Cairney, Trevor. *Balancing the Basics for Teachers of Reading (K-8)*. Sydney: Ashton Scholastic, 1983.

Caulkins, Lucy McCormick. *Living Between the Lines*. Portsmouth, NH: Heinemann, 1991.

Chall, Jeanne. *Stages of Reading Development*. New York: McGraw Hill, 1983.

Chambers, Aidan. *Booktalk: Occasional Writing on Literature and Children*. London: The Bodley Head, 1985.

Church, Susan. "Is Whole Language Really Warm and Fuzzy?."*The Reading Teacher* 47, February 1994.

Clay, Marie. *Reading Recovery: A Guidebook for Teachers in Training*. Portsmouth, NH: Heinemann, 1993.

___. *Becoming Literate: The Construction of Inner Control*. Portsmouth, NH: Heinemann, 1991.

Cleary, Beverly. *Henry Huggins*. New York: William Morrow, 1950.

Coles, Robert. *The Moral Life of Children*. Boston: Houghton Mifflin Company, 1986.

___. *The Call of Stories: Teaching and the Moral Imagination*. Boston: Houghton Mifflin Company, 1989.

Curry, Nancy and Carl Johnson. *Beyond Self-Esteem: Developing a Genuine Sense of Human Value*. Washington: National Association for the Education of Young Children, 1990.

Curtis, Bruce. *Building the Educational State: Canada West, 1836-1871*. London, Ontario: The Althouse Press, 1988.

Dearden, Robert.*The Philosophy of Primary Education: An Introduction*. London: Routledge and Kegan Paul, 1968.

___. *Problems in Primary Education*. London: Routledge and Kegan Paul, 1976.

Delamont, Sara, ed. *The Primary School Teacher*. London: The Falmer Press, 1987.

Dewey, John. *Democracy and Education: An Introduction to the Philosophy of Education*. New York: The Free Press, 1916.

___. *Experience and Education*. New York: Collier Books, 1938.

Doll, William. *A Post-Modern Perspective on Curriculum*. New York: Teachers College Press, 1993.

Edwards, Carolyn, Lella Gandini, and George Forman, eds. *The Hundred Languages of Children: The Reggio Emilia Approach to Early Childhood Education*. Norwood, NJ: Ablex, 1993.

Egan, Kieran. *Primary Understanding: Education in Early Childhood*. New York: Routledge, 1988.

Eliot, George. *The Mill on the Floss*. Oxford: Oxford University Press, 1980.

Elkind, David, ed. *Perspectives on Early Childhood Education: Growing with Young Children Toward the Twenty First Century*. Washington, DC: A National Education Association Publication, 1991.

Elkind, David. *The Hurried Child: Growing Up Too Fast Too Soon*. Reading, MA: Addison-Wesley, 1988.

___. *Miseducation: Preschoolers at Risk*. New York: Alfred A. Knopf, 1989.

Fogarty, Robin. *The Mindful School: How to Integrate the Curricula*. Palatine, Il: Skylight Publishing, 1991.

Fox, Mem. *Possum Magic*. San Diego: Harcourt Brace, 1983.

___. *Dear Mem Fox, I Have Read All Your Books Even the Pathetic Ones and Other Incidents in the Life of a Children's Book Author*. San Diego: Harcourt Brace, 1990.

___. *Shoes From Grandpa*. San Diego: Harcourt Brace, 1992.

___. *Radical Reflections: Passionate Opinions on Teaching, Learning and Living*. San Diego: Harcourt Brace, 1993.

Freire, Paulo. *Pedagogy of the Oppressed*. New York: Continuum, 1990.

Froese, Victor ed. *Whole Language: Practice and Theory*. Scarborough, Ontario: Prentice Hall, 1990.

Furlong, L. Dolores, *Natural-Ethical Decisions in Caring Relations*. Paper presented at the Learned Societies: Charlottetown, June 1992.

Gilligan, Carol. *In a Different Voice: Psychological Theory andWomen's Development*. Cambridge, MA: Harvard University Press, 1982.

Goodlad John, and Pamela Keating, eds. *Access to Knowledge: An Agenda for Our Nations's Schools*. New York: College Entrance Examination Board, 1990.

Goodlad, John. *A Place Called School: Prospects for the Future*. New York: McGraw Hill, 1984.

___. *Educational Renewal: Better Teachers, Better Schools*. San Francisco: Jossey-Bass, 1994.

Goodman, Kenneth, Lois Bridges Bird and Yetta Goodman, eds. *The Whole Language Catalog*. Santa Rosa, CA: American School Publishers, 1991.

Goodman, Kenneth. *What's Whole in Whole Language*. Richmond Hill, Ontario: Scholastic, 1986.

___. "I Didn't Found Whole Language." *The Reading Teacher* 46, November 1992.

___. *Phonics Phacts*. Richmond Hill, Ontario: Scholastic, 1993.

Graham, Carolyn. *Singing, Chanting, Telling Tales: Arts in Language Classrooms*. Englewood Cliffs, NJ: Prentice Hall, 1992.

Graves, Donald. *Writing: Teachers and Children at Work*. Portsmouth, NH: Heinemann, 1983.

___. *Investigate Nonfiction*. Portsmouth, NH: Heinemann, 1989.

___. *Discover Your Own Literacy*. Portsmouth, NH: Heinemann, 1990.

___. *Build a Literate Classroom*. Portsmouth: Heinemann, 1991.

Groome, Thomas. *Christian Religious Education: Sharing Our Story and Vision*. San Francisco: Harper and Row, 1980.

Hagerty, Patricia. *Readers' Workshop: Real Reading*. Richmond Hill, Ontario: Scholastic Canada, 1992.

Hargreaves, Andy and Peter Woods, eds. *Classrooms and Staffrooms: The Sociology of Teachers and Teaching*. Milton Keyes: Open University Press, 1984.

Harste, Jerome, Kathy Short and Carolyn Burke. *Creating Classrooms for Authors: The Reading-Writing Connection*. Portsmouth, NH: Heinemann, 1988.

Heard, Georgia. *For the Good of the Earth and Sun: Teaching Poetry*. Portsmouth, NH: Heinemann, 1989.

Hersh, Richard, John Miller and Glen Fielding. *Models of Moral Education: An Appraisal*. New York: Longman, 1980.

Hirsch, E.D. *What Your First Grader Needs to Know: Fundamentals of a Good First Grade Education*. Chicago: Delta, 1993.

Hollinger, Robert, ed. *Hermeneutics and Praxis*. Notre Dame: University of Notre Dame Press, 1985.

Hollingsworth, Sandra, ed. *International Action Research: A Casebook for Educational Reform*. London: The Falmer Press, 1977.

Houston, Susan and Alison Prentice. *Schooling and Scholars in Nineteenth Century Ontario*. Toronto: University of Toronto Press, 1988.

Hunt, David. *Beginning With Ourselves: In Practice, Theory, and Human Affairs*. Toronto: OISE Press, 1987.

Jackson, Philip. *Life in Classrooms*. New York: Teachers College Press, 1990.

Jones, Pat. *Lipservice: The Story of Talk in Schools*. Milton Keynes: Open University Press, 1988.

Jordan, Judith. "The Meaning of Mutuality." *Works in Progress* 23 Wellesley, MA: Stone Center Working Paper Series, 1985.

Kambeitz, Martha and Carol Roth. *Starting Points in Language Arts*. Toronto: Ginn, 1976.

Kelly, Michael, ed. *Hermeneutics and Critical Theory in Ethics and Politics*. Cambridge, MA: The MIT Press, 1990.

Kosnik, Clare and Clive Beck, "Does Involvement in Action Research Develop a Sense of Ownership for Student Teachers in their Preservice Programs?" Paper presented at the American Educational Research association meeting, San Diego, April 14, 1998.

Kosnik, Clare. "A Community of Learners: A Fresh Approach to In-Servicing Whole Language." *Orbit* 22, December, 1991.

____. "Everyone is a V.I.P. in This Class." *Young Children* 49, November, 1993.

____. "The Class as a Learning Community." *Orbit* 25, May, 1994.

____. *Nelson Spelling 4.* Scarborough: ITP Nelson, 1997.

____. *Spelling in a Balanced Literacy Program,* Scarborough: Nelson Canada, 1998.

Lickona, Thomas. *Raising Good Children: Helping Your Children Through the Stages of Moral Development.* Toronto: Bantam, 1983.

Lightfoot. Sara Lawrence. *The Good High School.* New York: Basic Books, 1983.

Livesley, Jack and Frank Trotz. *The Penguin Guide to Children's TV and Video.* Toronto: Penguin Books, 1993.

Loughran, John and Tom Rusell, eds. *Teaching About Teaching: Purpose, Passion and Pedagogy in Teacher Education.* London: The Falmer Press, 1997.

Lowe, Roy, ed. *The Changing Primary School.* London: The Falmer Press, 1987.

Luke, Carmen and Jennifer Gore, eds. *Feminism and Critical Pedagogy.* New York: Routledge, 1992.

MacLure, Margaret, Terry Phillips and Andrew Wilkinson. *Oracy Matters.* Milton Keynes: Open University Press, 1988.

Manning, Maryann, Gary Manning and Roberta Long. *Theme Immersion: Inquiry-Based Curriculum in Elementary and Middle Schools.* Portsmouth, NH: Heinemann, 1994.

Martin, Jane Roland. *The Schoolhome: Rethinking Schools for Changing Families.* Cambridge, MA: Harvard University Press, 1992.

McGowan, John. *Postmodernism and Its Critics: The Problem of Freedom in Postmodern Theory.* Ithaca: Cornell University Press, 1991.

McMahon, Ian. "Public Preschool From the Age of Two: The *Ecole Maternelle* in France." *Young Children* 47, July 1992.

Miller, Jean Baker. "What Do We Mean by Relationships." *Work in Progress* 22, Wellesley, MA: Stone Center Working Paper Series, 1986.

Miller, John, J. R. Bruce Cassie, Susan Drake. *Holistic Learning: A Teacher's Guide to Integrated Study.* Toronto: OISE Press, 1990.

Miller, John. *The Holistic Curriculum.* Toronto: OISE Press, 1988.

Montessori, Maria. *Dr. Montessori's Own Handbook.* New York: Schocken Books, 1965.

____. *The Discovery of the Child.* New York: Ballantine Books, 1967.

____. *The Absorbent Mind.* New York: Delta, 1967.

Nelson, Canada. *Waves.* Toronto: Nelson Canada, 1992.

Newman, Judith and Susan Church. "Myths of Whole Language." *The Reading Teacher* 44, September 1990.

Noddings, Nel. *Caring: A Feminine Approach to Ethics and Moral Education.* Berkley: University of California Press, 1984.

___. *The Challenge to Care in Schools: An Alternative Approach to Education.* New York: Teachers College Press, 1992.

Noddings, Nel and Paul Shore. *Awakening the Inner Eye: Intuition in Education.* New York: Teachers College Press, 1984.

Ontario College of Teachers. *Standards of Practice for the Teaching Profession.* Ontario College of Teachers: Toronto 1998.

Ontario, Ministry of Community and Social Services. *Children First: Report of the Advisory Committee on Children's Services.* Toronto, Ministry of Community and Social Services, 1990.

Ontario, Ministry of Education and Training. *Antiracism and Ethnocultural Equity in School Boards: Guidelines for Policy Development and Implementation.* Toronto: Ministry of Education and Training, 1993.

___. *The Common Curriculum — Working Document.* Toronto: Ministry of Education and Training, 1993.

___. *Computers Across the Curriculum: JK to OACs.* Toronto: Ministry of Education and Training, 1993.

___. *The Ontario Curriculum, Grades 1-8.* Toronto: Ministry of Education and Training, 1997.

Ontario, Ministry of Education. *Programme of Studies for Grades 1 to 6 of the Public and Separate Schools.* Toronto: Ministry of Education, 1960.

___. *The Formative Years.* Toronto: Ministry of Education, 1975.

___. *Education in the Primary and Junior Divisions.* Toronto: Ministry of Education, 1975.

___. *Personal and Societal Values: A Resource Guide for Primary and Junior Divisions.* Toronto: Ministry of Education, 1983.

___. *Science is Happening Here.* Toronto: Ministry of Education, 1988.

Open Court Publishing. *Open Court Reading and Writing.* Peru, Illinois: Open Court Publishing Company, 1989

Paley, Vivian. *You Can't Say You Can't Play.* Cambridge, MA: Harvard University Press, 1992.

Peterson, Ralph. *Life in a Crowded Place: Making a Learning Community.* Richmond Hill, Ontario: Scholastic Canada, 1992.

Peterson, Ralph and Maryann Eeds. *Grand Conversations: Literature Groups in Action.* Richmond Hill, Ontario: Scholastic, 1990.

Plowden, Bridget. *Children and Their Primary Schools: A Report for the Central Advisory Council for Education.* London: Great Britain, 1967.

Prentice Hall Ginn Canada. *Collections.* Scarborough: Prentice Hall Ginn Canada, 1998.

Purkey, William and John Novak. *Inviting School Success: A Self-Concept Approach to Teaching and Learning.* Belmont, CA: Wadsworth, 1984.

Purkey, William. *Self-Concept and School Achievement.* Englewood Cliffs, NJ: Prentice Hall, 1970.

Reimer, Joseph, Diana Pritchard Paolitto and Richard Hersh. *Promoting Moral Growth: From Piaget to Kohlberg.* New York: Longman, 1979.

Rorty, Richard. *Contingency, Irony and Solidarity.* Cambridge, MA: Cambridge University Press, 1989.

Schermann, Ada. "Reflecting on the Relationship." *Orbit* 25, May 1994.

Sergiovanni, Thomas. *Building Community in Schools.* San Francisco: Jossey-Bass, 1994.

Sharp, Rachel and Anthony Green. *Education and Social Control: A Study in Progressive Primary Education.* London: Routledge and Kegan Paul, 1975.

Sheehy, Gail. *Passages: Predictable Crises of Adult Life.* Toronto: Bantam Books, 1976.

Short, Kathy Gnagey and Kathryn Mitchell Pierce, eds., *Talking About Books: Creating Literate Communities.* Portsmouth: Heinemann, 1990.

Silverstein, Shel. *The Giving Tree.* New York: Harper Collins, 1964.

Smith, Carl and Karin Dahl. *Teaching Reading and Writing Together: The Classroom Connection.* New York: Teachers College Press, 1984.

Smith, Frank. *Reading Without Nonsense.* New York: Teachers College Press, 1985.

Spodek, Bernard and Olivia Saracho, eds. *Issues in Early Childhood Curriculum.* New York: Teachers College Press, 1991.

Statistics Canada, 1998 www.statcan.ca

Steig, William. *Sylvester and the Magic Pebble.* New York: Simon and Schuster, 1969.

Stevenson, Harold and James Stigler. *The Learning Gap: Why Our Schools are Failing and What We can Learn from Japanese and Chinese Education.* New York: Summit Books, 1992.

Strickland, Dorothy and Lesley Mandel Morrow eds. *Emerging Literacy: Young Children Learn to Read and Write.* Newark: International Reading Association, 1989.

Surrey, Janet. "Relationship and Empowerment." *Work In Progress* 30, Wellesley MA: Stone Center Working Paper Series, 1987.

Thornly-Hall, Carol. *Let's Talk About Talk.* Mississauga, Ontario: Peel Board of Education, 1988.

Turkle, Sherry. *The Second Self: Computers and the Human Spirit.* New York: Simon and Schuster, 1984.

Van Manen, Max and Bas Levering, *Childhood's Secrets: Intimacy, Privacy and the Self Reconsidered.* New York: Teachers College, 1996.

Walker, Decker and Jonas Soltis. *Curriculum And Aims*. New York: Teachers College Press, 1992.

Weaver, Constance. *Understanding Whole Language: From Principles to Practice*. Portsmouth, NH: Heinemann, 1990.

Weedon, Chris. *Feminist Practice and Poststructuralist Theory*. Cambridge, MA: Basil Blackwell, 1987.

Weininger, Otto. "Understanding Educational Play." *Orbit* 25, May, 1994.

Wells, Gordon. *The Meaning Makers: Children Learning Language and Using Language to Learn*. Portsmouth: Heinemann, 1986.

White, John. *The Aims of Education Restated*. London: Routledge and Kegan Paul, 1982.

___. *Education and the Good Life: Autonomy, Altruism and the National Curriculum*. New York: Teachers College Press, 1991.

Witherell, Carol and Nel Noddings, eds. *Stories Lives Tell: Narrative and Dialogue in Education*. New York: Teachers College Press, 1991.

Wood, George. *Schools That Work: America's Most Innovative Public Education Programs*. New York: Penguin Books, 1992.

Yardley, Alice. *Structure in Early Learning*. Oakville, Ontario: Rubicon, 1989.

MEMBRE DE SCABRINI MEDIA

Québec, Canada
2002